A British Soldier of the 18th Century

GEORGE TOWNSHEND

A British Soldier of the 18th Century

The Military Career of George Townshend
during the War of Austrian Succession
& The Seven Year's War

ILLUSTRATED

C. V. F. Townshend

A British Soldier of the 18th Century
The Military Career of George Townshend during the War of Austrian Succession
& The Seven Year's War
by C. V. F. Townshend

ILLUSTRATED

First published under the title
The Military Life of Field-Marshal George First Marquess Townshend 1724-1807

Leonaur is an imprint of Oakpast Ltd
Copyright in this form © 2017 Oakpast Ltd

ISBN: 978-1-78282-686-6 (hardcover)
ISBN: 978-1-78282-687-3 (softcover)

http://www.leonaur.com

Publisher's Notes

The views expressed in this book are not necessarily those of the publisher.

Contents

Preface	9
Dettingen 1743	11
Fontenoy 1745	52
Appendix	71
Rebellion in Scotland 1745–46	80
Appendix	95
Laffeldt 1747	97
Appendix	115
At Home 1748–59	118
Appendix	129
Quebec 1759	131
Appendix	216
Vellinghausen	231
Portugal 1762	257
Viceroy of Ireland	265
Appendix	269

This Book I Dedicate
To My Cousin
Lady Agnes Townshend

Preface

The late John, 5th Marquess Townshend, not long before he died, asked me to write the life of our common ancestor, for which purpose a large mags of family papers and letters, at Raynham Hall, appertaining to the 1st Marquess, was available.

The work has been carried on under many interruptions and difficulties. When I had visited all the European battlefields mentioned in the work, I was ordered out to India, back again to England shortly after, and then out to South Africa. A considerable portion of the writing was done on board ship, and I finished the book on my return from the Cape.

I have five large volumes of closely written letters from Townshend, when he was Viceroy of Ireland, to the Prime Minister, but I have had to confine myself to the military life of George Townshend, for if his political life were included the book would necessarily extend to two volumes.

The part of the work which describes the Expedition to Quebec will be found to give many military details which up till now have been wanting in all histories of that memorable epoch. It will be seen that the unexpected and surprising manner in which Quebec was taken was the plan of the brigadiers, and not of Wolfe.

That Wolfe put into happy execution the plan of others is no disparagement to his glorious memory—such things are not unknown to students of military history; and, moreover, it was Wolfe's martial spirit which at once adopted the plan, led the men up the cliff in the night, and compelled victory in the morning.

George Townshend, on the death of Wolfe, wrote to a friend the following letter expressing his sentiments on the death of his gallant chief:—

I am not ashamed to own to you, that my heart does not exult in the midst of this success. I have lost but a friend in General Wolfe. Our country has lost a sure support and a perpetual honour. If the world were sensible at how dear a price we have purchased Quebec in his death, it would damp the general joy. Our best consolation is that Providence seemed not to promise that he should remain long among us. He was himself sensible of the weakness of his constitution, and determined to crowd into a few years actions that would have adorned length of life.

My best thanks are due to the present Marquess Townshend for his kindness in placing all papers and documents at my disposal.

C. V. F. Townshend.

Shaft Barracks, Dover,
April 11th, 1901.

Dettingen 1743

The Honourable George Townshend was born on February 28th, 1724. He was the eldest son of Charles, 3rd Viscount Townshend, and his wife Audrey Harrison, daughter and heiress of Edward Harrison, Esq., of Balls Park, Hertford, and grandson of Charles, 2nd Viscount Townshend, the great statesman, known as the head of the Whig firm "Townshend and Walpole." George had three younger brothers—Charles, Roger, and Edward, the last dying very young.

Charles Townshend, the second brother, born in 1725, was the famous wit and orator in Parliament. He was Chancellor of the Exchequer in 1766, and Leader of the House of Commons; he then proposed and carried those measures of taxation which led to the rebellion of our American colonies; he was about to be entrusted with the formation of a ministry in 1767, when he died of fever. He was ranked as an orator with Pitt, and Burke called him "the delight and ornament of the House of Commons"; Macaulay speaks of him as "the most brilliant and versatile of mankind, who had belonged to every party and cared for none."

Roger Townshend entered the army, like his elder brother George; he was an officer of great promise, a lieutenant-colonel in the 1st Regiment of Foot Guards, and fell gloriously under General Amherst at the taking of Ticonderoga, in America, and there stands a monument to him in Westminster Abbey.

Amongst the mass of family papers in the library at Raynham Hall, in Norfolk—some of these of the greatest interest to the State—I can find but little bearing on the early boyhood of George Townshend; but as I am writing his *military* life, I do not think it matters if the usual fairy tales of early boyhood are omitted. He went to Cambridge University, where he matriculated from St. John's College, graduating M.A., and displayed the highest abilities, giving him a claim to the chances in life which his birth and alliances set within his reach. A spirit of enterprise in him, and a passion for military honour, surmounted every consideration of comfort and selfishness, and he volunteered for the campaign.

In 1742, when Townshend left St. John's College, Cambridge, the times were stirring, as now in 1901; the Emperor Charles VI. of Germany, the last male heir of the House of Austria, having died on October 20th, 1740, hostilities had commenced on the Continent, in consequence of the Elector of Bavaria and the King of France combining to deprive Archduchess Maria Theresa, the Queen of Hungary, of her hereditary dominions, which had been guaranteed to her, as the daughter of the late Emperor, by the edict known as the Pragmatic Sanction.

George II., the King of England, supported the claims of the House of Austria, and in April, 1742, a British force of 17,000 men was ordered to Flanders, under the command of Field-Marshal Lord Stair, who had under him Generals Honeywood, Cope, Ligonier, Hawley, and the Earl of Albemarle, and Brigadier-Generals Cornwallis, Bragg, Pulteney, Huske, Ponsonby, Frampton, Lord Effingham, and Lord Rothes. The troops ordered to take part in the expedition were as follows:—

3rd and 4th troops of Horse Guards.

2nd troop Horse Grenadiers.

Royal Regiment of Horse Guards Blue.

King's Regiment of Dragoons (now King's Dragoon Guards).

General Ligonier's Horse (now 7th Dragoon Guards).

Honeywood's Dragoons (now 3rd Hussars).

Campbell's Dragoons (now Scots Greys).

Hawley's Dragoons (now 1st Royal Dragoons).

Cadogan's Dragoons (now Inniskilling Dragoons).

Rich's Dragoons (now 4th Hussars).

Cope's Dragoons (now 7th Hussars).

Infantry

Three battalions of Foot Guards, *viz*. 1st Regiment of Foot Guards (now Grenadier Guards), the Coldstream Regiment of Foot Guards, and the 3rd Regiment of Foot Guards (now Scots Guards).

Cornwallis's Foot (now the 11th or Devonshire Regiment); Duroure's (now the 12th or Suffolk Regiment), in which young James Wolfe, the future hero of Quebec, was serving as ensign and acting-adjutant.

Pulteney's Foot (13th); Campbell's (Royal Scots Fusiliers); Pierce's (Royal Welsh Fusiliers); Handasyde's (31st); Huske's (32nd); Bragg's (28th); Ponsonby's (37th); Johnson's (33rd); Bligh's (the 20th).

I find by old lists that battalions at this time, with the exception of the Foot Guards, were seldom over 500 combatants in strength, though the complement of officers was generally as now.

The Guards marched on May 26th, 1742, from London to Woolwich, to embark for Flanders; the Guards Brigade consisted of the English Guards (1st Foot Guards), 1st battalion Coldstream Guards, and the 1st battalion of the 3rd Foot Guards (Scots Guards). On this day, over 16,000 men were embarking for Flanders, and London turned out its people in thousands to see the troops marching to the sound of fife and drum to Woolwich. Battalion after battalion of our famous red-coated British infantry was taken off in boats to the transports lying in the stream. There was great enthusiasm, for they were bound for Flanders, the cockpit of Europe, and England had been at peace for thirty long years. When night fell, the whole fleet was at sea, with the cliffs of the North Foreland on the starboard bow.

There was little for the private soldier—or the "private man," as he was then called—to look forward to in those days; there were no pensions; and, to quote Napier, they were "stretched as it were on the bed of Procrustes by a discipline which had no resource but fear"—and were badly fed.

There are many order-books of this campaign at Raynham; and in *Brigadier Frampton's orderbook* I read on this date, May 26th, 1742 (on which date his orders commence on board a transport), that—

> A return of each battalion be given in immediately in the following form;—captains' names, number of officers, sergeants, corporals, drums and private men. No more than five women per company be permitted to continue on board the transports. A commissioned officer on board each transport to see the provisions delivered to the men and that there is no waste made. The commanding officer of each transport is to take care that neither officer nor soldier lie on shore....
> A sergeant, a corporal and 12 men of each transport to be as a guard to keep things quiet and to place centrys on the officers'

FOOT GUARDS

baggage and to suffer no man to smoak between decks. To take care of the lights and to commit any man prisoner that is guilty of any disturbance and that man will be severely punished

The tattoo and revallee not to be beat on board any of the transports unless a gun is fired by a man of war or till further orders.

The parole is King George.

The troops landed at Ostend on June 12th; on the 13th they marched to Bruges, and the 14th to Ghent, where they were destined to pass several months of waiting in winter quarters before advancing to the Rhine. This delay must have been useful in the way of pulling brigades together; for the battalions were raw, and the commissariat arrangements wretched. The order-books show great minuteness of detail, the orders as a rule being very sound, and arrangements for alarm posts and so forth never omitted.

George Townshend was now eighteen years of age; he had persuaded his father to let him see this campaign as a volunteer, which was then the fashionable thing to do, as it is now in our own times, and matters were arranged for him by his uncle, the Duke of Newcastle, as the following letter from that nobleman to Lord Dunmore, commanding a division under Lord Stair, shows:—

My dear Lord

The goodness you have shewed me on all occasions and particularly upon your leaving England gives me great reason to hope that you will not refuse me a favour which will lay me under a very great obligation to you. Mr. Townshend who will have the honour to deliver this letter to you, is my Lord Townshend's eldest son and my nephew. He has an inclination to the army and intends to serve as Volunteer this campaign in our army in Germany.

The favour I have to beg is, that your Lordship would take him particularly under your protection and that he may have the honour and advantage of your advice and direction. I am sensible of the service it must be to a young man of quality, who may be desirous of coming into the army, to be assisted and favoured with your Lordship's countenance. My nephew is extremely well disposed and I daresay you will have all imaginable reason to be satisfied with his behaviour, whilst he is at the army. I therefore most earnestly recommend him to you

and am with great truth and respect
>My dear Lord
>>Your Lordship's
>>>most obedient
>>>>humble servant
>>>>>Holles Newcastle.

It will be seen that George Townshend began his soldiering at the same time as Wolfe, who was also serving in this campaign as an ensign in Duroure's Foot (now the Suffolk Regiment), having been transferred to that regiment from the Marines, in which he obtained his first commission. Townshend, however, began on the staff, and I am afraid that throughout his service he never learnt by experience the difference between the labours and the dangers of staff and regimental officers on active service, which are—as Napier has so truly said—generally in inverse ratio to their promotion.

Wolfe had no family interest or friends in influential quarters, but he was far ahead of the great bulk of officers in the army at that time as a student of his profession and in proficiency; and in this respect Townshend ran Wolfe very close. Townshend was possessed of great energy and determination in carrying out an enterprise; he was cool in action, and showed great abilities and qualifications for high command; and he had the strictest sense of honour and of the duties of a gentleman.

The withdrawal of General Maillebois with a French Army from the frontiers of Hanover enabled George II. to draw 16,000 excellent Hanoverian troops from that country, and march them to Brussels to co-operate with the allied army then in Flanders; and also, the services of some Hessian troops were utilised, the Hessians being taken into British pay, together with the Hanoverians, by Act of Parliament. Amongst some notes I find the following on the Hanoverian troops:—

> The Hanoverians are proportionable well bodied men and extraordinary good soldiers, bearing the most severe shock with all the calmness imaginable, seldom the least disorder to be perceived in their ranks; they march with as little concern to action, as if they were going to a banquet, and generally smoke tobacco, which is their common maxim in all intervals throughout an engagement; they are of the reformed religion, and appear very devout, being seldom addicted to any pro-

faneness, and have commonly prayers at the head of their lines twice a day, and sing hymns as they march to action; which intimates that good Christians seldom fail of being good soldiers.

The Seven Years' War, the Peninsular and Waterloo campaigns, testify to the bravery and discipline of the Hanoverian troops, and they have shared much in British glory.

Amongst the papers I found a list of George Townshend's outfit for this campaign, written out by his father Lord Townshend, with the prices of each item. His outfit was not a bad one; it came to about £400, which nowadays would mean, say, £800, and it included two horses and "a pair of silver mounted pistols." Apparently, his father did not much like having to pay for campaigning kits, for I find a letter to his son, dated September 26th, 1748:—

> I remember very well that it was about the time when you went over to Flanders from Scotland, and I had made a large disbursement for equipping you for that campaign when you was to serve as *aide de camp* to the Duke (of Cumberland).

About the end of February, 1743, the allied troops in winter quarters in Flanders began their march in divisions for the Rhine. The British and Austrian troops formed the vanguard, being joined on their march by the Hanoverians in British pay; the Hessians relieved the Austrian troops in garrison in the frontier towns, and they in turn were relieved by Dutch troops and ordered to join the allied army. These Hessian troops did not overtake the army till after the Battle of Dettingen.

The British cavalry, under General Honeywood, marched from Brussels on May 1st, and towards the end of the month joined the allied army near Hochst, on the Main, which place had been designated by Lord Stair as the rendezvous for the allied army. It had been very severe weather for marching, the roads being heavy with much snow and ice. The Rhine was crossed by our troops at Neuwied, below Coblentz; the route from that place was by Ehrenbreitstein and Ems, up the right bank by Cassel, and thence along the Main, until a junction with the Austrian and Hanoverian troops was made at Hochst, near Frankfort.

Lord Stair chose Hochst for the centre of his operations probably because the banks of the Main had often before been chosen in the wars of the Empire as a good base of operations, the river winding so far about as to secure the right flank and rear of his position. Lord Stair was the descendant of an honourable Scottish family; he had served with great distinction under the Duke of Marlborough in Flanders, and had been raised to the peerage for his services. He was known as a man of strict integrity and uprightness, but must at this period have been past work.

The French Court had taken alarm at the movement of the allies, and in order to prevent their junction with Prince Charles of Lorraine and his Austrian Army (which had defeated the Bavarians in Bavaria) ordered two large armies to be concentrated. The one under Marshal Noailles, of 60,000 men, was to oppose Lord Stair, while the other, of 50,000 men, under the Duc de Broglie, was to defend Alsace and the neighbouring provinces, and to oppose Prince Charles, if he attempted to cross the Rhine. Field-Marshal Lord Stair remained at Hochst in his camp, the French Army under De Noailles being in the Palatinate.

Lord Stairs force was computed on paper at 16,000 British, 16,000 Hanoverians, 12,000 Austrians—in all, 44,000 men; but after deducting sick and so forth, the actual fighting strength was only 37,000. The French army under De Noailles mustered about 70,000 men; 12,000 of these he detached under the Comte de Segur to cover the retreat of the over-cautious De Broglie, making De Noailles' force only 58,000 men, from which a considerable number of sick should probably be deducted.

On May 14th De Noailles crossed the Rhine at Rhine Turkheim, about six miles below Worms, and marched towards the Main with a view to seizing some high ground on the west side of the river that commanded Hochst. The intelligence department in Lord Stair's army would appear to have been very inefficient, and when that officer became acquainted with this move of the French he determined to advance. Accordingly, the allied army marched to Hellinback, between the edge of the forest of Darmstadt and the River Main, where Lord Stair formed, in the opinion of all the generals, an impregnable camp. Want of supplies, however, and the need of securing the communications of the River Main, forced him to move on again to Aschaffenburg, some twenty miles east of Frankfort, with a castle on the north side of the Main (right bank), where there was a large stone bridge, which same bridge is standing now.

Here, then, Lord Stair established his headquarters, and wrote to the Duc d'Aremberg, who commanded the Austrian force, to come on and join him. The two were not on good terms, there was much friction, and the Austrian general wrote back to say that "as his Lordship had brought himself into the scrape it was his business to get out of it as well as he could." Lord Stair's force alone without the Austrians was too weak to detach troops to occupy different posts of advantage along the Main, *viz.* Miltenburg, Klingenberg, and Wurtz; so, the French occupied them, thus cutting off the allies from their supplies at Frankfort, and in two days they were in great extremity.

It was June 7th, 1743, when Lord Stair reached Aschaffenburg and secured the bridge over the river. He had made a forced march to get there; but as the allies had had to take the bow, and the French had only the string, as will be seen by looking at a map, the French had not so far to go, and, reaching the wood near the bridge of Aschaffenburg the same day, encamped in it undiscovered by the allies, whose piquet on the bridge must have been only 400 or 500 yards off!

On the next morning, June 8th, Lord Stair rode across the bridge to reconnoitre, being escorted by 300 sabres British cavalry. They had no knowledge whatever of the French being in the wood, and Lord Stair narrowly escaped capture, getting a bullet through the brim of his hat. Some French hussars, having watched the approach of the party, attempted to cut them off. The cavalry escort of Lord Stair behaved badly, as the following account shows:—

> The detachment that escorted the British Field Marshal, on the first appearance of the French, retreated with great irregularity and precipitation, but, as soon as they came near a small party of the British Foot Guards, they halted and facing about, found that the French had not pursued them! . . . . When the escort halted Lt. General Cope and Brigadier Bland warmly upbraided them with the irregularity of their retreat, showing them the great danger the Marshal had been exposed to by their conduct, and the indignity which so ill a beginning would bring upon the army.

Three of the dragoons were killed.

The day after the famous reconnaissance King George, attended by the Duke of Cumberland and Lord Carteret, arrived at Hanau in three days from Hanover (seventy miles a day), escorted by 300 horse, and continued on to Aschaffenburg the same day, reviewed the troops in the afternoon, and assumed the supreme command. Townshend arrived at the same time, travelling with Lord Mordaunt from The Hague, and was at once appointed an extra *aide-de-camp* on Lord Dunmore's staff.

THE EARL OF STAIR.

The situation of the army was then regarded as most serious and critical; for, with its communications with Frankfort cut off, it had become in a way invested.

The allied and the French armies were encamped on the plains near the banks of the Main, opposite to and in sight of each other, the allies on the north and the French on the south side. A ridge of hills covered with woods enclosed the allied army to the north. In accounts of the battle I have seen these hills described as mountains; but, on seeing the place, I found them to be gentle hills covered with thick woods as far as the eye can reach.

The town of Aschaffenburg is twenty miles east of Frankfort, twelve miles south-east of Hanau, and six miles south-east of the village of Dettingen. The Main is about sixty yards broad; the banks are flat, with cultivation on the north bank, where the allies were, extending for a distance from the river of, say, 700 yards, and then the wood and bush commence. Between Aschaffenburg and Dettingen is the village of Klein Ostheim, but little altered since the time of the Battle of Dettingen, with its quaint old houses, tiled roofs, and wooden beams showing through the walls, and the paved main road passing through it.

On the south side of the Main and opposite Klein Ostheim is the village of Scockstadt; the village of Mainfling, 00 the south bank of the river, faces Dettingen, on the north bank; about two miles lower down the river (west) is the town of Seligenstadt. I noticed that the south bank of the river slightly dominates the north bank, and this is frequently mentioned in accounts of the battle as giving the command to the French artillery; but it is very slight, and nothing like the extent asserted by some writers.

Little is changed in the terrain since the time of the Battle of Dettingen, though there is now a small railway station near the village; and I gathered from a plan of the battle that this railway station now must be about the spot where the centre of the allied line rested in the first part of the battle. The high road between Klein Ostheim and Dettingen is bordered by a fine avenue of trees, at the end of which, when going from Klein Ostheim, one sees the church spire, houses, and orchards of Dettingen.

Beyond Dettingen village to the north one sees the village of Welsheim, at the foot of the hills, a mile and a half distant.

The camp of the allied army extended from the town of Aschaffenburg westward as far as Klein Ostheim village, about two miles in

A View of the Glorious Action of Dettingen June 16/28 1743, between the Forces of the Allies Commanded by the KING of GREAT BRITAIN and the French Army under the Marshal Noailles.

length, at a distance of, say, 250 yards from the river. The camp was covered by piquets thrown out in front of their regiments, between them and the river. The Austrians were the farthest west, then the Hanoverians, and the British in the outskirts of the town of Aschaffenburg. George II. had his quarters in the old castle which overlooks the stone bridge of Aschaffenburg. The allies had a chain of posts between Hanau and Aschaffenburg, to ensure the safety of the passage of convoys; and the bank of the river was indifferently patrolled by our cavalry.

The French Army extended on the south bank of the Main from near the Aschaffenburg bridge westward as far as Seligenstadt. De Noailles had already, as described, seized various posts on the river; and if he also seized Welsheim and Seligenstadt, he would cut off all supplies. This he proceeded to do without delay, and the situation of the allies became alarming.

George II. issued very stringent orders against looting, which were read at the head of every regiment on parade. All men caught straggling beyond the limits of their camp without passes, or caught in the act of looting, were to suffer immediate death at the hand of the provost-marshal; and these orders had the desired effect.

The king and Lord Stair received news, on June 11th, that 6,000 Hessians and 6,000 Hanoverians, under the command of Prince George of Hesse, coming to reinforce the allied army, had arrived within two days' march of Hanau. The allies were short of provisions and unable to procure forage, and it was felt that the French would most certainly endeavour to prevent the junction of these reinforcements and the allied army at Aschaffenburg. Orders were sent accordingly to Prince George of Hesse to halt at Hanau. De Noailles, unlike the allies, had a very good intelligence department, and was excellently informed as to the intentions of the enemy.

He determined to prevent the junction of these reinforcements, and to shut up the allies in a trap by seizing the mouth of the defile at Dettingen (west of this hamlet the valley broadens out), and also blocking the end of it at Aschaffenburg. In this way, he hoped to compel the surrender of the allied army; for, by all accounts, there was no retreat through the impassable woods to the north. There was a road, however, as we shall see later; and from looking at the country casually I should say that the task of retiring an army northward through the woods would not be a very difficult one. The defile in which the allied army found itself was exposed also to the fire of the French artillery, which was safe on the south bank of the river; moreover, the allies would be subject for a long time to the fire of the French guns before they could emerge from the defile.

The river was sixty yards broad, and the space of ground over which the allies must move was only from 700 to 800 yards across. The plan of De Noailles was good, but he did not allow for De Grammont's mistake, thus exemplifying in himself what so many other generals have done before, and will do in the future—that the greatest warriors are the very slaves of fortune.

On June 13th, the French moved south into the woods (this was to enable them to march with greater ease to Seligenstadt, to cross the river there and to occupy Dettingen); and that evening great quantities of wood and straw were being burnt in the French camps, which led to the supposition that they were going to march; but in the morning the sight of numbers of the French soldiers at work entrenching raised fresh doubts.

For some time previous the French cavalry had been very active on the side of the river held by the allies. French hussars forded the stream near Dettingen constantly, and harassed our foraging parties. Under cover of this De Noailles was busy laying a couple of bridges over the Main at Seligenstadt. One might well ask what the allied cavalry was doing. Not only were the scouting and work generally of the mounted arm contemptible during this campaign—taking the famous reconnaissance of June 8th, for example—but in the battle of Dettingen even the spirit of our cavalry was brought into question.

Not before the bridges had been completed were they discovered by our dragoons, and Lord Stair and the king decided that it was time to move out of the defile; but their information led them to believe that the French would attack from the Aschaffenburg side.

The following orders are in Lord Stair's orderbook on the "15th June, 1743, Aschaffenburg":—

> General officers for the day tomorrow: for the Horse, Lt. General Ligonier, Major General Lawley, Brigadier Grant; for the Foot, Lt. General Hilton, Major General Monroy, Brigadier Pulteney.
>
> Majors of Brigade for the Horse, Gothart and Beaumont, and for the Foot, Blakeney and Dopost.
>
> For the piquet this night: for the Foot Guards, Lt. Colonel Corbet; for the foot, Lt. Colonel Bashfos, Maj. General Greenwood;

GEORGE II.

Horse Guards, Lt. Colonel Driven; Horse and Dragoons, Major Bogoust; for the detachment of 250 foot for the security of convoys, Lt. Colonel Whitemore; for the detachment of 600 foot, Lt. Colonel Waite.

After Tattoo this night, the tents of the whole army to be struck without any noise, and all the baggage and artillery to hold themselves in readiness to march; likewise, all the army to remain under arms in front of their encampments.

Tomorrow at break of day every regiment to march into their new ground; and as soon as the army are arrived in their new camp, they are to remain under arms in front of their new ground in the same manner as they did the night preceding till further orders, keeping a profound silence, no fires be suffered in the camp.

When the army marches, the camp on the left (east) forms the rear guard of the army, the advanced posts of the foot to remain there till further orders.

The baggage of the British troops to remain behind till the artillery marches, and then follows the artillery till further orders. Every regiment leaves 1 sergt. and 12 men with the baggage as a guard, and besides the British foot leave a detachment of one captain and two subalterns as a guard to the said baggage.

Four cannon will be sent from the Hanoverian camp to the head of Genl. Campbells regiment of dragoons, to remain there till Genl. Hilton sends for them, sentries from the standard guard of the said regiment to take care of them—the guards of the dragoons and foot to be immediately taken off

It is the Earl of Stairs orders that the dragoons sent back from the French Army are not to be employed on any service by ill they are exchanged by other prisoners which to their respective regiments.

erting from the French to be brought to headquarters to be examined, and if it is found that they have robbed their masters they are to be sent back to the French camp.

That as information has been given, that several deserters of the regiment of *cuirassiers* and one of the *carabiniers* who came over from the French camp some days ago had stolen several horses besides their own, orders to be given that strict enquiry should be made after such horses, and if they are found they shall be brought to the headquarters, in order to be sent back to the

French camp; all the above points to be given out in orders.
  (Signed)   Stair.
Aschaffenburg 15 June 1743.

The following is also an extract from Lord Stairs order-book:—

N.B. On June 16th 1743 was fought the Battle of Dettingen.

Marshal Noailles knew on good intelligence that the allies would march on the night of June 15th; he therefore ordered the Duc de Grammont to cross the Main at Seligenstadt with 30,000 men, and to entrench himself at the village of Dettingen, and so block the road of the allied army. De Noailles arranged also to throw 12,000 men into Aschaffenburg directly the allies should leave it. The extraordinary thing is that the allies did not blow up the bridge at Aschaffenburg; but one must suppose that, as they were operating in a friendly country, they did not wish to destroy property and so forth. On the night of the 15th, then, the French General ordered the camp fires to be lit as usual; but it was overdone—such an unusual illumination was seen by the allies that night as to arouse suspicion that the French meant to move.

It was a clear starlight night, and the approach of De Grammont's troops to the river at Seligenstadt was discovered by an allied patrol on the opposite bank, a report being sent to Colonel Gee, who commanded an infantry post beyond the village of Dettingen, that a great number of the enemy had already crossed the bridge, and were on our side of the river. Gee promptly retired with his party, instead of sending in a message and waiting to observe. On daylight appearing, the allies could see the French troops in movement towards Seligenstadt to cross the river.

About 4 a.m. the allied army began its march in two columns west towards Dettingen. The British cavalry at the head of the leading column formed the vanguard; they were followed by Gleichen's Cuirassiers and other Austrian cavalry; next came the British infantry, followed by the Austrians. The rear-guard was composed of the three battalions of Foot Guards, four Hanoverian battalions, and the Hanoverian cavalry. King George had made up his mind that the French would attack our rear, and therefore he had placed the best troops in the rear-guard.

At 5 a.m. the king rode along the line of the Foot Guards, inspecting them. Soon after the march commenced, and it was discovered that the head and not the *rear* of the column was to be attacked; and

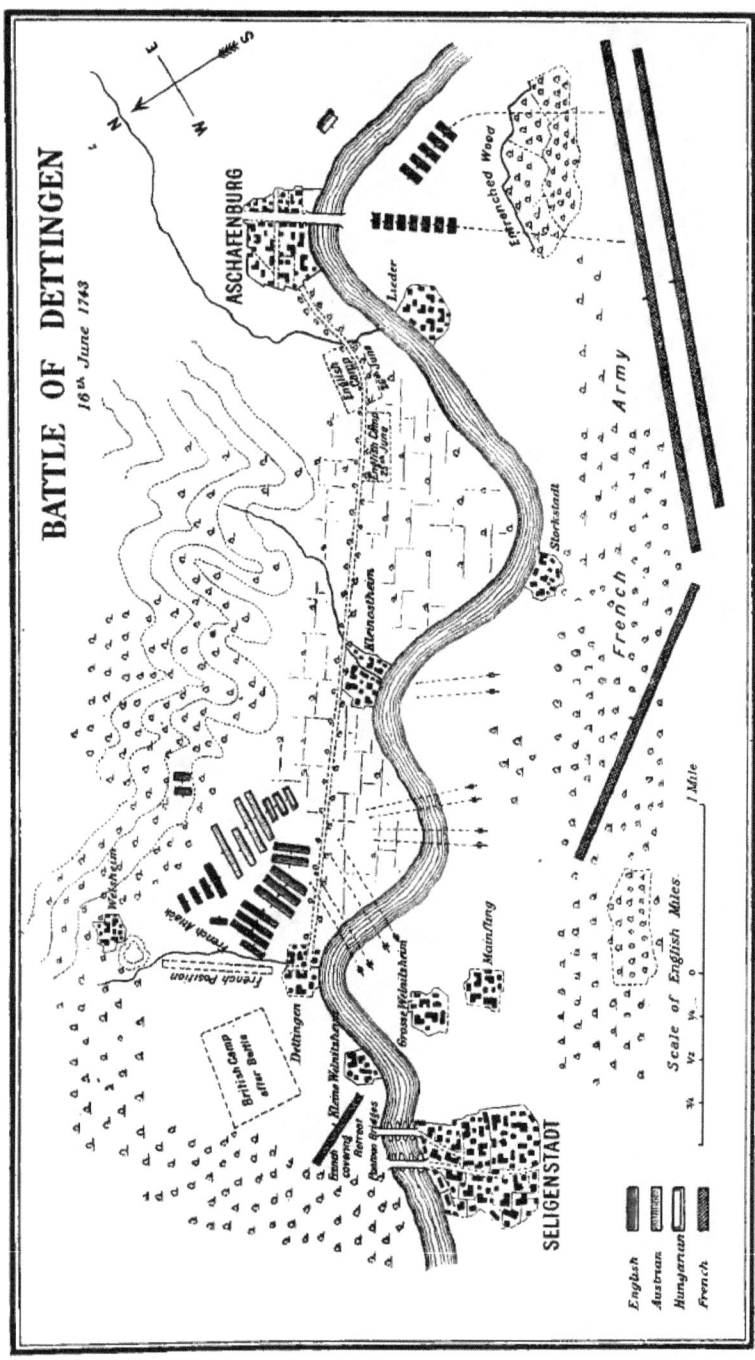

as there was no time to get the Guards to the head of the column, they were sent to occupy a hill on the right flank (north) of the line of march; this hill commanded a secure though narrow line of retreat. General Hilton commanded this detached force established on the hill in question, the force consisting of the Guards Brigade, a Hanoverian brigade, four guns, and twenty-six squadrons of Hanoverian cavalry. These hills are steep and covered with wood.

De Noailles had given ample instructions to De Grammont, and himself remained on the south bank to watch the effect of his artillery fire, from which he expected great things. His officer commanding artillery had placed five batteries on the south side of the river (which dominated the north bank) between Klein Ostheim and Dettingen.

At 7 a.m. the French battery posted at a little chapel west of Stockstadt village opened fire on the British cavalry passing through Klein Ostheim, and the allied artillery began to answer. Townshend says in his *Journal*:

> The generals were raised from their carriages by a severe cannonade!

The fire of the French guns soon put our baggage train into utter confusion and disorder; the drivers made off with their waggons into the woods, where it would seem that everyone, including the peasantry, looted the baggage and made off—nothing is mentioned about the conduct of the escort.

When the fire of the French artillery opened, George II. was at the rear of the column, and we are told the French guns fired continuously in that direction, as the news had gone round that he was there; but the king immediately moved up to the head of the column, riding between the river and the troops, and being cheered by the men as he passed along. On his arrival at the head of the column the French could be seen in position in front, between the villages of Dettingen and Welsheim. Lord Stair rapidly deployed into line and got into battle order; pouches were opened, and orders passed to "examine flints, ammunition, and priming."

The French, formed in two lines, were conspicuous from their gay white uniforms and white standards. On the other side were the red-coated British, with their buff, blue, or white facings, as the case might be; the large cuffs and long-skirted coats, the pale-blue breeches and white gaiters buckled up over the knee; the Guards in their conical grenadier caps, and the line in the three-cornered hats,—every private wore a sword in addition to his bayonet and musket, and every officer and sergeant carried a pike, except in the fusiliers, where the officers carried a light fusil.

Such was Tommy Atkins at Dettingen—a contrast indeed to his descendant in the dirty, stained khaki uniform of the present day! German cavalry in black cuirasses, helmets, and jack-boots; *Uhlans* in blue jackets and red breeches, armed with sabre, lance, and pistol; Hungarian hussars in green and red,—the allied lines at Dettingen must have been a very picturesque sight.

The presence of George II. in his famous red coat greatly animated our troops—the last occasion of the King of England being present in the field in command of a British Army.

James Wolfe, a lad of sixteen, was acting-adjutant of Duroure's Regiment (now the Suffolk), about to undergo his baptism of fire, with George Townshend, afterwards to be his second in command at Quebec in 1759. Townshend was with Lord Dunmore, who commanded the second line of the British; Amherst, who was to be the commander-in-chief in America, was also present. Wolfe, writing to his father, says that our army was drawn up in five lines, two of foot and three of horse, between a wood and the River Main, and Duroure's Regiment was in the centre of the first line; he says also that the French had thrown about 30,000 men across the river, and that we had opposed to them rather more.

The French were in two lines, extending from Dettingen village (which they held, having prepared it for defence), on the bank of the river, to the village of Welsheim, at the foot of the hills. The morning was cloudless, with a hot sun. It was twelve o'clock midday before the allies were ready to begin, and the French artillery across the river were firing all this time, and doing considerable execution (these guns were only 200 or 300 yards from our left flank) in our left wing, which was composed of British and Hanoverians, the Austrians being on the right. The first line of the allies was under General Clayton and the Duke of Cumberland; Lieut.-General Lord Dunmore and Major-General Earl of Rothes were with the second line.

The first line of horse was led by Generals Honeywood, Campbell, Ligonier, and Lord Albemarle; the second line by Generals Cope and Hawley; the British Life Guards, we are told, were on the extreme left.

In the meantime, the Duc de Grammont, the nephew of Marshal Noailles—who, as I have said above, was in command of the 30,000 men holding Dettingen—suddenly, to the general astonishment of the

Dragoons at Dettingen

allies, passed the defile behind which they were posted, and advanced into the small plain where the allies were in order of battle. Marshal Noailles, who had recrossed the Main with all his staff after inspecting De Grammont's position at Dettingen, was thunderstruck to see De Grammont foregoing all the advantages of his position. "Grammont," he exclaimed, "has ruined all my plans!"

This was about noon. Our guns were endeavouring to reply to the French artillery, but were greatly inferior in number and metal, and the continual strain was as much as our young and inexperienced troops could bear. Lord Stair, on seeing the French advancing, instead of remaining on the defensive, ordered his first line of infantry to advance under the Duke of Cumberland.

With regard to De Grammont's mistake I find in Townshend's *Journal*:—

> The Duke de Grammont happily for the British Army quitted his advantageous position, by passing the rivulet and its boggy borders and formed in the plain, leaving all the advantageous features of the ground in his rear.

Advancing halfway to the French position, the allied line was halted to give breath to the men, and after cheering the line advanced again. A French squadron of cavalry, which was in front of the French line of infantry, nearly opposite the left of the allied centre, still retained its position in spite of the advance, and drew the fire of the allied infantry. Wolfe relates to his father in a letter how the men began firing without orders, and thus led to a fire fight commencing before it was intended. However, they soon moved forward, the French advancing also; and the fire became general on both sides. The French Household troops, who were on the right of the French line, pressed forward, keeping up a disordered fire.

About this time King George II. rode down the line, brandishing his sword, and calling out to the British infantry:

> Now, boys, now for the honour of England advance boldly, and the French will soon run.

We are told that this greatly animated the troops, and no doubt it did so; it shows that His Majesty understood how essential it is to give men enthusiasm in action. The king then posted himself with the British infantry of the right wing; and as his horse became unmanageable from the noise of the firing, he dismounted, and continued on foot throughout the action.

The French line began to recede before the continued advance of the allies, and their cavalry were then launched into the fight, to take the pressure off the infantry. The allied cavalry took ground to the left of the allied line. The French cavalry came on boldly, and Bland's Dragoons were ordered by General Clayton to charge. They obeyed the order, but were themselves met by the French *gens d'armes* and utterly routed; and we are told that but for the fire of a battalion of infantry near the river taking the French cavalry in flank, and so stopping their pursuit, Bland's Dragoons, (now 13th Hussars), would have been cut to pieces; they lost forty-one killed and ninety-seven wounded, including one officer killed and nine wounded.

> Our cavalry were repulsed at first by the Maison du Roy, who attacked with great vigour—Townshend.

The battle now resolved itself into a succession of cavalry charges. The Black Mousquetaires, charging across, between the two fires of the opposing infantry, upon Hawley's Dragoons, who were supported by other allied cavalry, were very roughly handled and cut up, and their standard taken by a corporal of Hawley's Dragoons. The Prince de Montbelliard, the Marquis de Merinville, the Chevalier de Reville, and many noble French officers perished in this charge.

Ligonier's Horse, (now 7th Dragoon Guards), and the Kings Regiment, (now King's Dragoon Guards), now swept to the front, charging the French in turn, but were met and overthrown by the French cavalry, Ligonier's Horse losing twenty-one killed and thirty wounded, and Honeywoods eight killed and twenty-eight wounded. The Blues were now launched into the fight, supported by Rich's, (now 4th Hussars), and Cope's, (now 7th Hussars), Dragoons and two regiments of Austrian dragoons. The Blues galloped through the intervals of our infantry, and advanced against the French *gens d'armes*, but did not charge home; and Wolfe (who could see well from the central position of his battalion), in a letter to his father, comments severely on the Blues for using their pistols, and not closing with the enemy.

Altogether the British cavalry did not distinguish themselves, and were the subject of much comment—except Ligonier's Horse, who did splendidly; one reads that the men and horses of our cavalry were raw and untrained, so the result is not to be wondered at. The Blues retired in disorder: and the Grey Mousquetaires, following them, fell on the Scots Fusiliers, some of their men charging right through this battalion, the fusiliers losing thirty-eight killed and fifty-four wounded. Wolfe wrote that only about twenty cut their way through, and that many of the French cavalry were bayoneted by the fusiliers.

> Our cavalry met the enemy's which were formed part in our front, part on our left with an inverted angle, their rear to the river—our cavalry were repulsed at first by the Maison du Roy, who attacked with great vigour being aided by the rest who operated from the aforementioned position on our left—our infantry were just forming when this happened; a great part of the *musquetaires* and *gens d'armes* who pursued a part of our cavalry fell in with some of our British regiments of foot and Austrians and were received with great firmness and so great was the slaughter that they could not penetrate the 2nd Line which was supported by the Scotch Greys, but were obliged to scamper to the left between both lines, the first facing to the right about; they fell between the two fires. Happily, at that instant the French infantry had not been able to arrive to form in time over the plain which was chiefly high corn and on the left they were checked by the Hanoverians and Guards under General Hilton whom His Majesty had detached on the heights to the north to secure a retreat in case of a defeat—Townshend's *Journal.*

Twice after this the allied cavalry charged, and twice they were repulsed; however, they were again rallied and led forward, the French cavalry retiring behind their infantry. It is interesting to note that on the right of the British Brigade in the first line was Pulteney's (now the 13th), then Onslow's (8th), Sowle's (11th), Duroure's (12th or Suffolk), Welsh Fusiliers, and Scots Fusiliers, with Johnson's (33rd) on the left; these English regiments had broken the two lines of French infantry, and now Lord Stair placed himself at their head for a final effort, leading them himself against the third line of the French. Wolfe in a letter thus describes our last advance:—

> The third and last attack was made by the infantry advancing on both sides. We advanced towards each other our men in high spirits and very impatient for fighting, being elated by driving back the French cavalry. The major and I, for we had neither colonel or lieut.-colonel, before the French came near, were employed in begging and ordering the men not to fire at too great a distance, but to keep it till the enemy should come near

us; but to little purpose, the whole fired when they thought they could reach them, which had liked to have ruined us. We did very little execution with it. So soon as the French saw we presented they all fell down, and when we had fired they got up and marched to us in tolerably good order, and gave us a brisk fire which put us into some disorder, and made us give way a little particularly ours, and two or three more regiments who were in the hottest of it. However, we soon rallied again and attacked them with great fury which gained us a complete victory and forced the enemy to retire in great haste."

The third attack, then, was completely successful, and the French gave way on all sides.

> The ill success of the Maison du Roy and some feeble efforts of the French infantry occasioned a retreat before Mareschal de Noailles could attack the rear of the British Army as he proposed, after having passed the Mayne at Aschaffenburg, where the bridge over the river had been most injudiciously left undemolished; had he arrived in time and the Duke de Grammont kept his position as proposed by the French commander-in-chief, the British Army must have been invested. The French Army retired in great confusion, they had but two narrow passes the one near the Mayne the other at the head of the rivulet, near the vineyards at the foot of the hills—whilst they were in this dispersed situation they were to the surprise of everyone suffered to escape unmolested!
> The king halted and the scene of action and military ardour was suddenly turned into a court circle—His Majesty was congratulated by every military courtesan on horseback, on the glorious event—The Hanoverian generals galloped up with their reports—questions innumerable were asked and reports made; the British generals returning lamented the loss of so interesting a crisis, and some of them ineffectually represented upon it, yet the enemy was suffered to quietly repass their bridge over the Mayne! although 6000 Hessians were at Hanau in perfect order for action!—the greatest part of the British Army with great solemnity then passed the rivulet and encamped on the ground to the west of it where the Field Marshal Noailles had left his first position—Townshend's *Journal*.

This account of Townshend's explains clearly the conduct of the mounted arm, which from previous accounts is inexplicable—they were evidently not allowed to pursue!

Thus, ended the Battle of Dettingen: the French had been repulsed and thrown back across the river again, with a loss of 4,000 men killed and wounded; and the allies had lost over 2,000 killed and wounded. General Clayton had been killed by a spent bullet at the end of the battle, whilst riding by himself to give orders to the artillery to play on Seligenstadt bridge. General Monroy, of the Hanoverians, was mortally wounded; the Duke of Cumberland, in his first battle, was wounded in the leg; the Duc d'Aremberg, General Huske, Colonels Ligonier and Ponsonby were also wounded.

The French officers of importance killed and wounded were:— *Killed*: General de Chabannes Mariolles; Brigadier-General Vicomte de Coetlogon, Duc de Rochechouart, Marquis de Vaudevil and de Wargeomont; Messieurs De Pinon, Langeris, Charpentier, Boison, Bourquiran; Colonels Marquis de Sabran, De Fleury, and De Chavigney. *Wounded*: Lieut.-Generals Comte de la Motte Houdoncourt, Duc d'Harcourt, Comte d'Eu, De Cherify, and the Marquis de St. André; Major-Generals Marquis de Montjibault, Maquanes, Comte de Benoron, Duc de Bouffleurs, and Duc d'Ayen, the eldest son of Marshal de Noailles. Brigadier-generals wounded were Marquis de Gant, Messieurs D'Auger, Beaumont, etc.

I found in Townshend's *Diary* that he was near His Majesty George II. in the battle—

When His Majesty stood with great composure under a severe cannonade of the French from several batteries which raked our troops in forming the line.

The allies remained, then, masters of the field, with the empty marks only of a victory. The want of provisions necessitated their marching to Hanau, and most of the baggage had been lost; but I cannot understand why they abandoned their wounded to the mercy of a defeated enemy, marching off in haste at daybreak the next morning; yet this is what actually occurred. They passed the night on the field of battle. The attached list of casualties will show that the number of wounded was not very great; but nothing was done to collect them that night, and no excuse is given. It rained heavily the night after the Battle of Dettingen, and did not cease till eight o'clock the next morning. The sufferings of the wounded were great as they lay in the downpour, and the peasants murdered and plundered freely.

The same night Lord Stair urged that a fresh attack should be made on De Noailles early in the morning, but his advice was rejected. Probably the issue of the battle had been long doubtful, and the superior officers, impressed with the fighting power of the French and the rawness of their own troops, did not care to risk a battle again the next day; at any rate, the army marched for Hanau at daybreak, Lord Stair sending a trumpeter to Marshal Noailles to say that—

> His Britannic Majesty having thought proper to remove to Hanau, he had left an independent company in the field to take care of the wounded, who were strictly ordered to commit no hostilities, that therefore the marshal might send a detachment to bury the slain, and hoped he would treat with humanity those that were left behind.

The French marshal at once sent a body of French cavalry from Aschaffenburg, who removed all the wounded of their own and of the allies to their own hospitals. The French displayed the greatest generosity to our wounded—a very different story to their treatment of our people after Fontenoy, as will be seen.

In Lord Stair's order-book I find on June 17th, 1743:—

> The surgeon's mate of each regiment as have wounded men left behind to attend at Lord Stair's where they will receive their orders. This detachment was sent back to look after the dead and wounded we left behind us.

On the afternoon of June 17th, the allied army reached Hanau, and encamped between that place and Bergen, having joined the 12,000 Hessians and Hanoverians, making the total strength of the army up to 46,000 combatants, still 6,000 inferior to the army of De Noailles, which numbered 52,000.

Extracts from the order-book of Lord Stair after Dettingen:—

> *19th June* 1743. *Hannau Camp.*
> The commanding officers of troops to examine into the state of their troops and to make a return of what men and horses are now fit for service, what condition their arms are in, what camp necessaries they have lost the day of the action and are wanting in each troop. This examination to be made this day and the return to be given in by eight o'clock tomorrow morning to the adjutant.

20th June. Genl. Ligonier's regiment to do duty as a squadron only; Brigadier Bland's regiment to do no duty.

The king having been pleased to give an ox to each squadron of horse and dragoons as well as Life Guards, some men of each regiment are to be sent for them to the market place of Hannau this evening at six.

21 June 1743. Camp Hannau.

Regiments are to complete to 24 rounds a man.

Lt. General Clayton's effects are to be sold by auction at his house at Hannau tomorrow morning at nine o'clock.

Captain Marindin's effects to be sold at the head of General Honeywood's regiment in camp at 12 o'clock.

24 June 1743. Camp Hannau.

Te Deum to be sung next Sunday after prayers at the head of every regiment and all the army to be under arms at six in the evening, the Horse and Dragoons to be on foot, for a *feu de joie* for the victory. The fire to begin by the left of the front line; no cannon to be fired.

24 June 1743. Hannau Camp.

The standards and colours taken at the Battle of Dettingen to be carried immediately to Lord Carteret's quarters where those who have taken them shall receive 100 crowns reward for each.

De Noailles had marched to Offenbach—a town on the south side of the Main, at an equal distance between Hanau and Frankfort—where he encamped, his camp being in full view of the allies; and we are told that there was great dissatisfaction in the allied army that the victory had not been followed up.

Dettingen may be called a great political victory, for the consequences obliged the French to evacuate Germany.

The plan of De Noailles was a good one, and he was a well-tried and skilful general. He could not possibly foresee the blunder of De Grammont, who, ordered to remain in his trenches at Dettingen and hold the head of the defile, left his entrenched position and advanced against the allies in the open!

While the two armies continued facing one another at Hanau and Offenbach, Prince Charles of Lorraine—the brilliant Austrian soldier, who had finished his work in Bavaria, obliging the Duc de Broglie to repass the Rhine—marched with 64,000 Austrians to attack De Noailles in his encampment at Offenbach. De Noailles therefore retreated on the night of July 2nd, blowing up his magazines; he made a rapid march, recrossing the Rhine between Worms and Oppenheim, continued his march into Alsace, and occupied the famous lines of Lauterberg, which were formerly made by the Germans to protect their frontier. The allies did not move a yard from Hanau in pursuit.

Lord Stair now resigned his command; there had been great friction from the moment the king arrived and took over the command, and the old field-marshal, after modestly recapitulating his many services rendered to the British throne, concluded his memorial by adding:

> I hope your Majesty will now give me leave to return to my plough, without any mark of your displeasure.

His resignation was a great loss to the army and to England; he was a man who had possessed the confidence and esteem of the great Duke of Marlborough, and to whose inspection the illustrious Prince Eugene had submitted his military schemes. After his resignation had been refused more than once, Lord Stair was allowed to go on September 4th, and quitted the army in Germany just as it was retiring into winter quarters.

I take the following extract from the orderbook:—

> Camp Worms Wednesday September 4th 1743. This day His Excellency the Field Marshal Earl of Stair resigned his command of the army.

The following extract I take from a letter of young George Townshend's, written home about this time:—

> I really don't know any one thing of the least consequence since the morning after the affair of Dettingen, except dismissing my Lord Stair; if the general's advice had been followed we should have been half way to Paris by now, or had any of the pressing instances he has made against the measures which have been taken, met with the least regard, our armies would not at present have been locked up by an inferior force and defeated army. I could give such an account of the declining condition of our army and interests of Germany as would make the most indifferent person weep, as none more sincerely wishes its prosperity than myself, or is more thoroughly convinced how essential a mutual confidence and affection between the king and nation is, and how melancholy the consequences of our

disagreement must always be; so I would not upon any account aggravate the least circumstance in the description, but to give you my opinion in the most tender manner of this campaign and of the conclusion of it, the more I consider the situation of our armies and the temper of those who direct them, the conduct of the French from our first sight of them, the accounts I learn from the inhabitants of this country and the opinion of people in general, all seem to agree in the verdict inglorious.

In the same letter reference is made to the friction and the bad feeling between the British and Hanoverians. Jealousy and animosity seem to have been the order of the day between the troops of the two nations since the Battle of Dettingen, our people being jealous of the favour shown by King George to the Hanoverians, whom our soldiers regarded as mercenaries only. Apparently, the whole camp was in a flame, the English expressing their resentment deeply and loudly; while the Duke of Marlborough, who commanded the Brigade of Guards, resigned, in consequence of some insolence shown him by a Hanoverian general.

In pursuance of plans arranged between the allies at Hanau, whereby Prince Charles of Lorraine was to cross the Rhine into Upper Alsace, while King George II., at the head of the allied army, followed up De Noailles, the allied army quitted Hanau on August 4th, and, crossing the Rhine on the 27th above Mentz, proceeded to Worms, to await there the arrival of 20,000 Dutch troops under Maurice of Nassau, this junction being formed at Spires on September 25th. The Austrian irregular cavalry did some smart raiding work in Alsace. Although the total of the allies was raised to 70,500 men by the arrival of the Dutch, nothing was done.

The Duc de Noailles retired from the Lauterberg lines into Upper Alsace. Prince Charles of Lorraine was unable to cross the Rhine, so King George's army retired again to Spires, and on October 11th retired farther to Mentz; and soon after this they separated to go into winter quarters. The English, Austrians, and Hanoverians in our pay returned to Flanders, the Dutch to Brabant and Gelderland, and the Hessians and remainder of the Hanoverians into their own country. Our troops reached Ghent and Brussels in the middle of November.

George Townshend then went on leave to Switzerland, visiting on his way the Austrian Army on the Rhine, whither it had pursued the French. From Switzerland, he went by Besançon to Paris; from Paris, he went to The Hague, where he projected the raising of a regiment of two battalions of Irish for the service of the States. Lord Chesterfield warmly approved of the young officer's scheme, as did also the British Government, and it nearly succeeded. No doubt it would have been an excellent thing from a political point of view, but it was defeated by an unexpected interference. George Townshend had stipulated that after him there should be no colonel in future but a native of Ireland, although he was himself an Englishman.

A Scottish gentleman, however, had interest enough to obtain a commission of lieut.-colonel as second in command. Townshend thereupon, determining not to break his word or deviate from the principle of the establishment proposed, abandoned the scheme, after it had received the fullest countenance in England.

In this matter, he would have been better advised, I should say, had he consulted the public good rather than his own particular wishes; it was of the greatest importance to the country to have an Irish regiment, and of little matter if the commandant was English or Scotch or Irish.

The following printed pamphlet I found amongst Townshend's papers giving an account of the battle :—

Relation of the Battle of Dettingen
16.27. June 1743

The king having received certain intelligence that the Marshal de Noailles intended to endeavour to prevent the junction of the Hessian troops, under the command of Prince George of Hesse, and the eight Hanoverian battalions, under that of General Druchleben, to the main body of the army, sent orders Prince George of Hesse and the said general upon their march, to halt at Hanau, and determined to join them with the whole body of the army; Accordingly, on the 15th 26, in the evening, His Majesty gave orders that the army should hold itself in readiness to march the next morning early, and about 4. the troops began to file off in two columns, when the Duke de Noailles perceiving this motion.

He immediately ordered a detachment of his army to march along the Mayn towards Seeligenstadt where the infantry passed that river over two bridges, and the cavalry forded it a little above the said village, with a design to oppose with all its force the junction of our army; The artillery of the French Army forming the *arriere-garde*; and as soon as it was in reach of annoying our army, it begun to play upon

LOSSES OF THE ALLIES AT BATTLE OF DETTINGEN.

	Regiments.	Officers killed.	Officers wounded.	Men killed.	Men wounded.	Remarks.
Horse:						
	3rd troop of Guards	. .	Lt.-Col. Lamoloniere, Major Jackson, Lt. Willes	1	2	
	4th ditto	. .		2	2	
	and troop Grenadiers Horse	. .		3	3	
	Royal Blues	. .	Lt. Elliot.	8	11	
	Honeywood's	Capt. Meriden, Lt. Draper, Cornet Aldcroft	Cornet Davies	8	28	
	Ligonier's	Quartermaster Jackson	Maj. Carr, Capt. Sawrine, Capt. Smithy, Lt. Wallis Lieut.-Col. Ligonier, Capt. Stewart, Capt. Robinson, Lieut. Cholmondeley, and Cornet Richardson			
	Hawley's	Lt. ——	Lt. Preston	21	30	
	Scotch Greys			. .	. .	
	Bland's		Major Honeywood, Captain Brown, Lieut. Robinson, Cornets Monteith, Dawson, and O'Carrol—three Quartermasters	. .	. .	
Dragoons.	Rich's	. .		41	97	
	Stair's	. .		4	6	
	Cope's	. .		2	1	
	Howard's	Lt. Falconer, Cornet Hobey	Lt. Frazer, Cornet St. Leger —one Quartermaster	2	15	
	Onslow's	Maj. Barry	Lt.-Col. Keightley, Lt. Robinson.	3	3	
	Sowle's	. .	Maj. Greenwood and Capt. Lee	6	20	
	Duroure's	Capt. Phillips, Lt. Monroe	Capt. Campbell, Lt. Williams, and Ensign Townshend	11	28	
Infantry	Pulteney's	. .	Ensigns O'Grilby and Gray	26	65	
	Bligh's	. .		29	29	
	Scotch Fusiliers	Lt. Younge	Lt. Livingstone	1	1	
	Welsh		Col. Piers, Lt. Price	38	54	
	Handside's	. .	Brigadier Huske	15	27	
	Huske's	. .		. .	3	
	Johnson's	Capt. George Campbell, Lts. Strangeways, Maxwell, and Fletcher		. .	. .	
	Ponsonby's	. .	Capt. Debays	26	50	
	Artillery	. .		4	15	
	Austrians	. .		5	8	
	Hanoverians			307	643	
		8	19	170	347	
		7	—	—	—	
	Officers killed	30	Officers wounded 79	725	1488	Grand total, killed and wounded, 2322

us about half an hour past ten in the morning, and took us in flank. This fire lasted near two hours, and though we erected some batteries in order to silence those of the enemy, yet they did not discontinue firing, notwithstanding which our army continued its march, and by perseverance arrived in a little wood, behind which the French Army was ranged in order of battle.

Their right wing was covered by the Mayn, and supported by a battery erected near Maynfling on the other side of the river. The left extended itself towards the hills, and had behind it a little rivulet and the village of Dettingen. The French Army amounting to near 30000. men, was drawn up in two lines and an *arriere-garde*; It was commanded by the Duke de Noailles; The Duke de Chartres, and several other princes of the blood were present, and the Household troops made the centre, supported by the infantry.

The king, having given his orders to the respective generals of the army with the greatest calmness and resolution, placed himself, on the right wing, at the head of the British infantry, on foot, sword in hand. Our army drew up in order of battle, as well as it could, in the wood, and extended itself as far to the front of the enemy as the ground would allow of.

On the right of our army, at the entrance of the wood, the Hanoverians, erected a battery, which flanked the enemy, and did great service in the heat of the action; Another was erected by the English, on the left, and a third, by the Austrians, in the centre.

Such were the dispositions of die two armys, till about 12 o'clock, when, the army was advancing to charge the enemy, the troops of the French Kings Household attacked with great vigour our centre, which gave way a little but soon rallyed, repulsed them, and drove them before them 'till they beat them out of the field.

I send enclosed a list of the prisoners, many of whom are officers and persons of quality; a great number were killed and wounded, and some standards and colours taken; and a (2) list of people of consequence dead and wounded in the French camp, and after this defeat, the French Army, perceiving themselves attacked on all sides, quitted the field of battle, passed the rivulet behind them, posted themselves *en front de bandiere* upon an eminence commanding the plain, and notwithstanding this advantageous disposition, upon our troops marching towards them with resolution and in order, they abandoned that post, retired to Klein-Welsheim, and at last retreated in great disorder towards the village of Seeligenstadt, passed the Mayn with precipitation and confusion, several were drowned, and a great many died of their wounds in the pursuit; the great number of the killed, that were found dispersed on all sides, shews that their loss must be considerable, and it is computed to be about 4000, killed, wounded, drowned, and taken prisoners.

On our side, our loss is computed near 1500, killed and wounded; Among the first, Lieutenant-General Clayton, who was killed on the spot, equally regretted, by the king's officers and soldiers; among the last His Royal Highness the Duke of Cumberland, commanding with great bravery at his post of major general, received a musket ball through the leg, the Duke d'Aremberg another in the breast, but neither of the wounds are thought dangerous; Colonel Peers received a dangerous shot in the throat; Major General Monroy and his son had each a leg shot off by the same cannon ball, but none of the three are despaired of; Brigadier Huske was also shot in the foot, which, tho it broke the bone, is not thought dangerous.

As all these prisoners, whom we have sent back from the several corps, have been treated with all the humanity the circumstances would admit, so we must do the justice to the Marshal de Noailles that he has proceeded in the same manner, having taken the utmost care of all that fell into his hands.

This is the most authentick account that hitherto can be got.

LIST OF PRISONERS WHO FELL INTO THE HANDS OF THE ENGLISCH,

and have been sent back to Marshal de Noailles by His Majesty's Order.

Monsr. de Montgibaut, Marechal de Camp, Commandant la Compagnie d'Harcourt.

Monsr. de la Sale, Aide Major des Mousquetaires du Roy, Maitre de Camp de Cavalerie.

Monsr. de Chavoisi, Marechal de Logis des Mousquetaires, Maitre de Camp de la Cavalerie.

Monsr. de Thesy, Marechal de Logis des Mousquetaires, Maitre de Camp de Cavalerie.

Monsr. Bouillant } Sous Brigadiers des Mousquetaires.
„   du Fou

Monsr. de Vesin
," de Girardote de Malassy ⎫
," de Girardote la Sale
," de Gressy
," de Quesnay
," de la Fouchas
," Dupleissis
," d'Oleau
," de Varenne
," de la Gravene
," le Chevalier de Serteuil
," le Chevalier le Blanc
," d'Alberti } Mousquetaires.
," le Chevalier de Fenelon
," de Prunelle
," de Gascœn
," de Grave
," de Bailli
," de St. Aubin
," St. Cyre
," d'Erard
," de Tarnay
," de Suze
," de Redon ⎭

Un Tambour des Mousqetaires
Monsr. le Prince de Montbelliard.
," de la Pauperdiere, Mousquetaire noir.
," d'Orville, Sous Brigadier des Mousquetaires gris
," de Moubyon ⎱ Gens d'Armes.
," le Chevalier de Reville ⎰
," de Paniot, Brigadier des Chevaux legers.
," Bousons, Chevaux legers.
," de la Veille Ferte, Aide Major des Chevaux legers.

Monsr. de Brevons ⎫
," d'Epinoy
," de Breredan
," de Cochard } Chevaux Legers.
," le Chevalier de Fouchares
," d'Estreville
," d'Orville
," de Mouseur ⎭

Monsr. de Voine, Exempt des Gardes de Corps.
," du Lyon, Brigadier des Gardes du Roy.

Monsr. le Coq de la Vallée ⎫
," Perrin
," de la Mare
," de Bouhan
," de Clozel
," de Bois la Ville
," de Kerkessée } Gardes du Corps.
," de Montrail
," de Bois
," de la Merité
," de Formanville
," de Beauchambre ⎭

Monsr. de Rozé, Gardes du Corps.
   ,, de l'Enclos, Brigadier des Gardes du Corps.
Monsr. Ythier, Exempt des Gardes du Corps.
   ,, Bertran
   ,, de Hautolle
   ,, de Boisneux
   ,, Montamy   } Gardes du Corps.
   ,, Seaux
   ,, Boislonar
Monsr. de Chavagnac, Brigadier des Gardes du Corps.
   ,, le Marquis de Mirenville Guidon des Grenadiers de la Garde.
Monsr. de Montaign, Capitaine de Cavalerie.

                                      (Signé) Montgibaut.

Monsr. de Combes, Mestre de Camp, & Lieutenant des Grenadiers à
                                      Cheval.
   ,, de Vesan, Aide-Major en Chef de la Compagnie des Chevaux
                                   legers de la Garde.
   ,, de Mesmey, Capitaine du Regiment de Rohan Infanterie.
   ,, le Chevalier des Fontaines, Aide-Major des Chevaux legers.

LIST OF THE DEAD AND WOUNDED IN THE FRENCH ARMY

The Prince de Dombes wounded in the Thigh.
Monsr. le Duc de Boufleurs wounded in the Neck.
Monsr. de Sabran Colonel of Condè, his Thigh shot off, and since
                                       dead.
Le Petit de Boufleurs, his Thigh shot off.
Monsr. le Duc Rochechouart Colonel, Capitain of Grenadiers and
                                       Major, killed.
The Duc d'Harcourt   } dangerously wounded.
Monsr. Duchatel
Three Marshals de Camp missing.
Colonels de Montgiboult
       Chatenmaville   } killed.
       de Chavigni
       de Chatelet
Monsr. de Lambilli, Captain of the French Guards dangerously
   wounded ; and his Brother Lieutenant-Major killed.
   ,, de Rosting, First Captain of the Grenadiers of the King, both
      his Thighs shot off.
   ,, de Custine Colonel d'Hainaut   } wounded in the Jaw.
   ,, de Chabot
   ,, le Duc d'Eu, slightly wounded.
   ,, de Voubecourt, Colonel of Dauphinè wounded in the hand.
   ,, le Duc d'Ayen wounded in the Belly.
   ,, du Chaila received two Wounds in the Body.
   ,, de Beuvront, Major-General, wounded.
And several others of Distinction, as also many Officiers, and others of the Kings Household, killed, wounded, and missing.

LIST OF PRISONERS WHO FELL INTO THE HANDS OF THE AUSTRIANS, AND WHO HAVE BEEN SENT BACK BY THE D. D'AREMBERG

Monsr. le Marquis de Marignan, Marechal de Camp de Chevaux legers.
Le Marquis de la Vieuxville, Capitaine au Regiment de Noailles Cavalerie.
De Corcocal } Chevaux legers.
De Guislain }
Le Chevaliers de Vuilles } Mousquetaires.
Dorias }
De Marivat, Colonel-Lieutenant dans le Maitre de Camp de Noailles.
Dumont, Brigadier de la Lieutenance Colonel.
De Fricamps, Lieutenant au Regiment de Mortemar.

LIST OF PRISONERS WHO FELL INTO THE HANDS OF THE AUSTRIANS AND WHO HAVE BEEN SENT BACK BY MARSHAL NEIPPERG

Fait par le Regiment de Heister.
Alexandre du Regim. de Noaille Inf. de la Comp. de Massau.

Sans Soucy	Rouen. Inf.	de Dreux.
Va de bon Cœur	Turraine	Coussy.
Sans Chagrin	Chartres. Inf.	Flamain.
St. Jean	Rouen. Infant.	Menard.
La Rofé	Chartres. Infant.	du Roux.

Fait par le Regiment de Priè.

Jean Soucy	Condè	Collonelle.
Belle Cour	Vexin	Remont.
Lionnois	Dauphiné	Grenfac.

Consignes par les Hanoveriens.

| St. Marcelle | Pentievre Inf. | Lazerèes. |
| Sans Soucy | Rouen | Vignacourt. |

Fait par Wolfenbuttle.

| La Violette | d'Eux | du Plantin. |

St. Claud Valet dans le Regiment d'Artillerie.

Par les Compagnies Franches.

| St. Pierre | Royal Marine | du Vergier. |
| Olivier | Ditto | Ditto. |

Par le Regiment de Ligne Infanterie.

L'Arriez	Gardes Françoises	Bauloirant.
La Douceur	de la Marche	Boune.
Jolicœur	Tourraine	Maillard.
La Joïe	Chartres	Fertier.

19. Hommes.

Certifiè par sans Fouci de la Compagnie, Colonelle au Regiment de Condè Infanterie, & par Maturin Olivier de la Compagnie de du Vergier du Regiment Royal Marine.

Les Officiers & Gens de Dinstinction ont été envoyés le jours même de l'Action à S. A. Monseigneur le Duc d'Arenberg.

Wagenbucken, le 4 Juillet 1743.

List of French Standards Taken

1. A White Standard finely embroidered with Gold & Silver, a Thunderbolt in the middle, upon a Blue & White Ground.
    Motto. sensère Gigantes.
    NB. Both sides the same.
2. A Red Standard. 2. Hands with a Sword, & with a Laurel Wreath & Imperial Crown at Top.
    Motto. Incorrupta Fides & Avita Virtus.
    On the other side, the sun.
    Motto. Nec pluribus impar.
3. A Yellow Standard, embroidered with Gold & Silver. The sun in the Middle.
    No Motto.
4. A Green Ditto in the Same way.
5. The Mast of Another tore off, but appears to have been Red.
6. A White Standard, embroidered with Gold & Silver. In the Middle a Bunch of Nine Arrows tyed with a Wreath; All stained with Blood; The Launce broke; The Cornet killed without falling, being buckled behind to his Horse, and his Standard buckled to Him.
    Motto. Alterius Jovis altera Tela.
    NB. This Standard belonged to the Musquetaires Noirs, & was taken by a Serjeant of Lieutenant-General Hawley's, of the Right Squadron of the whole Line.

The aspect of affairs after the victory of Dettingen showed beyond doubt that England was equal to the task that she had undertaken. The real menace of the French to Europe was clearly exposed; the charge of quixotism by the Opposition party in Parliament against the Government was disposed of, and as the commencement of the war was vindicated, so the counsels of that great man the Earl of Stair, had they been followed, would have secured equal approbation for its close. But, as if Fortune had attached herself alone to his sword and Wisdom to his counsels, from the moment he left the army its affairs went backwards.

Field-Marshal Wade was appointed as Commander-in-Chief of our forces in Flanders in succession to Lord Stair. The Ministry thought that Wade would render greater deference to the Ministerial views than his predecessor could prevail upon himself at all times to pay. The Army destined to invade Flanders (for the French had decided to turn their arms on to the Low Countries in the next campaign) was concentrated in the neighbourhood of Lille, the capital of the French Netherlands, and numbered 120,000 men and 260 guns. Marshal Noailles had been superseded by Maurice, Comte de Saxe, "the first soldier of the age," though it is interesting to note that Napoleon did not think much of Saxe.

★★★★★★

Maurice Herman, Comte de Saxe, Marshal of France, born at Gotzlar, in Saxony, in 1696, and died at the Château de Chambord, November 30th, 1750. He was an illegitimate son of the Elector of Saxony, afterwards King of Poland under the title of Augustus II., and of the Comtesse Aurora of Koenigsmarck. Thanks to her beauty and imperious will, she captivated for some years this dissolute prince and made him recognise her son, and Maurice of Saxe was made a soldier.

★★★★★★

Marshal Wade, whose chief exploits seem to have been making roads and bridges in the Scottish Highlands, had under his command 22,000 British, 16,000 Hanoverians, 18,000 Austrians, and 20,000 Dutch—about 76,000 men.

Count Maurice of Nassau commanded the Dutch, and the Duc d'Aremberg the Austrians. Wade and the other generals imagined themselves too weak to attack the French, and waited for further reinforcements, whilst the French overran the country at their pleasure. The French, after taking Courtrai, were allowed to take Menin and Ypres successively; whilst Wade, instead of stopping them on the Lys, thought himself lucky in being covered by the Scheldt. Even then the Marshal did not think himself secure, for he sent away his plate to remain in safety with his guns at Antwerp. And thus, the first blow was given to the spirit of our army.

The difference in numbers which furnished Marshal Wade with the pretence for conduct which dispirited his troops was soon removed. He was reinforced by 18,000 Dutch under Ginkel, which brought the strength of the allies up to 90,000 on paper; and the French Army was reduced by detachments sent off to Alsace to fight Prince Charles of Lorraine, who with 70,000 men had crossed the Rhine and was in the lines of Lauterberg. Notwithstanding, however, the increase of numbers, our army still stuck to its camp on the Scheldt, until Wade was compelled by orders from England to quit it—orders which rebuked the disgrace of remaining so long idle with a superior army which could make him indisputably master of the field, while Saxe maintained himself in the heart of the country with an army little more than half the number of the allies.

Under compulsion then Wade advanced on July 20th, and after much painful marching the allies got into the enemy's country, where the commander-in-chief gave them a specimen of his military genius in his judicious manner of encamping; and all expectations of battle were only raised to be disappointed.

The allies advanced towards Helchin, and entrenched themselves between Hauterive and Avelghem, where Wade held a council of war on July 24th, in which it was held to be unadvisable to attack the French, owing to their advantageous position. It was resolved to try and make a diversion by entering the French Netherlands, and, by investing one of their fortified towns, to draw Saxe thither. Accordingly, the allies shifted their quarters, and on July 30th encamped four miles from Lille, where they foraged unmolested for several days. Count Saxe did not even trouble to move from his position behind the Lys, and contented himself with throwing reinforcements into Lille.

Generals Ligonier and Somerfeldt, moved to indignation at our scandalous inaction, were daily urging Wade to fight. They offered to take Maubeuge and Landrecy, two places of the greatest importance, opening a road into France, and they asked for twenty battalions and thirty squadrons to do it. Another plan they urged was to attack Saxe behind the Lys. Either of these plans was sound, the latter perhaps the better of the two; but Wade, always anxious to curry favour with the Ministry at home, became penurious in his economy, and refused the money to get horses to draw the siege guns required until the Dutch agreed to share half the expenses.

He objected to spend the £60,000 required for the horses, although Ligonier and Somerfeldt themselves offered to contribute £9,000. Wade would have nothing to do with their generous offer, and rested his merit on his parsimony, having no other merit to plead. But that did not avail him either, for he squandered the whole expenses of the year by applying them to no purpose; and not prodigal of money only, he squandered time, which, in war, is of all losses the most difficult to be repaired.

The French cavalry raids became bolder and bolder, and in one of them the old marshal was nearly carried off from his quarters; and they only discontinued, I suppose, on recognising that such an enterprise, if successful, would have been prejudicial to themselves.

On September 12th, the Austrian and Dutch commanders proposed to Wade to march back north again to Ghent, where they could get forage easily, resting their right flank on the Lys and their left on the Scheldt. Wade did not agree to this, saying it would end the campaign; however, the Dutch and Austrian commanders then informed him that they intended to march, which they accordingly did, leaving Wade to follow and retire into winter quarters.

A campaign so glaringly mismanaged obliged the commanders, who could not vindicate it from blame, to throw it on each other. Their recriminations succeeded, if their apologies did not; for everyone was convinced that they were all of them at fault and all of them utterly useless. Already the British laurels of Dettingen had begun to wither. The minister who directed this inglorious campaign was thrown from power; Marshal Wade, who conducted it, was recalled, and laid by in England to recruit a fresh stock of vigour for subsequent occasions, as we shall see a year or so after this, when at a most critical juncture—*viz*. the Rebellion of 1745—Wade was brought out of the infirmary and placed at the head of the army at home; and, as if all remembrance had been lost of his behaviour in Flanders against the French, he was picked out to save the nation from the rebels. The same cause produced the same effect; but in the north of England he was destined to become the dupe of the local militia instead of Marshal Saxe.

Fontenoy 1745

As Wade, who was old and had seen service, had succeeded so badly, the British Ministry had hopes, it may be supposed, in opposite qualities, as if from age and experience mismanagement had proceeded, and not from a want of capacity, which no age or experience could have improved. Therefore, the Duke of Cumberland, to whom with no degree of justice these objections could be made—for he was as young in years as in experience—was selected to succeed Wade.

On April 10th, 1745, the Duke of Cumberland arrived at Brussels, and took over the supreme command of the allied army, which he found in a high state of order and discipline. Saxe was engaged at the time in besieging Tournay, one of the keys of Flanders, a town on the river Scheldt, twenty-one miles west of Mons; he was pressing the siege with vigour, and the arrival of Louis XV. greatly stimulated the enthusiasm of the French troops.

The Duke of Cumberland was just entering the twenty-fourth year of his age, and he had plenty of personal courage. His army mustered 53,000 combatants, made up of 21,000 British, 8,000 village of Anthoin, on the west; his centre at the village of Fontenoy; his left wing was covered by the wood of Barri, extending nearly as far east as the villages of Gaurain and Ramecroix: there is a gentle eminence in the middle of the French position called Notre Dame de la Justice.

The villages of Fontenoy and Anthoin he had put in a thorough state of defence, entrenched and barricaded, the whole position being plentifully garnished with batteries and redoubts, and there was a large redoubt at the point of Barri Wood (see plan), and an entrenched camp on the above-mentioned eminence Notre Dame de la Justice.

The allies had to ascend a gradual slope, on the crest of which were the French—"entrenched up to their necks," one reads; but, on viewing the ground, I find this deep trench mentioned by writers was simply a hollow road, which runs from east to west along the French position, and which the French utilised.

Anthoin was occupied by the brigade of Piedmont, supported by Crillon's brigade.

The brigade of Beltens extended from Anthoin to Fontenoy, about half a mile; then came the brigade of Aubetone; then four battalions of French and two of Swiss Guards.

The 5th and 6th battalions of French Guards and the 3rd Swiss Guards were entrenched at the bridge thrown over the Scheldt.

The Irish Brigade (consisting of Bulkeley's, Clare's, Dillon's, Ruth's, Berwick's, and Salby's regiments) and two battalions of Swiss Guards were north of the wood of Barri.

The brigade of Vaisseaux held Ramecroix, and behind them was the battalion of Angoumois in the chateau of Bourquembray.

The brigades of Normandy and Royal were entrenched at Ruvignies.

Count Lowendahl, with the Auvergne brigade and three battalions of the regiment of Touraine and thirteen squadrons of horse and dragoons, was between the village of Ruvignies and Mont Trinité.

The infantry of the centre was supported by two lines of horse, the first consisting of six and the second of five regiments. The Royal regiment of *Carabiniers* was in reserve behind Leuse; the Household Cavalry, thirteen squadrons, were behind the *carabiniers*.

A battalion of D'Eu's regiment occupied the two redoubts of Barri Wood.

On viewing the terrain, one is struck by the admirable nature of the position taken up by Saxe. Curving convexly towards the allies, it displays a gradual and easy slope, so as to give a grazing fire for his 200 guns. There were no houses or trees in the interior of his position to impede communications; while to the north, to conceal and shelter his reserves, were slopes descending to the Scheldt, which to all intents and purposes is a large canal of, say, thirty yards broad. The great defect in his position was that, in case of defeat, Saxe's army would have been driven into the Scheldt.

The hamlet of Vezon, with its orchards and gardens and thick trees in the ravine in front of the French position (see plan), would break up all formation of the allies advancing, and a rivulet also runs through this hamlet. We shall, however, see afterwards that this ravine, sheltered as it was in some measure from the French artillery fire, enabled the repulsed and disordered battalions of the allies to reform.

1st Foot Guards at Fontenoy

The wood of Barri is a very large one, and was a serious drawback to Saxe; it was too large to occupy, and the allies could form their battalions for attack behind it (south). Saxe therefore took up a position in rear, treating the wood as a defile, and defending the exit—quite according to modern ideas. For this purpose, he established two redoubts to guard the exits, and planted the wood thickly with skirmishers.

Fontenoy now (and it is very little altered since 1745), like most villages in Flanders, is a large hamlet of white cottages, with the red-tiled roofs characteristic of Flanders. The church, a very old one, with its quaint tower, surrounded by the usual walled enclosure, from 3 feet 6 inches to 4 feet high, forms a natural *réduit*, and must have been the landmark for the British line to march on. The environs consist of the usual clusters of gardens and hedges.

Looking south from the village of Fontenoy, I identified Baugnies and South Baugnies, where the allies were encamped before the battle; also, the village of Moubray, from which the Dutch infantry advanced to assault Fontenoy and Anthoin, and I am not surprised at their repulse; it is all very well to blame the Dutch, but the villages of Fontenoy and Anthoin were too strongly fortified to be carried by direct assault unprepared by artillery bombardment. The village of Vezon is about 1,200 yards to the south of Fontenoy, in the valley or depression, with its numerous enclosures, trees, and orchards, its tall church steeple making an excellent landmark.

My impression was, that Saxe had taken up an *excellent* position, even in accordance with modern requirements; its weak point was the wood of Barri, which the Duke of Cumberland should have utilised; and I could not understand, in going over the country here, why the duke had not marched to relieve Tournay over the country *east* of the main road from Ath to Tournay, where the terrain was much more favourable, and thus compelling Saxe to quit his chosen and prepared position. Frederick the Great would have executed his famous flank movement, and attacked Saxe from the east. It is interesting to note that Napoleon had no great opinion of Marshal Saxe:—

> *Le Maréchal de Saxe fait voir comme la France était alors pauvre en bons généraux. Je ne lui connais que Lawfeld et Fontenoy. Un bon général n'est pas un homme commun. Saxe, Luxembourg sont de second ordre. Saxe n'était pas un aigle mais il avait du caractère et se faisait obéir.*

The Duke of Cumberland, on his arrival at Baugnies and Moubray,

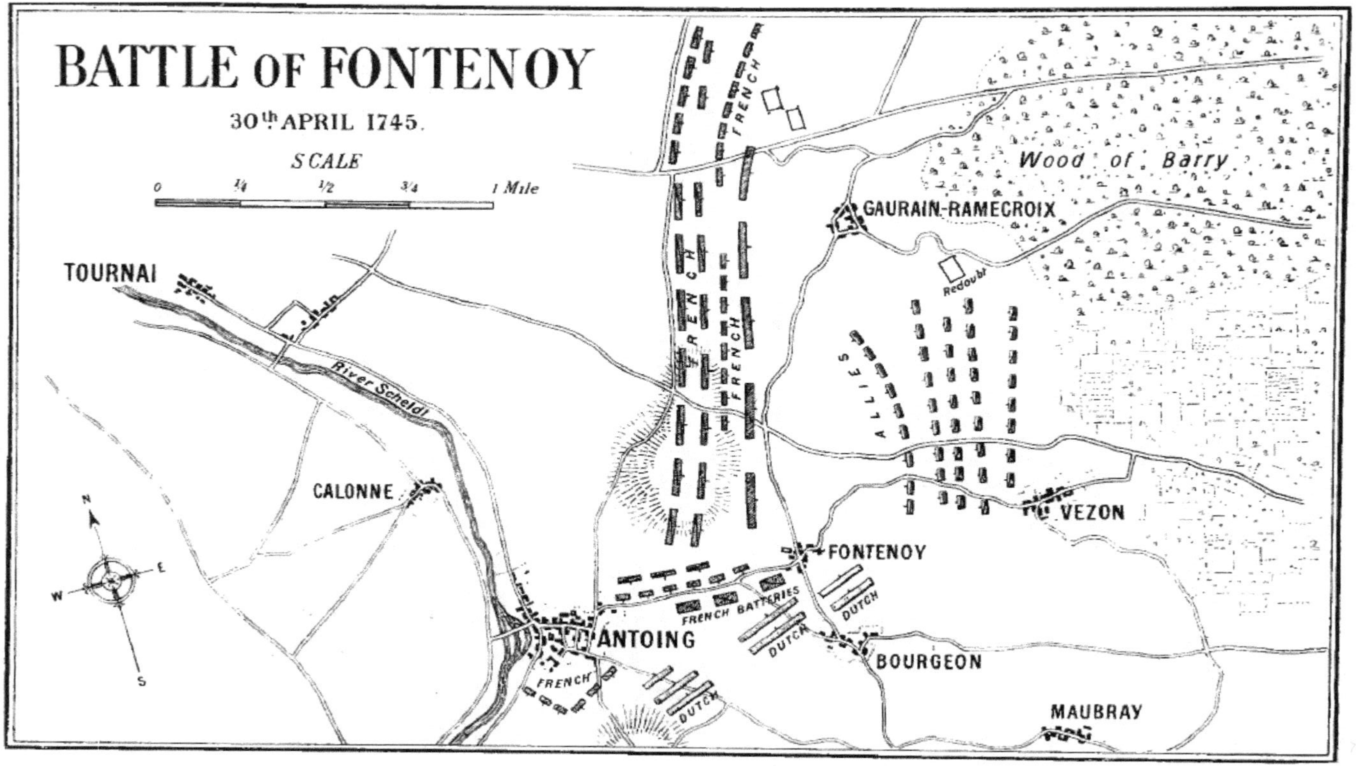
BATTLE OF FONTENOY
30th APRIL 1745.
SCALE
0
1/4
1/2
3/4
1 Mile
TOURNAI
River Scheldt
CALONNE
N
E
S
W
FRENCH
FRENCH
FRENCH
FRENCH
GAURAIN-RAMECROIX
Wood of Barry
Redoubt
ALLIES
VEZON
FONTENOY
DUTCH
DUTCH
DUTCH
FRENCH BATTERIES
ANTOING
FRENCH
BOURGEON
MAUBRAY

had formed the allied army in two lines in order of battle, with cavalry on both flanks and infantry in the centre.

First line. The three battalions of Foot Guards, forming the first brigade, under General Churchill, were on the right of the line. Ponsonby's and Onslow's brigades came next. The Hanoverians were on the left.

On the extreme left were the Dutch and a few Austrians (2,000 men). The British cavalry was on the extreme right.

Second line. The British brigades of Howard's (in rear of the Guards), Bland's, and Skelton's.

Brigadier Ingoldsby, with two battalions (*viz.* Duroure's and Pulteney's regiments), was echeloned on the right for a special object.

Two days were spent by the Duke of Cumberland in reconnoitring the French position, whilst Saxe took advantage of the delay and completed his entrenchments. The result of the reconnaissance was, that the allied generals were eager to attack, but Marshal Koenigseck, the Austrian general, urged caution.

On April 29th six battalions and twelve squadrons drove in the French outposts, the French retiring to their main position on the plateau of Fontenoy.

With reference to this reconnaissance, I find the following in the Duke of Cumberland's orderbook:—

Camp Château Buffoel 29 April 1745.
Six battalions and 12 squadrons from the right wing are to parade at 10 o'clock with 500 Pioneers with their arms and waggons and tools at the head of Duroure's regiment, with six 3 pounders and 2 *hawbitzers*. Lt. Genl. Campbell commands this detachment, with Major Genl. the Earl of Albemarle and Brigadier Roseleger and Earl Crawfurd. The 1st battalion of Guards, Howard's, (the Buffs), Onslow's, (8th King's, the Liverpool Regiment), and Sowle's, (11th, Devonshire Regiment), compose the battalions.

The reconnaissance was a most imperfect one. It is said that General Campbell suggested that the wood of Barri should be occupied (it was unoccupied by the French at the time); this was not done, and the next day it was full of French skirmishers.

The Duke of Cumberland decided on a costly frontal attack. Prince Waldeck, with his Dutch troops, was to undertake the carry-

1ST FOOT GUARDS AT FONTENOY

ing of Anthoin and Fontenoy. Brigadier Ingoldsby was to carry the redoubt d'Eu, at the edge of Barri Wood. General Ligonier, with the British and Hanoverians, was to assault the French main and centre position between Fontenoy and the wood of Barri, covered by the British cavalry on the right flank under General Campbell.

After Orders

The army to be ready to march tomorrow morning one hour before day. No tents to be struck, and as few men as possible to be left to take care of the tents and the baggage.

Two o'clock struck at Anthoin Church as the allies moved forward in two columns; it was still quite dark; the infantry, in heavy marching order, stumbled over hedges and ditches, and the troops formed up in battle order in the small plain where the afternoon before the French outposts had been driven in. The British and Hanoverians formed in four lines before the village of Vezon. The yellow-coated Dutch and the Austrian contingent were drawn up in two lines, extending to the left (west) as far as the wood of Peronne. Ingoldsby had orders to carry the redoubt d'Eu, at the edge of the wood of Barri and north of the village of Vezon; he was given two extra battalions (the 42nd and a Hanoverian battalion) in addition to the three he had already. As soon as Fontenoy was in the hands of the Dutch, and Ingoldsby had got the redoubt d'Eu, Ligonier was to assault the French entrenchments between Fontenoy and the wood of Barri.

About four o'clock the French artillery opened fire ("the French kept up a brisk artillery fire, which did a great execution "). General Sir James Campbell, commanding the cavalry—a veteran of Marlborough's wars—was knocked over and killed by a round-shot quite at the commencement of the action. Owing to his death, we are told the cavalry did not carry out the orders assigned to them.

Ligonier, a cool and able officer (who afterwards saved the British from destruction at Laffeldt, as we shall see), formed his two lines of British infantry under a heavy artillery fire, the duke ordering up seven guns to take the fire off them, and by 4.30 a.m. the artillery fire was general on both sides. About this time the Duc de Grammont, who at Dettingen committed the error which lost the French the battle, was mortally wounded by a round-shot. At 9 a.m. General Ligonier sent an *aide-de-camp* to the duke to say that he had been delayed by the enclosures and orchards of Vezon, but that he was now ready to attack as soon as Prince Waldeck should advance against Fontenoy.

The Dutch were then ordered to advance against Anthoin and Fontenoy, and Ingoldsby to carry the redoubt d'Eu. He advanced, however, very slowly and with no dash; and on being received by a biting fire from Barri Wood, garnished with French skirmishers, he fell back to a hollow way and sent for artillery. The Duke of Cumberland, finding that Ingoldsby made no progress, galloped across to him in a great rage, and, addressing him in very heated terms, ordered him to advance, and reinforced him with three guns. Meanwhile, the Dutch had been repulsed at Fontenoy and Anthoin villages, and with heavy losses were falling back in disorder. They had reached the first entrenchments, where they were enfiladed by a 25-gun battery firing case- and chain-shot into their dense columns, and the result was a retirement in great confusion.

Ingoldsby, notwithstanding his three guns, did not go on. Jeffrey Amherst (the future Lord Amherst of Montreal and Louisbourg fame), then an *aide-de-camp* to General Ligonier, galloped to Ingoldsby with a message from Ligonier to know what he was doing and why he did not go on. He answered that he was carrying out the commander-in-chief's orders—*viz.* to advance when the main body pushed forward, and not till then.

The Duke of Cumberland, in a rage at the failure of the Dutch to take Fontenoy, swore that he would carry the position, cost what it might. He put himself at the head of the British and Hanoverians, with Ligonier, and advanced to assault the French entrenchments between Fontenoy and the redoubt d'Eu. It was now about 10 a.m. The French kept up a terrible artillery fire on them, making whole lanes through the English, who advanced in the most steady and determined manner in spite of loss and necessary disorder, and actually reserved their fire till thirty paces from the French, although being fired into on all sides.

The power to restrain the men from firing back when under such a heavy fire and so close gives an idea of what the discipline must have been; such a thing would be impossible in our days. The British advance was not to be denied. The French began to retire; their guns on the crest of the eminence were in danger, the four battalions of French Guards advanced to the crest-line to save the guns, and the British and French brigades of Guards found themselves only fifty paces apart. At this conjuncture, there occurred an incident which has become famous in history. Lord Hay, of the 1st Foot Guards (Grenadier Guards), asked the French Guards to fire first, but the Comte d'Anterroche replied that the French Guards would not do so, not out of courtesy, as is imagined, but because their orders were to reserve their fire till the last moment.

Thereupon the British Guards opened fire, and 600 of the French Guards were killed and wounded at the volley (Larousse). The French Guards fell back in disorder, the British infantry continuing their advance. The French cavalry charged, but were repulsed by the cool and steady fire maintained by the English. But now a terrible artillery fire of canister and grape enfiladed the British infantry from the redoubt d'Eu; for Ingoldsby, who had at length advanced, was repulsed, and his brigade fell back, many of the men skirting the wood and joining the main body of the British. Ingoldsby is put down as having been wounded; but as I see by the orderbook that he was on duty the night after the battle, the injury cannot have been severe. Against this terrible cross fire (for the village of Fontenoy also played on them) the British could not make headway, and a retirement took place, in disorder, to the height by the fort near the wood, whence also they were fired into; but the duke, by great exertions, managed to restore order and get the troops into line again.

It was now 12 o'clock. The generals of the allies determined on another attempt. The British were to endeavour to carry the redoubt d'Eu, and Prince Waldeck and the Dutch to make a second attack on Fontenoy village. The allies advanced once more, the British infantry with such spirit and at such a pace that the Duke of Cumberland and his staff had to canter to keep up with them. Nothing stopped the advance of our splendid English battalions; they pierced no less than 300 yards past Fontenoy, most of the French infantry being broken again and again and retiring before them.

Their cavalry were repulsed by the British, now in one large square, and delivering their fire with admirable discipline and precision. The French accounts give all credit to the British, saying their fire swept everything away; the English officers could be seen directing the men's fire with their canes, and their guns were in the angles of the "square." Victory was ours, if only the Dutch had come up to give us the onward move again; but their second attack on Fontenoy was not even pushed home, and they retired from the fight, never to reappear—in short, leaving the British in the lurch (*vide* Larousse), as the French account states.

George Townshend in a letter, however, excuses the Dutch by saying that, although they could not be compared to the English or Hanoverians as troops, still, Fontenoy was too strong for them to take.

Although things were so bad for the French that Louis XV. was begged to leave the field, Saxe, carried about in a litter, made a supreme effort, bringing up the Irish Brigade, which had not been engaged. Our exhausted battalions, with ammunition fast giving out, were fighting over their own dead and wounded (always most trying for men), the French artillery pounding one flank, the other flank of the square charged also by the French Household cavalry and the *Carabiniers*. The British began to give way, and retired again to the ground between Fontenoy village and the point of the wood. They cannot have been in disorder, *as they were unpursued*, except by artillery fire. The French cavalry charged to break them, we are told, and met with a bloody repulse from the British Guards and the Hanoverian troops under General Zastrow; the regiment of Noailles was almost destroyed, and the *Carabiniers lost thirty-two officers killed*.

Townshend, in his *Diary*, clearly explains the defeat.

> In front of the British line was Fontenoy; on the left of the British, the village of Anthoin bordering on the river Scarpe, on the right of the British, the Bois de Barry, in which Colonel Forbes, Deputy Quartermaster General, an active and very intelligent officer, had observed the French posted with a preparation of flanking artillery to gall the right of our line, and he solicited a force to dislodge them on its approach. Warned as the noble commander was of this obstacle he marched on, on the following morning and no sooner had formed the line than he was harassed on his right flank and in the midst of his career in which he had beat the enemy in his front—and the Irish Brigade remained the last obstacle.
>
> The powerful effect of the enemy's artillery on his right flank and the havock on the *left* of the British line from the village of Fontenoy in front, from whose severe fire both artillery and musketry on the 2nd regiment of Guards which composed the left of our line (a battalion of Highlanders excepted which had flung itself into a hollow way parallel to the village), the line was so raked that H.R.H. found it necessary to halt and to detach against the enemy's batteries in the afore mentioned wood (De Barri); this occasioned a pause in a critical and deciding moment of success, during which our troops suffered grievously though in possession of the enemy's front ground, our left flank

fell back from the heavy fire on their left and our right wing fell back before an equally heavy fire on their right; thus our line formed to the enemy apparently 2 faces of a square which Voltaire had learnt was really the hollow square, but which did not exist in form, as unnecessary (not being surrounded) but was merely the effect of the pressure or rather heavy loss on its two flanks;.

In this order after so severe a slaughter our army retired preserving its two oblique fronts till it passed a small rivulet, leaving the Dutch on its left, who had been idle spectators of our gallant though injudicious exertions on their right and by which we should nevertheless certainly have penetrated and obtained the victory, had a proper disposition been previously made to divert the enemy's fire on our flanks at the moment we carried everything before us in front; so circumstanced and enfiladed, our progress in front was destructive in the extreme.

In no other account have I seen the square formation of the British, when they penetrated the French centre, explained. Another point is now clear also, and that is that our repulse was due as much to a heavy cross fire of artillery and musketry as it was to the advance of the Irish Brigade, which was supported by some fresh French battalions.

It is worthwhile here to quote the French account of this second assault of the French position by the British infantry, as it amply testifies to the magnificent bravery shown by our troops in this battle; I suppose never in any battle have our troops surpassed the bravery shown by Ligonier's battalions on this day:—

> *C'est alors que Koenigseck, s'inspirant d'un résotion hardie, conseilla au Duc de Cumberland de masser en une colonne épaisse l'infanterie Anglo-allemande, et de charger le centre de l'armée Française entre le Bois de Barry et Fontenoy. L'entreprise était audacieuse; mais il fallait la tenter ou se résigner à une retraite humiliante. Les Anglais et les Hanovriens s'avancent donc, trainant leurs canons à bras par les senders, franchissent intrépidement le ravin qui les séparait des Français et marchent sous les feux croisés de Fontenoy et d'une des redoubtes de Barry. Des rangs entiers tombaient foudroyés à droite et à gauche; mais ils etaient aussitôt remplacés, et les canons qu'ils amenaient vis-à-vis de Fontenoy et devant les redoubtes répondaient à l'artillerie Française. Entre cette colonne et le centre de notre armée, dont les gardes Fran-*

çaises formaient la première ligne, le terrain allait en s'élevant et dérobait à la vue la plus grande partie des Anglais. Les officiers des gardes Françaises se dirent alors, 'allons, prendre leurs canons,' et ils se jetèrent en avant. Ils furent bien étonnés d'avoir sous les yeux une masse compacte, formidable, dont rien ne semblait pouvoir arrêter la marche lente, mais irrésistible.

Les Anglais approchèrent jusqu'à 50 pas de distance; puis leurs officiers ôtant leurs chapeaux, saluèrent les Français. Le comte de Chabannes, le duc de Biron, qui s'étaient avancés, et tous les officiers des gardes Françaises, leur rendirent leur salut. On sait le singulier échange de courtoisie qui eut lieu entre les deux camps. Lord Charles Hay, capitaine aux gardes Anglaises, cria: 'Messieurs, des gardes Françaises, tirez.' Le comte d'Anteroche, lieutenant de grenadiers, répondit: 'Messieurs, nous ne tirons jamais les premiers; tirez vous mêmes.' Les Anglais ne se le firent pas répéter; ils exécutèrent un feu roulant qui emporta notre premier rang tout entier: 600 soldats et 52 officiers tombèrent morts ou blessés.

Au premier d'abord, ce raffinage de politesse, cette invitation à se faire passer par les armes, semble une quintessence ridicule de l'ancien esprit chevaleresque; mais il ne faut pas accuser ici les officiers Français d'une civilité puérile et par trop honnête, dont ils n'étaient pas coupables; une ordonnance de la fin du XVIIe siècle prescrivait à nos troupes d'essayer le premier feu, et c'est à cette ordonnance seule qu'il faut attribuer la courtoisie, devenue proverbiale, dont l'Anglais et Français usèrent les uns à l'égard des autres à Fontenoy.

La première ligne ainsi emportée, les autres tournèrent la tête en arrière, et ne se voyant appuyées que par une cavalerie éloignée de plus de 600 mètres, faiblirent aussitôt et se débandèrent, Les Anglais avançaient à pas lents, et comme s'ils eussent été sur un champ de manoeuvre; on voyait les majors appuyer leurs cannes sur les fusils des soldats pour les faire tirer bas et droit. Ils débordèrent Fontenoy et se trouvèrent bientôt au centre de l'armée Française: les divers incidents qui se produisirent imprimerent à la masse ennemie la forme d'une colonne carrée à trois faces pleines, lançant la mort de tous côtés. Son feu, violent et perfaitement soutenu, renversait tous les corps de cavalerie ou d'infanterie qui venaient vaillamment, mais sans ordre, se jeter sur elle les uns après les autres.

Plus la colonne Anglaise avançait, plus elle devenait profonde et redoutable, à cause des troupes nouvelles qui venaient sans cesse la renforcer, elle marchait toujours serrée à travers les morts et les blessés, *paraissant former un seul corps d'environ 14,000 hommes. Le sort de la journée paraissait donc fort compromis, et le maréchal de Saxe, que l'on voyait presque mourant, porté d'un corps à l'autre dans une petite carriole d'osier, envoya prier le roi de se mettre en sûreté. Vainement on lança contre la redoutable colonne les escadrons les plus éprouvés; le défaut d'ensemble dans ces attaques les rendit inutiles.*

Si les Hollandais, passant entre les redoutes établis de Fontenoy à Anthoin, étaient revenus à la charge pour donner la main aux Anglais, la victoire eût été certainement le prix de ce mouvement; mais il fut impossible de les ramener en ligne.

The Duke of Cumberland now had no choice but to order a retreat.

Howard's Regiment (the Buffs) and Sempill's (the Black Watch) were posted in the churchyard of Vezon to cover the retirement, and the cavalry were brought forward; but the French *did absolutely nothing to disturb the retirement of the British*, (yet Marshal Saxe was the man who laid down that "in pursuit all manoeuvres are good"), who retired to their camp at Bruffoel. At 11 p.m. they marched again to Lessines, near Ath, twelve miles north-west of Mons, leaving most of the wounded at Bruffoel upon the confidence of the cartel and the usual behaviour of European armies on such occasions. Notwithstanding this, the French treated our wounded brutally, and in consequence many officers and men died who would otherwise have recovered.

The loss of the allies in this battle was as follows:—

British	...	4,074 killed and wounded,	also 629 horses and	21 guns.
Hanoverian		1,762 ,, ,, ,,	,, 475 ,,	
Dutch	...	1,554 ,, ,, ,,		19 ,,
		7,390 killed and wounded.		40 guns.

Larousse gives the French losses as *at least* 7,000 killed and wounded.

Fontenoy was a glorious defeat for the British. Never in our military history have British soldiers fought more heroically; they had been pounded for more than three hours by the continuous fire of three large batteries, and then drove the French from their entrenchments. The infantry was unsupported by the British cavalry, who never came up and took the pressure off, as they were ordered to do, a blunder of which I cannot find any explanation. The Duke of Cumberland (in whom the troops never for a moment lost confidence, in spite of defeat, and who was as gallant an officer as ever wore the British uniform) then rallied them after the first repulse, and actually made them do the same work all over again; and the victory would have been won by sheer bravery but for the bad conduct of the Dutch troops, who, from all accounts, behaved disgracefully.

Fontenoy, however, is only one of the many illustrations of the uncertainty of war. As the Duke of Wellington said, he had fought a sufficient number of battles to know that the result of any battle was never certain. If the Dutch had behaved with the ordinary qualities of disciplined troops, the Duke of Cumberland would have ranked as a great leader; "for success in war," as Napier remarks, "like charity in religion, covers a multitude of sins."

The highest testimony of all that has ever been paid the British infantry for Fontenoy was by Marshal Saxe himself, in a letter published in the *Traité des Légions*, 4th edition, published at La Hague, 1757:—

> *Je ne sais s'il y a beaucoup de nos généraux qui osassent entreprendre de passer une plaine avec un corps d'infanterie devant un corps de cavallerie nombreuse et se flatter de pouvoir se soutenir plusieurs heures avec quinze ou vingt bataillons au milieu d'une armée comme ont fait les Anglais à Fontenoy, sans qu'aucune charge de cavallerie les ait ébranlé ou fait dégarnir de leur feu. Ce sont des choses que nous avons tous vu, mais l'amour propre qu'on ne veut point en parler, parce qu'on sait bien qu'on n'est point en état de les imiter.*

The principal British officers killed or who died of wounds afterwards were: General Sir James Campbell (colonel of the Scots Greys), who had distinguished himself at Malplaquet; General Ponsonby. Wounded: General Earl of Albemarle, General Howard, Brigadier Churchill, and Lord Ancram and Lord Cathcart, A.D.C.'s to the duke; also, Lord George Sackville, in Bragg's Regiment (28th), was wounded.

★★★★★★

Lord George Sackville was tried by court-martial after the Battle of Minden in 1759 for his inaction when in command of the British cavalry, and found unfit to serve His Majesty in any military capacity.

★★★★★★

In the appendix to this chapter I attach a list of casualties in the British force.

The French lost, according to their own account published at Lille, about 6,000 killed and 3,000 wounded. The Irish Brigade lost very heavily: Colonel Dillon and Lieut.-Colonels O'Neil and Manners, 13 captains, and 9 lieutenants killed; wounded, Colonel Lalley, Lieut.-Colonel Higerry, 2 majors, 19 captains, and 28 lieutenants; and in Fitz James's Horse 25 officers killed and wounded!

Our losses in the present day are nothing as compared to this battle. A list of casualties of 600 or 700 in the campaign in South Africa (combats, as a rule, fought at extreme long range—long-range-fire fights) is called a "desperate battle" in the headlines of London newspapers.

> Camp Aeth, May 1st, 1745, (the day) after the Battle of Fontenoy. Parole St. Bavon et Gand.
> A return to be carefully made as soon as possible of the number of men left behind wounded, the number of men wounded that are now here, the effective men on the spot and what number are now missing that marched out with us to the field of battle."
> A return to be given in as soon as possible of the officers killed or wounded with their ranks as likewise a list of the non-commissioned officers, soldiers and troop horses, killed or wounded or missing.
> That surgeons mates of each regiment be ordered to attend at the hospital, there not being a sufficient number of hands on the establishment, notwithstanding the supernumeraries.

The allies entrenched themselves at Lessines, near Ath, as the only means of covering Flanders. The following reinforcements soon reached the Duke of Cumberland—*viz*. Rich's Dragoons, Barrel's Regiment (4th King's Own), Fleming's (36th), Ponsonby's (37th), Ligonier's, Price's (14th), Royal Irish, and two battalions of Hanoverians.

Tournay surrendered to Saxe on May 21st, 1745.

On the news of Fontenoy reaching England, there was the greatest indignation at the conduct of the Dutch, and Brigadier Ingoldsby was very severely commented upon. Whilst at Lessines Brigadier Ingoldsby and Captain Watts were tried by a court-martial, presided over by General Lord Dunmore.

Brigadier Ingoldsby was found guilty of not carrying his orders into effect, "and was sentenced to suspension of pay and duty during the Duke's pleasure," and he was given three months in which to leave the army. I find in the Duke of Cumberland's order-book:—

10 August 1745 Camp Villevorde, Brigadier Ingoldsby is to remain suspended for three months.

On May 8th, 1745, I find in army orders at Camp Lessines that Captain Townshend, Captain Barrington, Captain Monckton, (afterwards commanded a brigade under Wolfe at Quebec), and Lieut.-Colonel Mostyn are appointed *aides-de-camp* to Lieut.-General Lord Dunmore.

On May 29th, also George Townshend is given his company in Bligh's Regiment (20th, now the Lancashire Fusiliers). The commission is signed by William, Duke of Cumberland. (See Appendix.)

Beaten into experience, the allies now changed their measures. From attacking the enemy in his chosen post, they retired to choose a post for themselves; and the camp of Lessines furnished a good one. There the enemy might have been received with advantage; and there Flanders could have been preserved, while Brabant was covered; for the enemy must either have offered their flank, if they marched against it on the same side of the Scheldt, or have marched against it on the other side, and left the allies masters to defend all the towns on it.

The drafts from England and reinforcements from Holland soon repaired the loss of the battle, but spirit returned not with numbers, for apprehension preponderated after the Battle of Fontenoy, as much as presumption had done before it, and showed that true judgment and courage were wanting to turn the balance. When Tournay had surrendered, the French advanced towards the allies, who at once put the Dender River before them; and though the allies had drained the magazines at Brussels and reserved those in Ghent, they now resolved to cover Brabant and abandon Flanders. Ghent, however, was not entirely forgotten; for after the enemy had turned off towards Oudenarde, and were nearer Ghent than the allies, then, and not till then, was General Moltke detached with four British battalions—Welsh Fusiliers, Royal Scots, Bligh's (20th), and Handasyde's (16th)—and Rich's Dragoons to reinforce the garrison of Ghent.

The remnant only of one of the battalions (the Royal Scots) found its way into Ghent, and were surprised in that city with the rest of the garrison next morning, whilst the remainder were surprised at Melle by 10,000 French in ambuscade, chiefly through the misconduct of General Moltke. Rich's Dragoons (now 4th Hussars) were almost cut to pieces, and the force only got away with difficulty, seeking refuge at Dendermonde.

20TH REGIMENT FOOT

******

Order-Book, May 6th, Camp Lessines:—

The three battalions of Duroure's, Welch, and Scotch Fuzileers to march tomorrow morning at 5 o'clock to Alost and the next day to Ghent.

The Welch Fuzileers are to go into the castle there and as soon as they have relieved the King's Regiment of Foot (8th) that regiment is to march to Alost and the next day to join the army. The Scotch Fuzileers to relieve the late Ponsonby's regiment at Bruges and Duroure's to relieve Ligonier's regiment at Ostend where Duroure's is to remain till further orders.

******

Immediately after the success of this ambuscade Count Lowendahl surprised Ghent at night with 4,000 men by getting over the ditch with fascines and letting down a drawbridge. The garrison was surprised asleep, and surrendered almost without an effort. The citadel was held by about 700 British, detachments of various regiments, who made only a very faint show of resistance before hanging out the white flag and surrendering. It appears to have been a very disgraceful affair. General Moltke, who had got into the city, as related above, with the Royal Scots and the remnants of Rich's Dragoons, galloped off with the dragoons and fled to Sluys, twenty-one miles north-west of Ghent, where he was refused entrance by the governor; finally, the fugitives reached Ostend.

the loss of this brigade, and unhinged by the surprise and Ghent, the allied army fled from the Dender to the car ls, where they encamped at Anderlecht; and this likewise would have been abandoned, had not the enemy had too much generosity to suspect the degree of the panic of the allies, and so saved them from further shame by not advancing, and were contented to employ the remainder of the year in reducing the many towns the allies had abandoned to them.

As soon as our generals had collected themselves, they turned their attention to strengthening their position in rear of the Brussels canal by works in a manner which put their future security behind the canal beyond doubt. This ended the campaign of 1745, both armies going into winter quarters. In the last year's operations, an army superior by half attempted nothing in open places: in this campaign, an army in the same proportion of inferiority attacked entrenchments.

Appendix

LIST OF REGIMENTS AND LOSSES AT BATTLE OF FONTENOY, APRIL 30TH, 1745

Regiments.	Officers killed.	Officers wounded.	Officers missing.	Men killed.	Men wounded.	Men missing.
British Cavalry.						
3rd troop Horse Guards	—	1	—	4	14	—
4th ditto	—	2	—	2	12	—
2nd troop Horse Grenadiers	—	4	—	4	10	—
Blues	—	5	—	10	39	—
Honeywood's	—	1	—	7	4	1
Ligonier's	—	1	—	3	4	1
Dragoons.						
Hawley's Dragoons	—	4	—	14	31	—
Scots Greys	—	1	—	14	11	—
Bland's Dragoons	—	2	1	9	14	7
Cope's ,,	1	5	—	10	35	3
Stair's ,,	1	—	—	3	11	—
Infantry.						
1st Foot Guards	4	7	—	85	142	—
2nd Foot Guards	3	8	—	112	116	—
3rd Foot Guards	4	7	—	105	131	—
1st battalion Royal Scots	—	8	—	87	83	8
Howard's (the 3rd Buffs)	1	2	—	11	32	8
Onslow's (8th)	—	7	—	16	83	31
Sowle's (11th)	4	2	1	49	112	46
Duroure's (12th)	6	10	—	153	149	—
Pulteney's (13th)	1	4	—	37	41	10
Maj.-Genl. Howard's (31st)	?	8	—	17	70	13
Bligh's (20th)	1	5	—	28	35	—
Scotch Fusiliers (21st)	2	9	3	201	144	15
Welsh Fusiliers (23rd)	4	10	8	185	77	39
Bragg's (28th)	1	9	1	27	76	12
Handaside's	4	5	1	139	100	12
Skelton's	—	5	1	16	100	17
Johnson's	6	12	—	42	84	30
Cholmondeley's	—	6	—	18	55	28
Lord Sempil's Highlanders	2	3	—	30	88	13
Artillery	1	—	—	4	23	—

Total British Troops 4074
Total loss, Hanoverians . . . 1742
    ,, Dutch . . . 1554

British, Hanoverian, and Dutch total loss . 7370

NAMES OF BRITISH OFFICERS KILLED AND WOUNDED OF DIFFERENT REGIMENTS AT BATTLE OF FONTENOY

3rd troop Horse Guards.—*Wounded:* Lieut.-Col. Lamoniere.
4th troop Horse Guards.—*Wounded:* Capt. Hilgrave; Cornet Burdett.
2nd troop Horse Grenadiers.—*Wounded:* Major Brereton; Captains Elliot and Burton; Adjutant Thacker.
Blues.—*Wounded:* Lieut.-Col. Beake; Captains Lloyde and Migget; two Quartermasters.
Honeywood's.—*Wounded:* Lieutenant Brace.
Ligonier's (7th Dragoon Guards).—*Wounded:* Quartermaster Heath.
Hawley's Dragoons.—*Wounded:* Lieut.-Col. Nason; Cornets Hartwell, Desmerit, Creighton.
Scots Greys.—*Wounded:* Cornet Glasgow.
Bland's Dragoons.—*Wounded:* Captain Wade; Quartermaster Corberidge. *Missing:* Cornet Bland.
Cope's Dragoons.—*Killed:* Cornet Potts. *Wounded:* Lieut.-Col. Erskine; Captain Ogilvie; Lieutenant Forbes; Cornet Maitland; Quartermaster Smith.
Stair's Dragoons.—*Killed:* Quartermaster Baird.
1st battalion of Foot Guards (Grenadier Guards).—*Killed:* Captains Harvey, Brorerton, Berkley; and Ensign Sir Alexander Cockburn. *Wounded:* Colonel Lord Hay; Captains Hildesley, Parker, Pearson, and Beckland; Ensigns Nash and Vane.
2nd battalion of Foot Guards (Coldstream).—*Killed:* Colonel Needham; Ensigns Cathcart and Molesworth. *Wounded:* Colonels Corbet, Kellet, Moyston, and Lord Bertie; Captains Townshend and Caesar; Ensigns Burton and Vanburgh.
3rd battalion of Foot Guards (Scots Guards).—*Killed:* Colonels Carpenter and Douglas; Captain Ross; Ensign Murray. *Wounded:* Colonels Waldegrave and Fraser; Captains Laurie, Kucoit, and Maitland; Ensigns Haldins and Nail.
1st battalion Royal Scots.—*Wounded:* Captains Thompson and Edmonson; Lieutenants Cockburn, Nairn, Elliot, Aburnathy, and Grant; Ensign Jones.
Howard's (3rd Buffs).—*Killed:* Quartermaster Cummins. *Wounded:* Lieutenant Tanner and Ensign Paunceford.
Onslow's (8th).—*Wounded:* Lieut.-Col. Keightley; Major Gray; Captains Dailons, Loftus, and Ekins; Lieutenants Cooke and Thompson.
Sowle's (11th).—*Killed:* Captain Browne; Lieutenants Capel and Mawbray; Ensign Farrington. *Wounded:* Lieut.-Col. Tullikins; Major Montagu. *Missing:* Lieutenant Hawkshaw.
Duroure's (12th).—*Killed:* Lieut.-Col. Whitford; Captain Campbell; Lieutenants Bockland and Lane; Ensigns Cannon and Clayton. *Wounded:* Colonel Duroure; Major Cassalow; Captains Sandford and Robinson; Lieutenants Murray, Townsend, Millington, Delgarne; Ensigns Dagers and Pierce. *Missing:* Captains De Cosne and Goulston; Lieutenant Salt.
Pulteney's (13th).—*Killed:* Captain Queenchant. *Wounded:* Captains Daniell, Nichols; Lieutenants Jones and Edhouse.
Major-General Howard's.—*Killed:* Lieutenant Le Grand; Ensign Gibson. *Wounded:* Maj.-Gen. Howard; Major Pettetot; Captains

Cockran and Douglas; Lieutenant Coote; Ensigns Cheap, Martin, and Porterfield.

Bligh's (*20th*).—*Killed:* Lieut.-Col. Gee. *Wounded:* Captains Meyrae and Maxwell; Lieutenants Bouchitere and Vicars; Ensign Mutley.

Scotch Fusiliers (*21st*).—*Killed:* Lieutenants Campbell, Austin, and Sergeant. *Wounded:* Major Colville; Captains Nantz, Oliphant, and Knatchbull; Lieutenants Colvil, Bellindon, Maxwell, McGaiken, and Townsend.

Welsh Fusiliers (*23rd*).—*Killed:* Lieutenants Weaver, Price, Foster, and Isaac. *Wounded:* Captains Hickman, Cary, Bernard, and Drysdal; Lieutenants Izard, Awbry, Clarke, Eyre, Roberts, and Rolle. *Missing:* Major Lort; Captains Taylor, Sabine, and Johnson; Lieutenants Berner, Gregg, Haws, and Lort.

Rothes'.—*Killed:* Ensign Bouvilette. *Wounded:* Lieut.-Col. Kennedy; Major Dalrymple; Captains Worge and Lucas; Lieutenants Livingston and Hall; Ensigns Cockburn and Jones.

Bragg's (*28th*).—*Killed:* Lieutenant Cliffe. *Wounded:* Lord George Sackville; Captains Fitzgerald, Jocelin, and Holt; Lieutenants Wright, Edgeworth, and Gradon; Ensigns Harman, Michelson. *Missing:* Captain Sailly.

Handasyde's (*31st*).—*Killed:* Lieut.-Col. Montague; Captains Baird and Pollok; Lieutenant Dolway. *Wounded:* Lieutenants Stafford and Porter; Ensigns Worsley, Bromley, and Freeman. *Missing:* Ensign Atkinson.

Skelton's.—*Wounded:* Lieutenants Lindsay, Meoler, Banks, Hows Prescot. *Missing:* Captain Farquhar.

Johnson's (*33rd*).—*Killed:* Lieut.-Col. Clements; Lieutenants Green, Colly, Houghton, and Oatway; Ensign Nesbit. *Wounded:* Major Mure; Captains Godfrey, Lacy, Eccles, and Tyghe; Lieutenants Gardiner, Gore, Burrough; Ensigns Collis, Rayner, Sampson, and Descury.

Cholmondeley's (*34th*).—*Wounded:* Lieutenants Cranmer, Forrest, Mure, Courtney, and Hargraves; Ensign ——.

Lord Sempil's Highlanders (*25th*).—*Killed:* Captain John Campbell; Ensign Campbell. *Wounded:* Captain Richard Campbell; Ensigns Reynold and James.

Artillery.—*Killed:* Lieutenant Bennett. Twenty-one guns were left behind, the drivers having fled.

Amongst Townshend's commissions is the following :—

" WILLIAM AUGUSTUS Duke of Cumberland and Duke of Brunswic Luneberg &c. &c. &c. Captain General of all His Majesty's Land Forces raised or to be raised and employed within the Kingdom of Great Britain, or which are or shall be employed abroad in conjunction with those of His Majesty's Allies:

"TO GEORGE TOWNSHEND ESQR.

" By Virtue of the Power of Authority to Me given and granted by His Majesty I do hereby constitute and appoint you to be Captain of that Company whereof . The Lord Cathcart was late Captain in the Regiment of Foot commanded by Colonel Thomas Bligh. You are therefore to take the said Company   into your Care and

Charge and Duty to exercise as well the Officers as Soldiers in Arms and to use your best Endeavours to keep them in good Order and Discipline : And I do hereby command them to obey you as their Captain . . . And you are to observe and follow such Orders and Directions from time to time as you shall receive from His Majesty Myself or any other your Superior Officer according to the Rules and Discipline of War. Given at the Camp of Lessines the Twenty Ninth Day of May 1745 O.S. In the Eighteenth Year of His Majesty's Reign.

"WILLIAM.

" By His Royal Highness's Command
"EVRARD FAWKENER.

" Townshend Esqr. to be Captain in the Regiment of Foot commanded by Colonel Thomas Bligh."

The following extracts from the Duke of Cumberland's orderbook for this campaign may prove interesting to military readers when punishments in the field in the present day are compared:—

Camp Villevorde August 30th 1745

Henry Treton of Genl. Blands Regimt. in Lt. Col. Honeywoods troops is to receive a 1000 lashes by sentence of the genl. court martial at what time and in what manner the commanding officer of the regiment shall think proper.

Mathieu Colquehoun tryed for clipping and condemned by the sentence of a genl. court martial to suffer death to be hanged at 8 o'clock tomorrow near Pont Bruele.

Daniel White tryed for endeavouring to seduce men to desert to receive 100 lashes with a cat of nine tails at the head of every brigade of the line and never to appear either in camp or in garrison on pain of being hanged to begin to receive his punishment tomorrow which is to be continued as the provost shall find him able to bear it.

Corporal Thomas Erwyn of Monro's Regiment to be shot tomorrow at the head of the said regiment by the 4 men of that regiment returned from desertion at the same time; his Royal Highness having been pleased to pardon them though condemned on condition they afterwards go to the West Indies to serve his Majesty in the troops there.

Alexander Tweedal of Genl. Cornwallis's Marines lately returned from desertion to be send to England in irons to serve in the said corps.

Camp Villevorde 1 Sept. 1745.
It is Genl. Ligonier's orders that the Foot put themselves in the best order possible to be seen by His Royal Highness on Thursday that their cloaths and lace be mended their hatts new cocked and everything in repair.

Camp Villevorde 5 Sept. 1745.
The right wing to be in readiness to be reviewed tomorrow morning by His Royal Highness who will be on the right of the Austrians at 10 o'clock from which the left may regulate themselves so as not to be too long under arms; the Guards not to be relieved till after the review a sergeant and 12 men of each regmt to be left as a Guard to the camp and 2 men of a company to take care of the tents.

If the weather is fine the men to open and dry their tents.

The quarter masters and camp colour men of the right wing to parade at 12 o'clock at the head of Cholmondeley's Regimt. and receive their orders from Lt. Genl. St. Clair.

A field officer of the piquet with 50 or 100 men to march immediately to Eppingham and collect all the forrages there posting proper Guards upon it and take care that the Foot Guards with the rest of the infantry and artillery take an equal proportion of the said forrage an officer of each corps giving a receipt for the quantity he takes the British begin 10th the Foot Guards after them the brigade of Barrell and so in their turns oats at Malines.

Disposition for the Genl. Officers taking their post tomorrow at the review:—

At the head of the Foot Guards:
    Earl of Dunmore
    Lt. Genl. St Clair
    M. Genl. Churchill
At the Head of Barrells:
    Lt. Genl. Ligonier
    M. Genl. Poultney.
    Brigdr. Fleming
M. Genl. Campbell at the Head of Sowl's.
Sir Robt. Monro as Col. at the head of his Regt.
At the head of Lt. Genl. Howards:
    Lt Genl. Earl Albemarle

Brigdr. Douglas
Brigdr. Price at the head of Wolfs.
At the head of Poultneys:
    M. Genl. Skelton
    Brigdr Cholmondeley
At the head of Gl. Greys:
    Lt. Genl. Hawley
    M. Genl. Bland
M. Genl. Earl Crawford at the head of the Horse Guards.
M. Genl. Rothes at the head of the Blues.
The Majors of Brigade to post themselves on horseback upon the right of the Grenadier Companeys of those regiments that their brigadiers are at the head of.
The *aids de camp* to post themselves at the Majors of Brigade do.
The General Officers of the Infantry to salute on Foot.
Orderly time tomorrow at half an hour after 8.

Notes After Fontenoy

There were many ugly stories as regards the treatment of our wounded left at Bruffoel after Fontenoy. The French soldiers were accused of knocking several of our people on the head who were left on the field of battle. Immediately after the battle Marshal Saxe sent to the allies to desire they would carry off their wounded, upon which the Duke of Cumberland sent 105 waggons to bring them away. Both waggons and men were detained.

At last the British surgeons were permitted to pass to their regiments, and on arrival in camp at Lessines they waited on the Duke of Cumberland, and laid before him the treatment of the British and Hanoverian prisoners by the French; they presented H.R.H. with a bag of chewed bullets, points of swords, pieces of flint, glass, iron, etc., which they had extracted from the wounds of our men; upon which a trumpet was sent from the allied army to the King of France, with a coffer sealed with the arms of the Duke of Cumberland, Marshal Koenigseck, Prince Waldeck, and Baron Wendt, filled with pieces of thick glass, brass, and iron buttons, all bloody, which were taken out of the wounds of General Campbell and other officers, accompanied with a letter from H.R.H., pointing out that the French had violated all the usages of civilised war.

In the Duke of Cumberland's order-book, just after the battle of Fontenoy, appear the following orders:—

Camp Lessines, May 7th.—Whatever hats or caps belonging to the brigade of Foot Guards are brought to their camp, the person who brings them shall receive 2 shillings reward for each. There is lost a fine grey gelding with a demi peak saddle, a brace of pistols mounted with silver and red furniture laced with gold belonging to an officer of the Grays. Whoever brings him or the furniture to the adjutant of the regiment shall receive 10 *ducats* reward or in proportion for what is brought.

Camp Lessines, May 9th.—The present General Court Martial is to continue sitting to examine Lt. Collins and Lt. Sampson of Brigadier Johnson's regiment at their own desire on a report spread by Mr. Crosby, surgeon's mate of their own regiment to their disadvantage, these two gentlemen and the said Mr. Crosby to attend the General Court Martial at 8 o'clock at the headquarters with their witnesses.

Camp Lessines, May 15th.—The sentence of the General Court Martial relating to John Crosby late surgeon's mate in Brigadier Johnson's regiment will be put in execution tomorrow at 8 o'clock, he having unjustly and injuriously aspersed the character of Lieuts. Collins and Sampson, he is sentenced to be cashiered and drummed out of the regiment along both lines of the British Army with a halter about his neck and not to return to the army again in camp or in garrison on pain of the severest punishment.

Camp Lessines, May 17th.—The Majors of Brigade and surgeons are desired to collect all the grape shot and the irregular balls and pieces of metal which were fired by the French and are now amongst the troops, and to bring them to headquarters as soon as possible.

Camp Gramont, June 23rd.—Whoever is catched cutting the damms that form the fish ponds will be hanged.
Capt. Wolf, (afterwards General Wolfe, the hero of Quebec), is appointed Brigade Major to Pulteney's Brigade.

Camp Deigham, July 9th.—Henry Wells of the 1st Regiment of Foot Guards ordered to suffer death for desertion by sentence of the Genl. Court Martial to be executed this afternoon at 2 o'clock on the hill between the first regiment and Lt. Genl. Howard's, all the British piquets under the command of the field officers to be present at the execution.

Camp Villevorde, August 4th.—John Burrage of Captain Trappaud's Company in Lt. Col. Howard's regiment who was taken last night marauding with his arms to be hanged immediately at the head of that regiment without a court martial by order of His Royal Highness, the piquets of the right wing to be present at the execution.

Same place, July 30th.—Robert Booth of Major Gen'l Howard's to be hanged tomorrow morning at 7 o'clock at the head of Wolfe's brigade who are to be under arms to see the execution.

Same place, July 28th.—Complaints have been made to His Royal Highness chiefly against the sutlers he is on the first complaint determined to have them hanged immediately.

Same place, August 10th.—Two soldiers deserted from the Irish Brigade in red clothing faced with black to be secured immediately and sent to headquarters.

Same place, August 12th. Drunkenness.—It is recommended to commanding officers of corps to prevent as much as possible drunkenness by giving orders to break all bottles and stave all casks with Geneva. Pursuant to the above order the officers are required to assist to their uttermost in preventing the excessive use of gin and all sergeants and corporals are ordered, on pain of being broke and rendered incapable of serving in those stations more to prevent it by breaking of all bottles, casks, &c, that they meet with in the lines or on a march and making the sellers prisoners and all soldiers are for the future strictly forbid the selling of gin on pain of the severest punishment.

Same place and date.—The officers of the outposts are never to salute or rest their arms to any general officer, but always face the enemy with their Guards.

Same place, August 19th. Negligence of Regimental Officers.—Whereas it has been represented by the field officer on duty at Fort Montroy that several men of his detachment wanted many cartridges of their complement and others had them so ill made as not to fit their pieces, His Royal Highness orders when such neglect are found for the future that the commanding officer of such detachment shall report the same, naming the regiments they belong to and their numbers that the proper officers of such corps may be called to account for such shameful neglect. All commanding officers to see their men have 24 rounds and that the cartridges are well made and fit their pieces, the majors to visit the men ordered on outposts on the regimental parade before they march off.

Same place, August 14th. Camp Followers.—All English ladies who do not belong to some corps or other, and cannot produce a pass from the commanding officer shall be taken up by the provost in order to be sent to England.

Rebellion in Scotland 1745-46

In the spring of 1745 most of the regular troops of the United Kingdom were absent in Flanders; the King was in Hanover; and the adherents of Prince Charles Edward judged the opportunity good for that Prince to essay his meditated plan against the wealth and power of England. History tells us how near he came to winning the throne of Great Britain; but fortune was wanting—that luck without which, as Napier tells us, men's efforts are but as bubbles on the troubled ocean. The greatest generals are the greatest slaves of fortune. Napoleon won Germany, Italy, Austria—almost all Europe; but fortune was wanting, and he lost all. Charles Edward called a council of war at Derby—and it is well known in history that a council of war does not fight—and he was lost.

I will only give a slight sketch of events up to the period when the Duke of Cumberland went north to Edinburgh, to command; for my book is only concerned with George Townshend, who on the outbreak of the rebellion came across from Flanders, and joined his regiment, the 20th, in Scotland; therefore, Preston Pans and Falkirk do not properly come within the scope of my narrative. The news of the great disaster at Preston Pans, where Sir John Cope was utterly routed and his force annihilated, struck consternation in London.

He had not been surprised—he was a most excellent commander and a brave soldier; but his two newly raised battalions behaved in a dastardly manner, and fled in the most disgraceful panic when charged by the Highland clansmen; and the cavalry behaved even worse than the infantry. Cope demanded a court of enquiry, by which his character was completely vindicated, as were those of Colonel Lascelles and Brigadier Fowke. The court found that:

> The misfortune of the day and action was owing to the shameful behaviour of the private soldiers, and not to any misconduct

or misbehaviour of Sir John Cope, or of any of the officers under his command; and there was no ground for accusation against him, Colonel Lascelles or Brigadier Fowke:

And yet in popular opinion it has been handed down that Sir John Cope is responsible for the famous disaster of Preston Pans.

★★★★★★

Cope was offered up as a victim to a misjudging public, and a press with whom success is the only criterion of merit. Military history shows that our generals, brave in action personally as the wildest subaltern, are commonly overwhelmed with the fear of responsibility when left to themselves. They know that, however prodigal of their blood they may have been, their reputation and past services will wither with the first blight of misfortune; and this will always be the case with our British public, for though the most *warlike* public in Europe, they are at the same time the most *unmilitary*.

If conscription were brought in tomorrow in England, our British public would then become very *military*, but at the same time the most *unwarlike*, for "the man in the club" and "the man in the street" alike would have to march, and would learn by *experience* the difference between theory and practice and between criticism and execution. "Speak to me of a general," says Turenne, "who has made no mistakes in war, and you speak of one who has seldom made war."

★★★★★★

All the English troops in Flanders were ordered home at once; ten battalions reached Gravesend in September, consisting of three of Foot Guards, the Buffs, Sowle's (11th), Pulteney's (13th), Bragg's (28th), Douglass (32nd), Johnson's (33rd), and Cholmondeley's (34th). All these battalions, with the exception of the Foot Guards, were sent round by sea to join the command of the famous Marshal Wade, who, as might have been expected from his exhibition in Flanders in 1744, did absolutely nothing, contenting himself with a few small skirmishes and a pilgrimage towards Carlisle and back.

The Duke of Cumberland returned from Flanders on October 18th, the following regiments arriving shortly after: Ligonier's Horse (7th Dragoon Guards), Bland's Dragoons (3rd Hussars), Royal Scots, Harrison's (15th), Huske's, Beauclerk's, Handasyde's (31st), Skelton's, Bligh's (20th), Mordaunt's, Campbell's (Royal Scots Fusiliers), Lord

Sempill's Highlanders, and Lord John Murray's Highlanders. These troops formed a camp at Dartford, as there were rumours of a French invasion.

Admiral Vernon and a strong fleet lay in the Channel. Loyal addresses poured in to the king from all parts of England; volunteers and yeomanry were mustered in the same way as for the South African war in 1899-1901; large subscriptions were raised in different counties—£40,000 in Yorkshire alone for the defence of the Government, and the gentlemen of that county also formed themselves into a yeomanry corps called the Royal Hunters. Cheshire furnished 2,500 volunteers. Lancashire provided subscriptions to maintain 5,000 men; in particular the town of Liverpool raised, equipped, and clothed a battalion of volunteers as the city of London did for the South African campaign, proving that the idea of the C.I.V.s is not a new one. Norfolk, under the leadership of Lord Townshend, gave £10,000 in subscriptions; the city of Bristol £150,000. Owing to the vigilance of our cruisers, the French were only able to transport to Scotland 14,000 muskets and £80,000 in money.

Prince Charles Edward crossed the Border and invaded England in November, 1745, with 10,000 men. Carlisle, garrisoned by militia, surrendered almost at once—Wade, of course, starting from Newcastle too late to relieve the town. The Duke of Cumberland now proceeded to Lichfield (where that excellent soldier Sir John Ligonier had formed a camp), and took over the supreme command. The duke warned the king that preparations must be made for the defence of London, as the Scots might get past him; and, owing to their freedom from baggage and *impedimenta*, they succeeded in doing this, quite outmarching the duke's troops.

Prince Charles Edward, however, halted at Derby, held the fatal council of war, and beat a precipitate retreat north again, harassed by the Duke of Cumberland, who followed him up relentlessly. The Scottish rear-guard, under Lord George Murray, was overtaken at the village of Clifton, near Penrith, by Cumberland's mounted troops, including a battalion of 1,000 mounted infantry. (Principally raised from the Foot Guards.) Brigadier Honeywood dismounted his cavalry, Bland's and Mark Kerr's Dragoons and Ligonier's Horse, and carried the village by assault, after an hour's sharp fighting, with a loss of twenty-nine dragoons killed and wounded. Seventy Highlanders were taken prisoners.

This was the only occasion, however, on which Cumberland's

troops got in touch; and Prince Charles Edward, crossing the Border safely into Scotland, quartered his army in Glasgow, to rest and refresh it at the expense of the honest inhabitants, as a punishment for the city's having raised a corps of volunteers for the service of King George. Everything was requisitioned, horses, carts, clothing, food, and boots—much to the indignation of the burghers of Glasgow.

On January 5th, 1746, Prince Charles Edward closely invested Stirling Castle, which was held by that gallant old soldier General Blakeney. Edinburgh, which had been reoccupied by our troops, was placed under the command of General Hawley, with a force consisting of thirteen battalions of infantry and some local militia. (It must be borne in mind that our regular battalions in those days seldom mustered over 400 bayonets, instead of 1,000 men, as nowadays.)

Hawley having resolved to relieve Stirling Castle without delay, left Edinburgh on January 13th, and, marching rapidly, reached Falkirk on January 17th. I shall not give an account of the Battle of Falkirk, as it does not properly belong to these memoirs. The battle was disgraceful to our arms; there seems to be not much doubt that Hawley was surprised—the usual story in our military annals. He had a well-disciplined and admirably-appointed force, and had boasted at White's in St. James's Street that with two regiments of dragoons he would drive the rebels from one end of the kingdom to the other; but he seems to have been one of those men who, if they could be bought at the world's price, could be profitably sold at their own.

The only thing that can be said for him is that, like Braddock his contemporary, he was brave. But professional expertness and enterprise are not sufficient to constitute a good general; there are higher qualities required—he must have the intuitive sagacity which reads passing events correctly, he must be well read in military history, and he must study and work daily to keep up to date. No example can be shown in our military history of a great general who was not a well-read man.

★★★★★★

Young men on joining their regiments have all the temptations in the world to pleasure, none to study; and they someday find themselves compromised on service from want of *knowledge*, not of talent (Sir Charles Napier).

★★★★★★

On news of Hawley's defeat at Falkirk reaching London, the Government decided that more vigorous measures must be taken.

Six thousand Hessians were dispatched north, and all the troops in North Britain were ordered to concentrate at Edinburgh. The Duke of Cumberland arrived in Edinburgh, where his presence was badly needed, on January 30th, having done the journey in four days from London. His reputation as a stout and able soldier had been in nowise diminished by Fontenoy; he was very popular with the troops, although a very stern disciplinarian; and the one wish of all ranks was that he would lead them at once against the rebels, to wipe out the disgrace of Preston Pans and Falkirk.

Their zeal was not allowed to cool, for the army was put in motion for Stirling on January 31st, the day after his arrival. The duke's force consisted of twelve squadrons of cavalry and fourteen battalions of infantry—*viz.* Cavalry: Cobham's, Kerr's, Nason's, St. George's, and Hamilton's Dragoons, and the Duke of Kingston's Yeomanry. Infantry: Howard's (the Buffs), Wolfe's (8th), Barrel's (4th), Bligh's (20th), Scots Fusiliers, Blakeney's (27th), Cholmondeley's (34th), Fleming's (36th), Battereau's (since disbanded), Price's (14th), Sempill's (25th, K.O.S.B.'s), 2nd battalion Royal Scots, Pulteney's (13th), and some Campbells under the chief of their clan.

The regiments were much under strength, as I shall show, in the field state before Culloden. The total combatants in the duke's force amounted to about 7,800 men. George Townshend, who had been granted permission by Lord Dunmore to join his regiment, the 20th, in order to see this campaign, had crossed from Flanders, and joined at Edinburgh soon after the Battle of Falkirk. Wolfe was also present in this campaign, being now a captain in Barrel's Regiment (the 4th).

Prince Charles Edward at once abandoned the siege of Stirling, recrossing the Forth with great precipitation, and leaving wounded and prisoners behind. The duke continued his march to Falkirk, detaching Brigadier Mordaunt, with the mounted troops and some irregulars—*viz.* men of the clan Campbell—to follow up the retreating rebel army; and on February 2nd he entered Stirling, and thanked General Blakeney in general orders for his gallant defence.

The rebel army continued their retreat to Perth, but did not halt at that town, for Prince Charles Edward spiked his guns there, and continued his retreat north to Aberdeen. General Lord Loudoun, who was at Inverness, collected some loyal clansmen, and decided to hold Inverness against the rebels; but on the approach of Prince Charles Edward he abandoned Inverness, and retreated into Ross-shire. The prince entered Inverness on February 18th, and put his troops into quarters there.

In the meantime, the Duke of Cumberland, marching north with his army, entered Aberdeen on February 28th, occupying Perth and Stirling with Hessians, to hold these places in case Prince Charles Edward should try to march south again. At Aberdeen, many of the northern nobility and gentry came in to offer their services and prove their loyalty. The duke sent out detachments to the outlying districts round Aberdeen, to protect those who were loyal, and to raid and harass those who were against us. One of these detachments, consisting of seventy Campbells and thirty yeomanry (Kingston's Horse), was surprised at Keith at night by a far stronger force of rebels.

The detachment took post in the churchyard, and made a desperate defence to the last, being surrounded. A cornet and five men of Kingston's Yeomanry managed to escape; the remainder were all killed. Another detachment of Campbells was attacked and cut to pieces near Mount Kanach; two other parties of these auxiliaries shared the same fate near Blair Castle. Lord George Murray attacked Blair Castle, his own home, which was garrisoned by Lieut.-Colonel Sir Andrew Agnew and 500 of his regiment, the Scots Fusiliers. The castle is a very strong one, twenty-four miles north of Perth; and although Lord George Murray pressed the siege vigorously, it was raised by some Hessian troops from Perth, and Murray retreated.

Fort Augustus, garrisoned by three companies of Guise's Regiment (the 6th, Royal Warwicks), surrendered to the rebels without a siege; but Fort William, under Captain Scot, of the same regiment, held out well, and the garrison made a most successful sortie, capturing a battery of eight guns and seven mortars, and this so discouraged the rebels that they retired. Lord Loudoun was surprised and defeated by 1,500 rebels, under the Duke of Perth, at Darnack, and retreated across to the Isle of Skye. The vigilance of the British cruisers off the coast placed Prince Charles Edward in a desperate plight for supplies and ammunition from France, several prizes being captured by the English ships.

The Duke of Cumberland having thoroughly rested his troops at Aberdeen, and collected supplies, again advanced, the ships coasting along the shores of Moray and Banff in view of the troops on the march. The Spey was crossed on April 12th at Fochabers, where it was thought the rebels would dispute the passage; but although a demonstration was made by about 3,000 of them, they retired without firing a shot. The troops forded the river, the current being strong and the water up to their waists, with the loss of one dragoon drowned, and encamped that night on the western bank of the river. The duke continued his march next day through Elgin to Forres, parties of the rebels falling back before our advanced guard; and on April 14th our troops arrived at Nairn, where the duke halted, receiving intelligence that the rebel army was concentrated and waiting to receive him about nine miles distant, on the road from Nairn to Inverness. Our troops halted the next day, and, being the duke's birthday, each man received a ration of brandy, biscuit, and cheese, at his expense.

Prince Charles Edward having blown up or burnt Fort Augustus and Fort George, had taken up a position at Culloden House, four miles east of Inverness (the house of Duncan Forbes, Esq.), in order to fight a pitched battle. He made an attempt to surprise the British by a night march on April 15th, and to attack them in their halting-place at Nairn; but the king's troops were very much on the alert, and the Duke of Perth, who had been given command of the operation, retired, as he saw no chance of effecting a surprise!

Night marches, says Napier, are seldom happy; and Wellington wrote that night operations could never succeed against really good troops. Where the Duke of Cumberland commanded there was always excellent discipline, as I can see well from his order-books in Flanders. His force had perfect confidence in him; the men respected and loved him, not because they thought him a genius (they had most of them suffered defeat at Fontenoy under his command), but because they knew he was brave, and would lead them into the fire, so to speak, himself; and a fighting general will always keep the confidence of the men.

The Highlanders had been successful at Preston Pans, and to a lesser degree at Falkirk, but the spirit animating Cumberland's English regulars was very different to that of Cope's two untrained battalions at Preston Pans; they were a picked body of highly disciplined troops, well seasoned in the campaign in Flanders, and led by a man they had confidence in; they were well fed, full of fight, and burning to avenge their loss of prestige at Preston Pans and Falkirk.

To give the men confidence in the bayonet against the claymore, the duke had instructed the troops in an entirely new bayonet exercise, to cope with the Highland claymore and target. As far as I can gather, the soldier was ordered to deliver his point, not at his adversary in front of him, but at his opponent on his right or left as the case might be. One reads of this in all accounts of Culloden, and there is no doubt that the drill was carried out; but it is obvious that the object was to give the soldiers confidence.

On April 16th, the troops marched from Nairn at 5 a.m., in three brigades, three columns in mass of five battalions each, the artillery and baggage following the first column. The cavalry moved along as a flank guard on the left (west), also in column.

After marching eight miles, the advanced guard, consisting of Kingston's Yeomanry and the Argyll clansmen under General Bland, Q.M.G., sighted the rebels some distance away on the left. The duke at once formed his force up in three lines, each column deploying; but finding the enemy did not advance, the force moved on for another half-mile in three lines with bayonets fixed, and after passing a morass came in full view of the rebels, who were drawn up in line of battle behind some huts and old walls on Strathgallen Moor, near Culloden House.

The first line of our troops consisted of six battalions, under General Lord Albemarle: Barrels (on the left); Dejean's, Scots Fusiliers, Price's, Cholmondeley's, Royal Scots (on the right); Cobham's Dragoons on the right, and Kerr's Dragoons on the left. Two guns were placed in the intervals between each battalion.

Second line, under Major-General Huske, five battalions: Wolfe's, Conway's, Sempill's, Bligh's (with which was Townshend), Flemings—so disposed as to front the openings of the first line, with three guns between the exterior battalions of each wing.

Third line, in reserve, under Brigadier Mordaunt: Blakeney's, Battereau's, Pulteney's, Howard's (the Buffs), and Kingston's Horse. The baggage was guarded by the Campbell clansmen.

★★★★★★

It will be noted that the three-line formation for the attack—which is the most modern idea of distributing large bodies of troops in the offensive—was used by the Duke of Cumberland as far back as Culloden. There is nothing new in the present day, except distances enormously increased.

★★★★★★

The Duke of Cumberland had on parade on this day 7,649 combatants of all ranks; and Prince Charles Edward mustered about 8,350 combatants.

The Scottish Army was formed in two lines, the clans under their respective chiefs. On the right of the line were forty of the principal gentlemen, who "dismounted themselves because of the differ-

A Plan of *CULLODEN* Battle, April 16th 1746

Park Wall broken down by the *Campbells*.

Lord GEORGE MURRAY.

||| Athol 500
||| Lochiel 600
||| Appin 200
||| Cluny 300
||| Lovat 500
||| M'Intosh 400
||| Farquharson 200

Right Flank 400. Pickets, by *Stapleton*.

Third Column 800. Colonel *Roy Stuart*'s, and those who have only Guns.

Col. Lord ANCRAM.
Mark Kerr's Drag. *Barrell*'s.
430   373

Wolfe's
491

Conway's *Sempill*'s *Blighs*
386   477   467

Lieutenant-General Earl of ALBEMARLE.

Major-General HUSKE.

Brigadier MORDAUNT.

The KING's ARMY.

The REBEL ARMY.

Lord JOHN DRUMMOND.

The Young PRETENDER.

Fitz-James's Horse.

Second Column 800. Lord *Lewis Gordon*'s, and *Glenbucket*'s to be ready to succour, when needful.

The Duke of *Perth*'s Regiment, and Lord *Ogilvie*'s, not to fire without positive Order, and to keep close as a fresh Corps de Reserve, 800.——In all 8350.

Sc. Fusil's *Price*'s *Cholmond.*
432   359   459

||| M'Intosh 300
||| M'Lean 100
||| M'Lean 100
||| Clanronald 250
||| Keppoch 300
||| Glengarry 600

Duke of PERTH.

Fleming's
425

Pulteney's *Howard*'s
474   463

Battereau's
423

Blakeney's
356

Kingston's Horse.
120

N. B. *Argyleshire* Highlanders on the Baggage Guard.

Kingston's Horse.
120

Major-General BLAND.
Royal. *Cobham*'s Drag.
481   430

Left Flank 400. Lord *John Drummond*'s Guards, Hussars, and *Perthshire* Squadron.

First Column 800. Those who have only Guns, and *Kilmarnock*'s Guards.

ence between their horses and the dragoons." The Atholmen, 500 strong, were the next on the right; then the MacLaughlans (150), the Camerons of Lochiel (600), Steuarts of Appin (200), Steuarts of Gardentilly (300), the Frasers of Lovat (500), the MacIntoshes (400), the Chisholms (150), the Farquharsons (300), the Gordons of Glenbucket (300), the MacInnons (200), the MacLeods (300), the MacLeans (100), the MacDonalds of Clanronald (250), the MacDonalds of Keppoch (300), the MacDonalds of Glengarry (400). (I cannot answer for the spelling, as the names are taken from old papers, where spelling was evidently of no consequence.—C. V. F. T.)

Four guns were placed in the centre, which was commanded by Lord John Drummond. The right wing was under Lord George Murray, and the left under the Duke of Perth.

Second line. On the right a battalion, under Lord Lewis Gordon, of 500 men; next to that a battalion of 500, commanded by Lord Ogilvie; then a battalion under Lord Lewis Drummond, 500 men; and the remainder, on the left, consisting of 500 men, under Lord Kilmarnock. They had a body of men in the park to keep the wall, which covered their right flank. In rear of the second line were posted the rebel cavalry to the number of 150 horsemen only. The rebel army amounted to about 8,350 men.

The Duke of Cumberland rode along the different regiments, and made the following address to the officers and men:—

> Gentlemen and fellow soldiers, I think proper to acquaint you, that you are instantly to engage in defence of your king and country, your religion, liberties and properties, and all that is dear to you; through the justice of the cause I make no doubt of leading you to a victory; stand but, and your enemies will soon flee; but if any amongst you are diffident of their courage or behaviour, which I have not the least reason to suspect; or any who through conscience or inclination, cannot be zealous or alert in performing their duty, my desire is, that all such would immediately retire; and I declare they shall have my free pardon for so doing; for I would rather be at the head of a 1000 brave and resolute men, than 10,000 amongst whom some, by cowardice or misbehaviour, might disorder or dispirit the troops and bring dishonour on the whole command.

He was received by the men with much cheering and shouts of "Flanders! Flanders!" At about 500 yards from the rebel army the

Duke of Cumberland at Culloden

Duke of Cumberland found that the morass which covered his right flank ended; he therefore recalled Cobham's Dragoons from the left flank, where they had been posted by Hawley, on the surmise that the right flank was safe, and he likewise ordered up a squadron of Kingston's Horse from the reserve, also to cover the right flank of the first line. By the time he had made this alteration it was almost one o'clock. The duke having sent forward Lord Bury, one of his A.D.C.'s, to see what some object which looked like a battery really was, the Jacobites commenced an artillery fire, which was very badly directed; the English artillery replied with great effect, using grape, inflicting heavy loss on the Highlanders, and putting them into the greatest confusion.

Goaded by the artillery fire, and not understanding this mode of fighting, the Highlanders clamoured on all sides to be led to the charge, and bodies of them began to move forward without orders; this forward move gradually developed into a charge, swarms of them doubling forward in a disorderly manner to close with the red-coated infantry, who, drawn up in perfect order, received them with a steady and regular fire. The Duke of Cumberland had himself taken post with Cholmondeley's Regiment on the right of the first line.

The Highlanders who attacked this part of the English line did not charge home; they could not face the steady fire being poured into them, and they fell back in disorder. In the meantime, however, the left of the British line had been enveloped and charged in the same way; the Atholmen, Camerons, and Frazers outflanked Barrel's Regiment (on the left of the first line), and rushed in, in spite of the perfect fire and steadiness of this regiment and Monro's (the 37th). The combat was short and sharp—a regular "bludgeon" fight of sword against bayonet. Barrels and Monro's were broken up, but they did not give ground. Many Highlanders broke their way through, only to be bayoneted afterwards by those in the second line. In the meanwhile, General Huske wheeled up two battalions of the second line—Bligh's and Sempill's—outflanking the Highlanders; and their fire, which was rapid and sustained and enfilading, at once stopped the Highland advance, and turned it into a flight.

> While the regiments of Barrell, (4th), and Monro, (37th, Dejean's), were briskly engaged with their bayonets in the front, where they did incredible slaughter, each man, according to instructions, directing his bayonet to his right hand man of the rebels, instead of pushing to the man directly opposite, a

Battle of Culloden

method meritorious of being registered among the brightest military inventions; for the rebels, whose ideas extended no further than to become offensive, never thought of the defensive; they never considered while they lifted up their broadswords with their right arms, how open they exposed their sides to receive the mortal stroke from the bayonet. The rebels so obstinately rushed on to death that there was scarce an officer or soldier in Barrell's regiment or in that part of Monro's which was engaged who did not kill one or two men each with their bayonets or spontoons—*Bigg's Military History*.

Barrel's Regiment had six officers killed and wounded and 119 N.C.O.'s and men killed and wounded: that is to say, 125 killed and wounded—in other words, about one-third out of a total only of 373 combatants, for that was the strength of the regiment before the battle. So, Wolfe must have been in the thick of it.

About this time General Hawley, who commanded the mounted troops, had got round the right flank of the rebels with Kerr's Dragoons and the Argyllshire men, and had broken down part of the park wall. The detachment guarding this wall took to flight, and the dragoons came through the gap, and, having formed up, charged furiously on the centre of the rebel army—"where they made a prodigious slaughter." Our mounted troops on the right had also got round the left wing of the Highlanders by now, and charged in the same way.

It was now two o'clock, and the battle was over. The rebels fled in the greatest rout and confusion, and Prince Charles Edward rode off the field with a small following. The pursuit of the mounted troops after the battle was close, and little quarter was given. The rebels lost about 2,500 killed and wounded. About 1,500 Highlanders were left dead on the field; 326 were taken prisoners, exclusive of 222 French who surrendered to General Bland and the cavalry at Inverness; 22 guns were taken, and over 2,000 muskets. The English loss was 52 killed and 251 wounded, according to the official list. Townshend's regiment, the 20th (Bligh's), which played an important part in the battle and was closely engaged, only lost 1 officer wounded, 4 men killed and 16 wounded.

No doubt very severe measures were taken after the battle, it being determined to take such steps as would ensure the country against a repetition of rebellion. Residences of the gentry and farms were burnt and cattle raided in those districts in which the inhabitants did not come in and surrender their arms; but it must be remembered that the country had been badly frightened, and it was not the first rebellion, that of 1715 having preceded it.

I was told, on visiting the battlefield, that very little is altered since the day of Culloden. The desolate moor, with the solemn green mounds marking the resting-places of the different clansmen who fell, stretches far away in the distance. Looking to the eastward, one sees the town of Inverness and the sea. I could picture the dawn breaking on the comfortless bivouac of the Highlanders in the bare, bleak heather; the news coming in of the advance of the English troops from Nairn; the Highlanders mustering half-starved and without hope; the columns of Cumberland gradually coming into sight; the redcoats, black-gaitered with white cross-belts, deploying into line with beautiful precision, with drums beating and colours uncased; and I wondered who had advised Prince Charles Edward to fight on such ground, eminently favourable to regular troops, with cavalry and artillery.

To my mind the battle was lost from the moment Prince Charles Edward determined to fight on Culloden Moor; by doing so, he gave the battle to the Duke of Cumberland. The terrain is like a billiard-table, and was the very ground for cavalry and artillery that Cumberland would have selected. Had Charles Edward only retired to the mountains and maintained a guerilla warfare, it is difficult to see how the duke could have attained success.

This decisive victory at Culloden extinguished the hopes of the Jacobites for ever, but the joy amongst loyalists in England and Scotland was great. The Duke of Cumberland received the thanks of both Houses of Parliament; and the Commons, sensible of his great service to England in crushing the rebellion, voted him £25,000 a year for life, in addition to his former revenue of £15,000; and on his return from the North he was accorded a great reception in London, the City being lined with crowds anxious to cheer the deliverer of the nation.

Appendix

RETURN OF REGIMENTS AT CULLODEN
ON APRIL 16TH, 1746

Showing the number of officers and men in each regiment of cavalry and infantry on the morning of the battle

Infantry.

	Officers.	Men.
2nd battalion Royal Scots (now 1st Foot)	26	455
Howard's (now 3rd Buffs)	16	448
Barrell's (now 4th Foot)	20	353
Wolfe's (now 8th Foot, King's Liverpool Regiment)	22	352
Pulteney's (now 13th Foot, Somerset Light Infantry)	22	352
Price's (now 14th Foot)	23	336
Bligh's (now 20th, Lancashire Fusiliers)	20	447
Campbell's Scots Fusiliers (now Royal Scots Fusiliers)	19	393
Lord Semple's (Black Watch)	23	392
Blakeney's (now 27th, Inniskilling Fusiliers)	20	336
Cholmondeley's (now 34th, Border Regiment)	24	435
Fleming's (now 36th)	26	389
Battereau's (since disbanded)	27	396
Dejean's (now 37th Foot)	23	468
Conway's (now 48th, Northamptonshire Regiment)	24	362

Cavalry.

Kingston's Horse (yeomanry raised by Duke of Kingston)	—	240
Cobham's Dragoons	—	430
Lord Mark Kerr's Dragoons (11th Hussars)	—	430
Argyll Highlanders (Irregulars), say 300		
	335	7014

Total Combatants . . . 7649

CASUALTIES AT CULLODEN

Regiments.	Officers killed.	Officers wounded.	N.C.O.'s and Men killed.	N.C.O.'s and Men wounded.
Cavalry.				
Cobham's Dragoons	—	—	1	—
Mark Kerr's Dragoons	—	—	3	3
Kingston's Horse (Yeomanry)	—	—	—	1
Infantry.				
2nd batt. Royal Scots	—	—	—	4
Howard's (the Buffs)	—	—	1	2
Barrell's (4th)	Captain Lord Robert Kerr.	Lt.-Col. Rich; Capt. Romer; Lt. Edmonson; Ensigns Campbell and Brown	16	103
Wolfe's (8th)	—	Ensign Bruce	—	—
Pulteney's (13th)	—	—	—	—
Price's (14th)	Capt. Crossette.	Capt. Simpson	—	2
Bligh's (20th)	—	Lt. Trappaud	4	16
Scots Fusiliers	—	—	—	7
Semple's (42nd)	—	—	1	13
Blakeney's (27th)	—	—	—	—
Cholmondeley's (34th)	—	—	1	2
Fleming's (36th)	—	—	—	6
Dejean's (37th)	—	Capt. Kennier; Lts. King and Lort; Ensigns Dally and Mondork	14	63
Conway's (48th)	—	Capt. Spark	1	4
Battereau's	—	Capt. Carter	—	2
Lord Loudoun's	Capt. J. Campbell	—	6	2
Argyll Highlanders (Irregulars)	Capt. Colin Campbell.	—	—	—
Artillery	—	—	—	6
			48	236

Laffeldt 1747

After the defeat of the rebels at Culloden, George Townshend embarked with Lord Albemarle at Leith for Ostend, having been appointed to the personal staff of H.R.H. the Duke of Cumberland who had now taken up the supreme command of the allied armies in Flanders. His victory at Culloden had confirmed public opinion in England that the defeat at Fontenoy had really been occasioned by the Dutch.

The allied army consisted of 8,000 English, 18,000 Hanoverians, and 6,000 Hessians, under the Duke of Cumberland; the Dutch at Breda, under Waldeck; and the Austrians and 4,000 Bavarians at Venloo, on the east side of the Meuse, under Marshal Bathiani; but though on paper the total was 140,000, only 126,000 could be mustered.

As the French had obtained manifest advantage in the last campaign from taking the field early and before the allies, the Duke of Cumberland now determined to get the start of the French, putting the troops in motion in the severe month of February; but he was very soon taught by experience that the opposite of wrong is not always right. Although the siege train was not yet disembarked, the army was marched towards Antwerp to besiege that city; but scarcely had the troops taken the field when the dream of glory vanished; for before the allies had marched half-way there, it was found that the army could proceed no farther for want of subsistence, someone having forgotten to provide wheeled transport to carry the forage!

So, our troops remained on the bleak and barren heaths about eleven miles south-east of Breda for six weeks without moving, exposed to the inclemency of the weather and the derision of the French; while Saxe, as if he affected to despise us, continued to keep his army in quarters in the country between Bruges, Antwerp, and Brussels for a long time afterwards. The famous marshal is reported to have said that:

> When the Duke of Cumberland had sufficiently weakened his army, he would convince him that the first duty of a general was to provide for its preservation.

As soon as the severity of the winter was over, Saxe concentrated his army between Antwerp and Mechlin, having at his command 136,000 combatants. He detached Count Lowendahl, with 27,000 men, on April 16th, to invade the Dutch territory, while he covered Antwerp and watched the motions of the Duke of Cumberland, who at last, after lying inactive for fourteen weeks, overcame the difficulties of rations and transport in time to find that Antwerp was too tough a morsel for him, and that an attack on it was equally contrary to the rules of prudence and of war. But though he abandoned this enterprise, Saxe proceeded at his leisure to execute his, and after the reduction of Dutch Flanders he proceeded towards Maestricht. The Duke of Cumberland, apprehending from the movements of the French that they intended to invest Maestricht, resolved to march with all expedition and put himself between the French and that place, and thus came about the battle of Laffeldt.

The allies decamped from behind the Demer on June 16th, marched all night, and next day encamped at Zorrork; on June 19th, they arrived at Laffeldt, and marched in three columns to Lonaken, (this movement obliged the French to halt near Tongres), two miles north-east of Maestricht, encamping the same night between that place and Ghenck, about two and a half miles south of Lonaken. The Austrians had already formed a junction with the English and Dutch. The Duke of Cumberland was in supreme command, Marshal Bathiani being in command of the Austrian troops, and Waldeck of the Dutch. As the two armies were quite near each other now, frequent cavalry skirmishes took place, in which General Trip and his Austrian hussars rendered a very good account of the French cavalry.

However, Count Thermont continued to occupy a position at Tongres, and this showed that Saxe was going to support him with his whole force, and if possible gain the camp at Bilsen. That situation seemed so advantageous that the Duke of Cumberland, on reconnoitring the country, resolved to possess himself of it. Accordingly, on June 20th the troops marched at daybreak, and about 4 a.m. the enemy were perceived in motion to the south in large columns. The allies then endeavoured to gain the heights of Herdeeren, but were forestalled by the French cavalry; and so the allies extended their line from Bilsen to Wirle, a mile to the west of Maestricht and about three from Herdeeren, occupying all the villages on that line, the right still holding Bilsen as in their former position, the allied cavalry out in front covering them.

The remainder of the day (June 20th) was spent in getting the allied army into position; it was decided to act on the defensive, if the French appeared eager to attack.

The villages of Great and Little Spawe were occupied by the Austrians (see plan). Towards evening a cannonade on both sides began.

During the night, the Austrians on the right and the Dutch at Wirle on the left entrenched themselves, while the British, Hessians, and Hanoverians, who occupied the centre of the line at Laffeldt hamlet, under Sir John Ligonier, did not entrench, nor did they put Laffeldt in a state of defence. According to George Townshend's notes they did not seem to know whether this village in front of the line should be occupied or not. Several contradictory orders were given; it was once ordered to be burnt, and twice to be evacuated and reoccupied; and when at last it was decided to occupy it, nothing whatever was done towards strengthening it for defence. The British, however, got some guns into position here to rake the French as they descended from the heights of Herdeeren.

The following British regiments, under Sir John Ligonier, were present. Cavalry: Scots Greys, Rich's, Rothes, and Copes Dragoons, and Cumberland's Hussars. Infantry: 2nd battalion of 1st Foot Guards, Wolfe's, Pulteney's, Howard's, Scots Fusiliers, Welsh Fusiliers, Crawford's, Douglas's, Johnson's, Fleming's, Dejean's, and Conway's. As soon as it was daylight on June 21st, the Duke of Cumberland, with his staff, rode along the line; Marshal Saxe put his troops in motion, and at 9 a.m. a heavy column of ten French battalions made a determined attack on La Veldt or Val hamlet, a small enclosure, consisting of five houses, and constituting the key of the allies' position.

The British regiments of Crawford, Pulteney, and Dejean, and Frendeman's Hanoverian battalion, occupied the village; the British guns continued a well-nourished fire the whole time the French were advancing, doing terrible execution. The famous Irish Brigade led this French column, and Fontenoy was renewed between them and the three British battalions in the village. The struggle was fierce and slaughtering, the Irish being hurled back with great loss; but brigade after brigade of the French pushed on to take the village, which had,

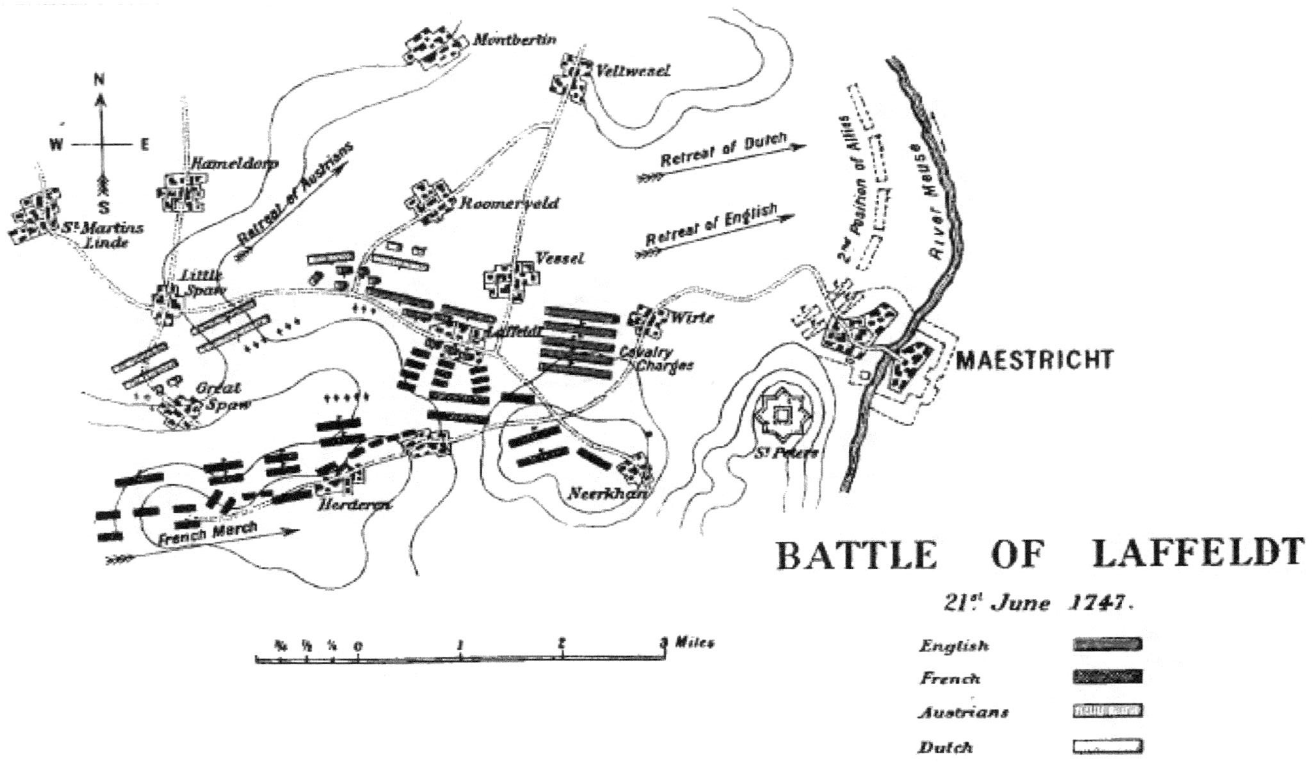
BATTLE OF LAFFELDT
21st. June 1747.
English
French
Austrians
Dutch
N
S
W
E
Montbertin
Veltwezel
Hameldorp
Retreat of Austrians
Roomerveld
St. Martins Linde
Retreat of Dutch
Retreat of English
2nd Position of Allies
River Meuse
Vessel
Little Spaw
Laffeldt
Wirte
Cavalry Charges
MAESTRICHT
Great Spaw
St. Peters
Neerkhan
Herderen
French March
¾ ½ ¼ 0 1 2 3 Miles

from sheer stupidity, not been prepared for defence. It was a desperate struggle, the hamlet being taken and retaken several times; Saxe kept pushing on one column after another against the village, which the passive attitude of the Austrians on the right enabled him to do.

Crawford's battalion lost about 50 killed and wounded and 187 men taken prisoners, Dejean's 6 officers killed and wounded and 128 men, Pulteney's 4 officers and 125 men, and Howard's (the Buffs) 10 officers and 139 men killed and wounded and about 30 prisoners, in this bludgeon fight in and about the small hamlet. Baron Ziggesaer, the German *aide-de-camp* to the Duke of Cumberland, was killed; another *aide-de-camp*, Captain Scheiger, was killed by a round-shot, Major Scott being also killed; and Wolfe, now a brigade-major, was also wounded (he received his brevet lieutenant-colonelcy for this battle).

For a long time, the battle raged round La Val. At last the regiments holding the village, unable to withstand the constant supply of fresh troops brought against them, were forced out, the houses and enclosures being occupied by the French. Ligonier then sent forward the Buffs, Conway's, and a Hanoverian battalion to retake it. These battalions went forward, scrambling over the hedges (for no communications had been made!); they carried out their orders, and the French were cleared out again. Again, was it retaken by the enemy, making the fifth time, our weakened battalions not being able to stand against the overwhelming numbers of the French. We are told that the French brigades of Navarre, La Marque, Monaco, and Royal des Vaisseaux were decimated, and the Irish Brigade had long ago been taken off the field completely shattered. However, Saxe was determined to take the village of Val, and pushed forward fresh troops time after time.

When the French first attacked La Val, the Duke of Cumberland had sent an *aide-de-camp* to Marshal Bathiani to say that the enemy were devoting all their efforts to that place, and asking for support. Bathiani said he would send nine battalions under Count Daun and five battalions from the reserve. Part of the nine battalions arrived, but none of the reserve. The British and Hanoverians stood well, and the French had gained no other advantage than taking La Val. The Dutch and the Austrians were ordered to advance by the duke, whereupon a large body of Dutch cavalry in the centre, on being ordered to charge and take the pressure off our weary infantry, who were hard pressed, suddenly turned, and fled in a disgraceful panic at full gallop through our battalions, trampling the men underfoot.

The Duke of Cumberland galloped to the head of the retreating

BATTLE OF LAFFELDT

Dutch, and endeavoured with the Dutch general of cavalry (General Cannenberg) to rally them, but in vain—the whole centre began to retire; the French had broken the allied army in two halves. No attempt was made to rally, and a precipitate retirement on Maestricht commenced; this retreat would have speedily degenerated into a flight, had not Sir John Ligonier, with what might, in the words of Napier, be well called a felicitous example of intuitive genius, entirely in accordance with the modern theory of the role of cavalry, charged at the head of the British cavalry and some Austrian squadrons, to sacrifice themselves in order to gain time for the retreat of the army.

It was a splendid charge; the British cavalry overthrew all before them, the French cavalry being checked; but the usual thing happened—there was no rallying, the men went too far in pursuit, and in turn they were cut up, in the same way as the Union Brigade at Waterloo. Sir John Ligonier, whose horse was killed under him, was taken prisoner by a French *carabinier*. The Scots Greys alone lost 140 men killed and wounded, Rothes' Dragoons 125 killed and wounded, but Rich's and Copes very few. Nevertheless, the object was gained; just as the charge of the Austrian reserve cavalry at Koeniggratz saved their army and enabled them to retreat, so Sir John Ligonier saved the allies on this day. Alluding to the conduct of the Scots Greys in this charge, Townshend speaks of them as the heroes of the campaign.

The Austrians retreated northwards in perfect order, the allies taking shelter under the works of Maestricht on the north side. The French did not make any serious attempts at pursuit, but were content with their victory, and with occupying the position the allies had been beaten out of. The allies lost in all 5,680 men killed and wounded, of which the heaviest share naturally fell on the English, Hanoverians, and Hessians, who had held La Val, the English losing 2,110 killed, wounded, and prisoners, the Hanoverians 2,435, the Hessians 385, the Austrians 600, and the Dutch 150. The Austrians and Dutch were practically unengaged. The British lost four colours and sixteen guns, and the Hanoverians one colour. The principal British officers killed were Lieut.-Colonel Williams, of Howard's (the Buffs), and Lieut.-Colonel Ross, of Douglas's. The wounded were: General Bland, Lord Glasgow, and Lieut.-Colonels Martin, Macdougall, Lockhart, Deane, Stanhope, and Jackson. Sir John Ligonier, Colonel Conway, and Lieutenant Robert Sutton were taken prisoners.

In George Townshend's *Private Book* the following anecdote of the battle is given:—

SIR JOHN LIGONIER.

Soon after break of day on the morning of the battle the Duke of Cumberland went to Marshal Battiani's quarters. Captain Townshend's horse, as well as Captain Scheiger's not being got ready so soon as the others of H.R.H.'s suite, they followed as soon as they could, but on their arrival found H.R.H. had left the marshal; on their return to join him they fell in with the regiment of dragoons to which Captain Scheiger belonged, in a vale, where it had halted, and the officers were taking a little refreshment on a Drum Head and invited them.

They stopped for a few minutes, when one of the officers said, 'Scheiger, you look grave today.' Scheiger drank a glass to their healths and said, 'I take my leave of you.' and on their returning immediately to join the Duke, Captain Townshend asked him what he meant by taking his leave, 'Why,' says he, 'I shall be one of the first men killed, if not the first today.' On overtaking the duke, and anxious to be seen as the action was beginning they rode up pretty close to His Royal Highness who turning round ordered one of the regiments to reinforce the village (of Laffeldt).

Scheiger being nearest received the order and Captain Townshend pulled up his horse and turned round to observe (as the former spoke broken English) if he delivered it right, when the first cannon shot cut Scheiger almost in two, the horse ran into the front of the battalion and Captain Townshend delivered the order and told the soldier near the colours (who secured the horse) to whom he belonged. (It is related that George Townshend remarked, on seeing Captain Scheiger's head blown to pieces, "I never thought he had so much brains before.")

After the battle Townshend was sent home with His Royal Highness's dispatches, and landed with them at Solebay, where he was informed that he had been elected member of Parliament for Norfolk. In connection with the battle he relates in his *Diary* how the Duke of Cumberland was under a very heavy fire throughout the action, and "saw many respectable officers, to his great concern, brought out on horses' backs slain or badly wounded." He speaks of the feeble resistance made by the Dutch, and he says that the general opinion was "that, had the Austrians attacked the French on their left in the beginning of the action, the Allies might have succeeded—but why this was not done has always remained a secret."

British Infantry at Laffeldt

No military events resulted from the Battle of Laffeldt. The allies crossed the Meuse into the duchy of Limburg, where they encamped; and though they lost the battle of Laffeldt, they secured Maestricht. On the other hand, another result of the defeat was the fall of Bergen-op-Zoom, which was invested by Count Lowendahl with 36,000 men as soon as the allies had crossed the Meuse. After nine weeks' siege Lowendahl carried the city by assault. The Dutch garrison numbered 3,000 men, including Lord John Murray's Highland regiment, which especially distinguished itself, the French losing several thousand men in the assault. Both the French and the allied armies now retired into winter quarters, and thus ended a series of campaigns in the Low Countries which did not reflect credit on the strategy of the allies, though the British troops not only maintained, but, as at Fontenoy, raised their reputation for bravery and coolness under fire.

The following is an extract from a French account of Laffeldt:—

Un corps de troupes placé sous les ordres du Conte de Clermont fondit sur le village fortifié que le Maréchal Saxe à la tête de quelques regiments, assaillait sur un autre point. Les retranchements furent vaillamment défendus et ce ne fut qu'après six attaques meurtrières que les positions furent enlevées. Les Anglais se distinguèrent surtout par une opiniâtre résistance; eux seuls balançaient encore la victoire lorsque des cris de triomphe retentissent tout autour d'eux leur annoncèrent la prise de Lawfeld. Ils se résignèrent enfin à battre en retraite, mais en bon ordre, et se retirèrent sous les murs de Maëstricht. La cavalerie Anglo-Hanoverien se signala par des charges brillantes, qui furent accueilliés par nos soldats avec la plus héroïque impassibilité; elle finit par être rompue et écrasée, mais sa vaillante conduite donna au Duc de Cumberland le temps d'opérer sa retraite avec le gros de l'armée et repasser la Meuse. Le Comte d'Estrées poursuivit les ennemis et leur fit un grand nombre de prisonniers, parmi lesquels se trouvait le général Ligonier né sujet Français.

The following letter of George Townshend's to a friend of his throws light on the manner in which the battle of Laffeldt was lost:—

We had in this battle every advantage we had ever wished for; we found the French uncovered by entrenchments, unsupported by batteries, in a plain, and on the march; and yet we suffered them to gain the Battle of Laveldt. For (not to mention neglecting to cut off twenty thousand men, which was in our power for two days together) it seems, we knew not, whether a village in front of the line, ought to be occupied or no: for, a little before the battle, it was once ordered to be burnt, and twice to be evacuated and repossessed; and when at last some wiser than the rest prevailed upon the R—— C——, to make use of so capital an advantage, nothing was done to add to the strength of the village, by *fortifying* it towards the enemy, and nothing to procure means of supporting the troops in it, by *laying it open towards our line*—but this was not all.

A space was left *unoccupied* which one of the battalions, which had been ordered out, had never returned to possess; and by that the enemy found at once an easy unopposed entrance into the village; which enabled them by attacking in flank and in rear, to dislodge the troops, that were defending it. So that, from the first, they were as much masters of the village as we; nor ever could be thoroughly driven out of it, though several of our battalions scrambled over hedges (for no communication had been made) to support their companions: and then though the enemy had gained no other advantage, though all the troops both on the right and on the left (Austrians and Dutch) stood firm and unattacked, without one attempt to rally, a *precipitate retreat* was made by the infantry towards Maestricht, a retreat which would have been made with as little safety, as it was with little *order*, if Ligonier s ever memorable attack with the cavalry had not secured it, and given time to the army to reach Maestricht in safety.

Ligonier, Curtius like, sacrificed himself to save the army, by leaping into the gulf, with what was most valuable in it. It may not be incurious to observe, that this attack of cavalry so beneficial to us and so much honoured by the enemy—an attack, wherein the British squadrons of the first line and a few Hanoverians adjoining them, put a whole wing of the enemy in such confusion, as obliged them to think of their own security, instead of disturbing our retreat—this attack, I say, was openly condemned in our army, before Ligonier's return from captivity. *The honour of saving the army was envied him, by those who had reaped none themselves.* But the service was too glaring not to establish its own merit. Nor was the testimony of the enemy wanting to acknowledge and admire what had checked their pursuit.

In February, 1748, George Townshend was gazetted to a company in the 1st Regiment of Foot Guards, and so became at the same time a lieutenant-colonel in the army, as the commission is worded, "and to take your rank as Lieutenant Colonel of Foot." On returning from England to Flanders, he found the enemy retiring; and his account of the march from Roermonde to the neighbourhood of Grave gives an idea of the arrangements and orders for marching, and makes it clear that there was still much room for improvement, even after" all the lessons given to our allied generals by Saxe, which one would have thought would not all have been thrown away. As an example the march from Roermonde to the neighbourhood of Grave is thus described by Townshend in a letter:—

> What might have been performed in three days with ease, was scarce performed in eleven. The destined ground for the camp, after marching two days towards it, could not be got at, at all. The cavalry was obliged on the eighth day, to leave the infantry, and make a forced march to approach the forage; and the infantry to follow and abandon the artillery, and yet this march was immediately directed by the general himself.

It only remained now to transport the troops to England as expeditiously as possible, for peace had been concluded; but many delays took place, and our troops were kept suffering from the cold in Dutch barns till the depth of winter.

> Letter from my son George with the allied army in Flanders," endorsed by the 3rd Viscount Townshend, dated Eindhoven, when he was still A.D.C. to the Duke of Cumberland:—
> It is certain here that H.R.H. the Duke will soon set out for England but what day or who he will take with him remains still a most profound and impenetrable secret. Our army is here in the most perfect state of inaction, the beauty, address, discipline and spirit of our troops is really a most melancholy object. The other day we used to only ruminate the enemy's irresistible superiority and now the greatest party only ruminate the reduction the nation will soon be obliged to make, and in one day discharge a number of men from her service that no other nation in Europe would be glad to engage and entertain in a time of the most settled peace.
> P.S. I hope my sister Audrey is well and also 'the captain' (his brother Roger).

SERGEANT 1ST FOOT GUARDS

On August 16th, 1748, dated Eindhoven, George Townshend writes to his father, saying that he hoped to have the honour of attending H.R.H. the Duke of Cumberland to England.

P.S. I have received from Norfolk the compliments and invitations of the gentlemen of the Constitution Feast for the 1st August. I hope they have given you the same notice on this occasion that the feast may have been attended with Rainham venison.

In a note-book of George Townshend's I find the following remarks on tactics, comparing Laffeldt to the Battle of Ramillies:—

One of the principal causes of the loss of the Battle of Ramillies by the French was that that village was not properly possessed by the troops—that it was too far from the line of battle, or rather the line of battle too far from it, to support it—nor were there proper *ouvertures* made for the communication of the troops destined for its defence, by which means the allies, attacked it with great advantage and says Trenquière 'What is more surprising is that *it was expected that this village was to cost the enemy very dear although at too great a distance to be properly supported by the line*, though in fact these troops were ill posted, and being neither supported soon enough or effectually, were soon forced by the flanks which were unprotected.'

The same fault was also one of the principal causes of the loss of the Battle of Lawfeldt in the year 1747, and every circumstance attended the same disposition except that difference which the superior in the firmness in the British Infantry to maintain a bad post longer than the French. It is remarkable that the attack which Mons. de Saxe made upon Lawfeldt was the same as the Duke of Marlborough made on that of Ramillies. The front of their attack which extended beyond the village took it in flank. Both the defensive generals saw without making any movement to interrupt the certain effect of this manoeuvre; as Trenquière observes '*ni l'officier ni le soldat étaient capables de redresser par leur seule valeur une affaire perdue par sa mauvaise disposition, de sorte que le desordre fut bientôt général par tout la droite, qui abandonna son champs de bataille et son canon.*'

The consequence of the loss of the village of Lawfeldt was so decisive, that the retreat of the greatest part of the infantry of the Left to Maestricht was near a general *deroute*; and having expended all their ammunition, they were saved only by a very judicious and well timed attack of Lord Ligonier with the cavalry of the left wing, whose impression covered their retreat.

On October 10th, 1748, dated Eindhoven, George Townshend writes to Lord Townshend:—

> I propose waiting on you in Norfolk within a few days after I arrive in England. I am afraid the service of Parliament will be such as will afford but little pretence for my absence being called a neglect of my duty to my country. His Royal Highness likes the greyhounds I gave him so much that he has desired me to secure him another brace not very nearly allied to the former that he may be able to secure the breed for Windsor.

I also find a draft of a letter from Lord Townshend to his son George, urging him most strongly to visit his constituents as soon as he arrives in England, "as you ought to do if you desire to be ever chosen again by the county."

The date of Townshend's return from Flanders and the end of the campaign is fixed by the following letter from him to Lord Townshend at Raynham Hall:—

> Craven Street, London,
> November 29th, 1748.
>
> As I have now gone through the ceremony of waiting on the Royal Family and kissing hands, attended this day the opening of Parliament and voted His Majesty an address of thanks for his speech, I shall wait on you in the country immediately.

The transports bringing the troops home met with awful weather; the ship bringing a part of the Scots Greys was lost, and many of the men perished.

A letter written by George Townshend after the campaign to a friend in Parliament seems such a true prophecy of the policy afterwards carried through successfully by Pitt, inasmuch as it finally crushed Napoleon, that I insert it here:—

> France has gained no acquisition, and has had her past experience confirmed, that she never can succeed in establishing Universal Monarchy, while we exert ourselves to oppose her; nor will she I dare say, ever resume a project, which had hitherto, to her cost, so often failed; unless she should be encouraged by the

establishment of a new system of *Politics* among us, to expect that we will no more thwart it. Let us then cease to give her that encouragement, by ceasing to declaim against *Land wars*, and *Foreign connections*. Let our interest direct us to watch every motion of that overgrown Power; let us interpose *our influence*, at all times, in behalf of those States of Europe, whose common interests join them with us in a *Natural Alliance* against it.

And if, at any time, any of them, especially if the Republic of *Holland* or *House of Austria*, should be in danger from it, let us interpose our *force* to defend those upon whom our own security depends. Nor let us, because one war has been carried on with as little conduct as economy, determine never to engage in another, though the preservation of the liberties of Europe (with which those of England are intimately connected) should require it.

Appendix

Townshend's Commission in the First Foot Guards

George the Second by the Grace of God King of Great Britain France and Ireland Defender of the Faith etc. etc. To our trusty and welbeloved George Townshend Esqr. Greeting: We reposing especiall trust and confidence in your loyalty, courage and good conduct, do, by these presents, constitute and appoint you to be captain of that company whereof Roger Townshend Esqr. was late captain in our First Regiment of Foot Guards commanded by our most dearly beloved son William Augustus Duke of Cumberland Captain General of our forces and to take your rank as Lieutenant Colonel of Foot.

You are therefore to take the said company into your care and charge and duly to exercise as well the officers as soldiers thereof in arms, and to use your best endeavours to keep them in good order and discipline. And we do thereby command them to obey you as their captain; and you are to observe and follow such orders and directions from time to time as you shall receive from us, your colonel, or any other your superior officer according to the rules and discipline of war in pursuance of the trust hereby reposed in you.

Given at our court at St. James's the twenty-fifth day of February 1747/8 in the twenty-first year of our reign.

By His Majesty's Command
Bedford.

Entered with the
Commissary General
R. C. Sovey.
Entered with the
Secretary at War
Edward Hoyd.
George Townshend Esqr. Captain in the first Regt. of Foot Guards.

A REGIMENTAL PLAN OF THE LOSSES OF THE ALLIES AT LA VELDT, alias VAL BATTLE

British Troops.	Regiments.	Officers killed.	Officers wounded.	Officers missing.	Men killed.	Men wounded.	Men missing.
	General Staff Officers	. .	Maj.-Gen. Bland; Majors of Brigade Leslie and Wolfe; Maj. Scott, the Duke's Aide-de-Camp; and Major Green, Engineers	Gen. Sir John Ligonier, with 2 Aides-de-Camp; the Hon. Capt. Keppel and Capt. Campbel; Capt. Heath, Engineer			
	Scotch Greys	. .	Lient.-Col. McDougal; Capts. Preston and Blair; Lt. Heron; Cornets Oglevie, Herrington, Ballantain, and Brown	Lts. Wauchope and Douglas; Cornet Hunt; Quartermaster Carlisle	112	28	
Cavalry	Rich's	. .	Cornet Scott		2	8	12
	Rothes'	Lt. Gordon; Cornet Hay		Cornet Simpson; Quartermaster Goodwin	80	25	2
	Cope's His Royal Highness's	Quartermaster Simpson	Lt. Armstrong; Quartermaster Seaman	Cornet Balmere Lt.-Col. Lord Robert Sutton; Capts. Otway, Hall, and Kirk; Cornet Kirton; Quartermaster Evans		8	5
	Second Battalion of First Regiment of Guards				3	13	63
	Ditto Third Reg. Old Buffs	Ensign Brown Capt. Hackett; Ensign French Capt. Meggot	Capts. Crosby, Stoyte, and Jocelyn	Capt. ——	5 7 40	32 19 85	37 20 26
	Wolfe's	. .	Lt.-Col. Martin; Maj. Lafausille; Capt. Chetewood; Lt. Conway; Ensigns Wilson, Webb, and Hamilton; Quartermaster Walwork.		11	89	25
	Pulteney's	Lt. Haddock	Capt. Stafford; Ensigns Nailor and Holyday		29	83	57

Infantry	Maj.-Gen. Howard's	Lt.-Col. Williams	Maj. Pettitot; Capt. Masters; Lts. Goddard, Brown, Martin, and Phillip; Ensigns Dobson and Fuller	14	125	30
	Scotch Fusiliers Welsh ditto	Capt. Johnson	Capt. Leslie	7	17	12
			Capts. Fortescue, Izard, and Baldwin; Lts. Eyre, Rich, Gregg, Aday, McLaughlon, and Hewit			187
	Lord Crawford's	Lt. Knight	Capts. Scott and Laurice; Lts. Stephens and Gore	1	42	26
	Douglas's	Lt.-Col. Ross; Maj. Roper	Capt. Fuller; Lts. Rogers, Farquhar, and Ross	31	65	13
	Johnson's		Lt.-Col. Lockhart; Maj. Lacy; Capts. Lord Glasgow and Herrie; Lts. Gardiner, Edgmonstone, and Cope; Ensigns Monneypenny, Francombe, and Morris	4	67	5
	Fleming's	Maj. Petrice; Lt. Brodie	Lt.-Col. Jackson; Capts. Morgan, Dod, Gore, and Peckell; Lt. Aikland; Ensgs. Vaughan, Strong, Ebrington, and Potter	12	64	82
	Dejean's	Lt. Clement	Lt.-Col. Deane; Capt. Goddard; Lt. Gremes	Ensign Duncan	24	79	90
	Conway's		Lt.-Col. Stanhope; Capts. Chomley and Douglas; Lts. Bodyer, McQueen; Ensign Crimble	Capt. Boucher and Lt. Lord Col. Conway; Capt. Dobson; Lts. Ramsey, Ellis; Ensigns Waterhouse, Rimple	10	28	32
Artillery			Maj. Michelson; Lts. McCleod, Farrington, Dexter, Stephens, and Goguey		42	9	25
Hanoverians	Cavalry	Col., 1; Subs., 4	Lt.-Cols., 2; Majs., 2; Capts., 4; Subs., 8	Capts., 2 : Subs., 2	30	19	65
	Infantry	Lt.-Cols., 2; Capts., 5; Subs., 2	Lt.-Gen., 1; Brig., 1; Cols., 6; Majs., 3; Capts., 10; Subs., 26	Col., 1; Lt.-Col., 1; Capts., 4; Subs., 2	64	176	245
	Artillery	Capts., 2	Subs., 3		437	1250	5
					7	20	
Hessians		Lt., 1; Adj., 1	Lt.-Gen., 1; Maj.-Gen., 1; Cols., 2; Maj., 1; Capts., 6; Subs., 8	Maj., 1; Capt., 1; Subs., 2	38	258	98

Total loss, 5,140; the Imperialists and Dutch not inserted.

At Home 1748-59

On Townshend's return from Flanders he was quartered with his regiment of the Guards in London, and his time was passed in carrying out the ordinary regimental routine of an officer of the Guards.

He married in 1751 Lady Charlotte Compton, only daughter and heiress of the Earl of Northampton, and Baroness Ferrers of Chartley in her own right; and the marriage proved a very happy one. Townshend took Cranmer Hall, which is only three or four miles from Raynham Hall, where the family has owned the same land since the twelfth century.

George Townshend was passing now the happiest time of his life, married to the woman he was passionately in love with, staying a good deal at the old Hall, where his father was living, where he himself was born, and where he was to die. There is no fairer scene in England that I know of than Raynham Hall, standing amidst woods that are beautiful and a park which is magnificent—the lake, nearly two miles long, below the house being very picturesque. No place that I have seen is fitter than the beautiful old pink-coloured brick house to convey the idea of all that is old-fashioned and dignified.

Raynham Hall was built by Inigo Jones in 1630, and was enlarged by Charles, Viscount Townshend, the grandfather of the subject of this book. At Raynham is the celebrated Belisarius of Salvator Rosa, supposed to be the finest work of that master in England. It was presented by Frederick the Great to Charles, Viscount Townshend, and was valued about thirty years ago at £10,000; the frame is surmounted by the arms of Prussia. The collection of pictures at Raynham is of great interest, especially, to my mind, a gallery of full-length portraits of English soldiers who served in the Low Country wars under Horatio, Lord Vere, one of Queen Elizabeth's greatest captains. His daughter and heiress, Mary Vere, married Sir Roger Townshend, Bart., M.P. for

RAYNHAM HALL.

Norfolk, who died in 1636. There is a full-length portrait by Janssen of Mary Vere, who brought all these pictures into the Townshend family. The names of Lord Vere's lieutenants are painted on the pictures; they stand with their pikes at the order, with pointed beards, fierce moustaches, and the ridiculous trunks and hose of Elizabeth's time.

Sir Robert Carey, Capt.; Sir Jacob Astley, Capt.; Henry, Earl of Oxford; Sir Thomas Gates, Capt.; Sir Henry Paston, Capt.; Captain Milles; Sir Thomas Winne, Capt.; Sir Mich. Everid, Capt.; Captain Teboll; Sir Wm. Lovelace, Capt.; Sir John Burroughs, Capt.; Sir Simon Harcourt, Sergt.-Major; Sir John Burlacy, Lieut.-Col.; Sir Thomas Dalle, Capt.; Sir Edward Vere, Lieut.-Col.; Sir John Congreve, Capt.; Sir Thomas Dalton, Capt.; Sir Edward Harwood, Capt. These portraits are particularly mentioned in the preface to Vere's *Commentaries*.

There is a three-quarter length of the Duke of Alva in armour by Sir A. Moor. There is the celebrated full-length portrait of George Townshend himself as a field-marshal, by Sir Joshua Reynolds; his brother Charles, the brilliant Chancellor of the Exchequer, also by Sir Joshua Reynolds; Dorothy Walpole, Viscountess Townshend, whose ghost is still supposed to haunt Raynham—she was the grandmother of George Townshend, and sister of the famous statesman Sir Robert Walpole. There is the Roundhead Fairfax, and also Horatio, Lord Townshend, who was chiefly instrumental in restoring Charles II. to his own again, for he it was who came over from Holland secretly and arranged the affair with the terrible General Monk.

There are Pelhams and Harrisons; there is the Marquess of Montrose; there are Knellers, Vandycks, Lelys, and Reynolds; and all the old portraits, which are there now as they were when George Townshend was a boy, look at you in silence, and tell a tale of the past glory of the family. As a boy, I remember well the picture that used to fascinate me was the handsome young Colonel Roger Townshend, of the Buffs, in his scarlet coat and three-cornered hat, who fell gallantly against the French at Ticonderoga in America.

About this time differences arose between Townshend and his former general, H.R.H. the Duke of Cumberland, now commander-in-chief of the army. The cause of this is not quite clear, but it is believed that Townshend displeased H.R.H. by his outspoken criticisms on the late campaign in Flanders. The following letter gives some idea as to how serious the difference between the duke and his former *aide-de-camp* had become; it is endorsed on the outside:—

Captain the Hon. Roger Townshend to his father.

Micham, November 15th, 1755.

My Lord—I did not receive your Lordship's letter till yesterday on my return to this place after a week's absence and attendance on Sir John Ligonier who has acted a very sincere and friendly part towards me; I acquainted your Lordship with Sir John Ligonier's having appointed me one of his *aid(es) de camp* a favour I had no right to expect from him as I was scarcely honoured with his acquaintance the many advantages that must of course arise to me in my profession from the friendship and opinion of that great man made it of all other the most desirable post in our present situation of affairs.

It has always been customary for general officers to name and choose their own *aid(e) de camps* and I don't believe there is an instance of its ever having been refused before; to make the refusal the more cruel and severe the Duke (of Cumberland) has consented to Lord Loudoun's appointing Capt. Campbell who is in the same Regiment with me and of the same rank and did not apply till many days after me; thus my Lord am I deprived of the same means of recommending me in my profession which every other capt. in my profession enjoys.

What is the real cause of the duke's hatred to me I am not in the least able to guess. Sir John Ligonier asked him if my behaviour either in my profession or towards him had been disagreeable to his Royal Highness; he said he had no kind of objection to any part of my behaviour since I had been in the army but that I positively should not be his *aid(e) de camp*; Sir John has been extremely hurt at the usage he has been treated with and has several times endeavoured to dissuade him from such barbarous behaviour but without success.

The general is determined he will name no other person and the duke is determined not to consent. It is very hard that my brother's quarrel with the duke should be continued to me. I was in no way concerned in it nor did I ever say a word in the least tending to reflect or call in question any part of the duke's conduct, but yet he is determined I shall not rise in my profession. I can conclude nothing less from his cruelty towards me but an absolute scheme of driving me out of the army. How much more noble would it have been in a great man to have waited till he had caught me erring in me (*sic*) profession; he might then have employed all his hatred against me without drawing upon him(self) the odious names of cruelty and tyrrany.

Every independent person has condemned the duke extremely and several of his friends have declared they endeavoured to persuade him from it. It is a melancholy subject for me to think of, let me behave with ever so much bravery and conduct and deserve preferment, as long as he commands I shall remain in my present post. I honour and love the army and the only ambition I have in this world is to do my duty in my profession and (I) desire to be made an example of if I am guilty and neglect(ful), but to be punished when I am conscious I am innocent is treatment every man of spirit and honour must feel and complain of.

I have troubled your Lordship with a real state of my case, Sir John Ligonier will do me the justice to confirm it; I suffer so much at present from the duke's treatment and my disappointment that I am afraid my letter may be confused which I hope you will excuse; our regiment is ordered to march on Wednesday to East Grinstead where my company will be quartered it is in Sussex.

The House of Commons sat till six o'clock on Friday morning Mr. Pitt and many other members spoke against the address; I am much obliged to you for the £50 note you was so kind as to send me and am your dutiful son.

Roger Townshend.

The following letter refers to G. Townshend's famous Militia Bill, which had been introduced the previous year by his brother Charles, and had passed the Commons, but been thrown out by the Lords. The measure encountered great opposition from the court and the government, no one being more bitter against it than George Townshend's father:—

The Honble. George Townshend to Mr. Pitt.
Audley Square Fey. 14 1757.

Dear Sir,

I must beg leave to inform you that the militia comes on in the committee tomorrow. Perhaps you may not have heard that it is to be attacked and under a pretence of substituting another plan they have not prepared and never mean, they hope once more to evade the establishment of this their much dreaded constitutional force.

We hope no less on account of your health than for our own sakes that you will find yourself in a state to support this essential and indeed almost only remaining effort in defence of our liberties and ability as a nation. How far your assistance and force upon this or any other occasion in parliament is of weight, it would look like flattery in me, however signal it is, to attempt to give a just description of, I shall only conclude with assuring you of my best wishes and respects on all occasions. I am Sir with the greatest regard
    Your most obedient servant

                                      Geo. Townshend.

After mature deliberation, the bill passed the Commons, but underwent several amendments in the House of Lords, one of which was the reduction of the number of militiamen to one-half of what the Commons proposed. The bill had given great offence to the Government, as it was considered hostile to the Constitution of the kingdom; but being supported by some of the most influential and independent members, and by the most unremitting attendance, and particularly by the help of Lord Chatham (then Mr. Pitt), who at all times was consulted, even on his sick-bed, and when able would attend the committee, this great national measure was passed into law.

Townshend raised the first corps in Norfolk—now the senior Norfolk Militia battalion—in spite of all the prejudices and tumults which were excited against it. The part which Townshend played in Parliament, especially his support of the Militia Bill, increased the displeasure of H.R.H. the Commander-in-Chief, and was ultimately the cause of Townshend resigning his commission in the Guards in 1757, soon after the passing of the bill. On his going out of London to hunt with his friend the Marquess of Granby at Belvoir Castle, he was put under arrest by Colonel Drury, the commanding officer of his regiment. Townshend asked, on his return to London, why he was put under arrest, and was answered, "For leaving town without leave." He then answered that:

> As there was no instance of any officer's being thus noticed who had no immediate duty to do (that if he had, many officers would have mounted guard for him; and he had frequently, when not on the tour of duty, retired to his country house

near Staines without objection), he must consider himself as a marked person, and that therefore he must resign his commission.

This he accordingly proceeded to do, and devoted himself to Parliamentary work. That he played an important part in Parliament will be seen by the following letter:—

William Pitt to Colonel the Honourable George Townshend.
June 18th, 1757.
Dear Sir, Though I can have nothing to inform you of relating to the Duke of Newcastle's transactions in order to a junction, which you are not acquainted with from His Grace, I should be extremely happy of an opportunity to have some conversation with you, on a subject, which but just now has taken its final and conclusive turn, and must receive a negative or affirmative answer. The D. of Newcastle and Lord Hardwicke have repeatedly declared to Lord Bute and myself that they could add nothing to the efforts already made with regard to the points of difficulty, now immovable, and in their express opinions, necessary to be complied with, as neither they nor their friends are disposed to resist any further. I am obliged to be at home on business tomorrow morning, which, I hope, will be my apology for taking the liberty to propose to you so great a trouble, as that of calling at my house tomorrow between ten and eleven, if it be not inconvenient to you to do me that honour. I am ever with the truest esteem and respect
    Dear Sir
        Your most obedient and most humble servant
                W. Pitt.

This letter is endorsed with the following memorandum in the handwriting of George Townshend:—

Friday, 7 o'clock.
N.B. This was the first time for about a fortnight I had heard anything from Mr. Pitt, during which time the negotiation for a Ministry went on in his and Ld. Bute's the D(uke of) Newcastle's and Lord Hardwicke's hands.—On the Friday night June the 18th 1757, I received this letter and the next morning waited on him with my brother, and to our astonishment heard him avow the rediculous and dishonest arrangement of men which

is now to take place—not the least adoption of any publick system of measures being declared or even hinted at by him. Upon this occasion I without hesitation declared my resolution to be no part of it—my brother did the same.

Geo. Townshend.

In the following letters to his father the expedition to Louisbourg is mentioned by Roger Townshend. He says that an expedition to America in the spring is rumoured, and he expects that his regiment (the Buffs) will take part in the campaign:—

Winchester,
November 6th, 1757.

My Lord—I received your Lordship's kind letter with the enclosed Bill of £50 on Mr. Child, for which I beg you to accept of my most sincere thanks. The letter you was so kind as to write to me before I went on our late unfortunate and disgraceful Expedition (to Westphalia) with the enclosed note I did not receive 'til I was on board the man of war and had no opportunity of acknowledging the receipt of it. I appropriated it to the use it was intended for and discharged my servt, and I give your lordship my word of honour that I will in every respect adhere and keep to that scheme of Economy which I know is absolutely necessary for my own happiness and will I hope recommend me to your Lordship s favour and opinion.

I beg leave to declare myself entirely ignorant of my late servants conduct concerning the old chestnut horse, your kindness to me on every occasion if I have a spark of gratitude in my composition, must make it impossible for me to act so low and base a part; I hope extravagence has been my greatest crime, and as I have suffered and know that it was you alone that freed me from my misfortunes, it would be unpardonable conduct in me towards your Lordship, if the business of my life was not to follow that plan layed down by you and do everything in my power that was most agreeable to you.

I've parted with the 2 mares and the brown gelding. I did not recolect when I sent my servant your mentioning the chestnt horse was disposed off. I can easily furnish myself with a strong horse and that with the black colt will be all I shall keep.

An inquiry is much talked off into the conduct of our general (the Duke of Cumberland) that commanded our late expedition (in Westphalia) it was well named the Secret Expedition, for without a real and honest inquiry takes place it will ever remain a secret to me.

Our going to America early in the spring seems at present to be believed. I could wish for a better. A commission eight years a captain is being very much out of luck, but, however, if they will not prefer me I can't help it, and must be contented to go upon another expedition with the Buffs—Your dutiful son

Ro. Townshend.

On Board the *Namur*,
February 12th, 1758.

My Lord—The ships are ready and Admiral Boscawen came on board last night. We wait only for a fair wind; the ships orderd to sail with us are, *Namur*, Adml. Boscawen, *Royal William* 90 Guns, *Princess Amelia* 80, *Invincible* 74, *Lancaster* 74, *Vanguard* 74, to join us at Plymouth, *Prince of Orange* 64, *Centurion* 60, *Burford* 74. Eight winterd at Halifax (in Nova Scotia) several are already gone with convoys; when the whole fleet is collected together it will amount to 24 sail of the line besides frigates; a fleet superior to anything the French can fit out.

I have been applyed to by a friend of mine to sollicit your Lordship in his favour, for a scarfe, when your have a vacancy; his name is Derby he lives at Winchester. If you are not under engagements to any other person Mr. Derby will think himself highly honoured and infinitely obliged to your Lordship for the scarfe. I know him to be a worthy good man and I should be happy in obtaining him this favour of your Lordship.

Your dutiful son

Ro: Townshend.

The following letter, dated September 26th, 1758, from George Townshend's brother Charles to his mother is of interest, as it shows that his brother's militia scheme has been a success, and that George Townshend is trying to get a command on some expedition:—

My dear Lady Townshend—Your ladyship has heard from my Brother Townshend that he has been so kind to us as to call at Adderbury in his journey from Bristol to London; and, though his visit was short, it was long enough to manifest, what I was very happy to find, that he never was in better health or spirits. *The success of the militia in every county in which it has been at all countenanced, and the notorious opposition or contempt of the Ld. Lieutenant in every county in which it has been ill received or forgotten, fully proves how indifferent at least, if unfavourable, the general opinion of the kingdom is to the measure*; which I should hardly have mentioned to your ladyship, if the measure itself were not the child of your son; which I know from most pleasing experience, is a consideration of great and irrestable weight in your judgement. *George seems more intent upon his command in the army than ever I saw him; The retreat of his formidable and abdicated enemy (the Duke of Cumberland)* the disreputation of almost all the senior officers hitherto employed, and the infinite honour naturally bestowed upon commanders successful in this perilous time all unite in indulging and inflaming his original genius and uncommon talents for the army.

He seems also to be not a little urged and accelerated by the quick rise and very promising prospect of preferment and command now opening to Roger; whose situation must improve every day; as his ability grows from experience; opportunities occur from his situation; and advancement follows from his service. General Amhurst speaks of his dilligence, attention and capacity in the most favourable language, and I should do him injustice if I did not acknowledge, how much he is likely hereafter to make a very considerable figure in a profession, whose importance and necessity grows too fast upon us in this country.

I learn from Lady Essex's letters to Lady Dalkeith that she lives entirely with Lady Ferrers at Bristol: Lady Ferrers gives the same account of their intimacy in her letters; which I only mention without comment; entreating you not to construe my words, til I see you, and from a desire of obviating prejudice, not affecting disguise.

Last week we sent you some venison and two pineapples; did they arrive safe, or where (*sic*) they good? Lady Jane Scott left us on Sunday; as she came, she went, opprest, unintelligible, wretched, healthy and whimsical, a monstrous appetite; good nights; occasional unguarded cheerfulness, and premeditated spleen and despondency are certainly no proofs of real illness and yet these are all the symptoms of it she has. I wish she is not in danger of a complaint still worse than ill health.

A thousand thanks to you for the many gazetts you have sent

us; They are infinitely agreeable to us, and most so, as they are testimonies of your affection: which is, in the estimation of us both, the most valuable possession we have or can enjoy in life. If I have in anything a real satisfaction it is in acknowledging the happyness I have in your affection and in saying in return how sincerely and invariably I am—

Your most affectionate and faithful

C. T.

(*P.S.*) Lady Dalkeith bids me say for her whatever words can say in declaring her love and honour for you.

Upon Pitt again coming into office in 1758, he at once offered to restore George Townshend his commission as colonel in the army—an offer which was readily accepted, on the condition that Townshend was to be employed in the first expedition abroad, and to serve under any general officer who had seen service since his quitting it. The Duke of Cumberland had now resigned his post as commander-in-chief, being succeeded by Lord Ligonier. On May 6th, 1758, Townshend was given his commission as colonel of foot in His Majesty's forces, no regiment being mentioned in the commission signed by His Majesty George II. and Pitt.

Appendix

THE following notes on the Militia Bill amongst Townshend's papers may be of interest in these days, when the militiaman is utilised for active service abroad side by side with the regular soldier, and the question of an increase in our land forces is directing attention to the Militia and Volunteers :—

> "The following Encouragement is given to those whose Lot it shall fall to serve for the Term of Three Years as Militia Men, in the Defence of their Country.

DURING their Term of serving as Militia Men, they shall not be liable to do Personally any Highway-Duty, commonly call'd Statute-work, or to serve as Parish Officers, or be OTHERWISE liable to serve in any of his Majesty's Land Forces than they were before they were appointed Militia Men.

HIS Majesty is empower'd by the Act to appoint any Labourer or Common Man, if he shall think so fit, the Lieutenant of any County.

ANY Militia Man who shall change his Place of Abode without giving Notice thereof to one of the Deputy Lieutenants, shall forfeit and pay the Sum of Twenty Shillings ; and if he refuse IMMEDIATELY TO PAY such Penalty, and if no Levy can be made, he shall be committed to the House of Correction, there to be kept to HARD LABOUR for the Space of one Month.

NO Pay, Arms, or Cloathing to be issued till four Fifths of the Men have been appointed.

THE Militia will be Trained and Exercised in Regiments, Battalions, Companies, Half Companies, or in smaller Bodies, on the several and respective Days by this Act appointed, in any Place or Places within the County where the Lieutenant, or Deputy Lieutenants, or any Three of them shall think fit to appoint.

THE Justice of the Peace is required to fine every Militia Man who shall be absent at Exercise, whose Excuse he shall not allow of ; for the first Time of his being absent Two Shillings which if he refuses to PAY IMMEDIATELY he shall be set in the Stocks for one Hour ; and for the second Offence such Militia Man shall forfeit and pay four Shillings, and upon Refusal IMMEDIATELY TO PAY such Penalty, he shall by Warrant be committed to the House of Correction for the Space of four Days.

AND for the Third, and every other Offence, such Militia Man shall forfeit and pay six Shillings; and upon his Refusal TO PAY IMMEDIATELY THE SAID FINE, he shall by Warrant be committed to the House of Correction for any Time not exceeding one Month.

IF any Militia Man shall be drunk on his Duty, he forfeits ten Shillings. If he be disobedient or insolent to his Officer, for the first Offence he shall forfeit two Shillings and six Pence: for the second Offence five Shillings; and for the Third, and every other Offence forty Shillings; and upon his Refusal IMMEDIATELY TO PAY the several Penalties, he shall be committed to the House of Correction for the Space of four Days for the first Offence, seven Days for the second Offence, and for the Third, and every other Offence, for a Time not less than fourteen Days, nor exceeding one Month.

A Militia Man is likewise liable to pay THREE POUNDS, in Case he SELLS, PAWNS, OR LOSES his Arms, Cloaths, or Accoutrements, and to be sent to the House of Correction in Case he refuses IMMEDIATELY TO PAY such Penalty, for the Space of one Month, and until Satisfaction be made for the same, and if not of Ability to make such Satisfaction then for the Space of THREE MONTHS.

IF a Militia Man refuses or neglects to return his Arms, Cloths, and Accoutrements in good Order, on the Day of Exercise, or the next Day, to the Person appointed to receive the same, such Militia Man shall forfeit two Shillings and six Pence, and if he refuses TO PAY IMMEDIATELY such Penalty he shall be sent to the House of Correction for the Space of Seven Days.

IN Case of Invasion or Rebellion the King may order the Militia to be drawn out and embodied, and put them under the Command of General Officers, and direct them to be led to Scotland, or any Part of the Kingdom, and they are to receive the same Pay as the Soldiers in the Army, AND NO OTHER, and subject and made liable to the Articles of WAR, RULES, AND REGULATIONS, that are or shall be in Force for the Discipline and good Government of the Army, as well as to the PECUNIARY PUNISHMENTS AND IMPRISONMENTS above recited, and when they return again to their respective Parishes and Places of Abode, they shall be under the same Orders and Directions only, as they were before they were drawn out and Embodied."

Quebec 1759

Colonel George Townshend was down in Norfolk, at Raynham, with his wife, Lady Ferrers, in the winter of 1758. He had written to Mr. Pitt on August 27th, congratulating him on the taking of Louisbourg, and asked to be employed on some expedition being prepared against France. About Christmas he received a letter from the Adjutant-General at the War Office, Lieut. -General Sir Richard Lyttelton, K.B. The letter is addressed to "Brigadier-General the Hon. George Townshend," and is dated from Cavendish Square, December 21st, 1758:

> My dear George
> I beg you will lose no time, but come to town directly. I am not allowed to explain myself by this letter, but you may be sure my reasons are very cogent. I should not otherwise write in this manner, but it is highly important to you to lose no time.
> 	Your faithful friend
> 					Richard Lyttelton
> P.S. Lord Orford's game is not arrived.

> Sir R. Lyttelton to General Townshend.
> 			Cavendish Square, Dec. 28, 1758.
> My dear Brigadier
> Lord Ligonier was yesterday in the closet, your affair was mentioned and very graciously agreed to by His Majesty. I congratulate you most sincerely upon the honour this spirited, and magnanimous acceptance of yours, will do you in the world, as soon as it becomes known, and upon the glory you will obtain, and I flatter myself the short time you will be absent, and the small risk you will probably run, in this enterprise will in some degree reconcile Lady Ferrers to it. I pity her from my heart, but her religion and philosophy will I hope enable her to bear up under it, and that she will consider how different her lot is,

from the many widowed wives, who mourn from year to year the absence of their husbands. I hope you will let her know that in all this matter, I have had nothing more to do than to lend my hand to the marshal and as a friend zealous for your glory to applaud with all mankind the resolution that you yourself have taken.

 I am ever my dear George
  Your most faithful and affectionate
    Richard Lyttelton.

The above letters, and the following letter from Wolfe, explain George Townshend's appointment to command a brigade under Wolfe in the expedition to Quebec, and will also show James Wolfe's appreciation of the value of Townshend as an officer:—

 To Colonel the Honble. George Townshend.

Sir

I came to town last night and found the letter you have done me the honour to write. Your name was mentioned to me by the *maréschal* and my answer was, that such an example in a person of your rank and character could not but have the best effects upon the troops in America and indeed upon the whole military part of the nation; and I took the freedom to add that what might be wanting in experience was amply made up, in an extent of capacity and activity of mind, that would find nothing difficult in our business.

I am to thank you for the good opinion you have entertained of me and for the manner in which you have taken occasion to express your favourable sentiments. I persuade myself, that we shall concur heartily for the publick service—the operation in question will require our united efforts and the utmost exertion of every man's spirit and judgment.

I conclude we are to sail with Mr. Saunders' Squadron. Till then you do what is most agreeable to yourself. If I hear anything that concerns you to know—be assured of the earliest intelligence.

 I have the honour to be
 With the highest esteem Sir
  Your most obedient and faithful Humble servant
    J. Wolfe.

London 6 Jan. 1759.

The foregoing letter is interesting, as bearing testimony to the estimation in which Townshend was held by the leaders of his profession. Wolfe was far in advance of his age as regards the views he entertained on the necessity of a higher standard of professional education for a soldier. He studied hard all his life; his memory was retentive, his judgment deep, his comprehension quick and clear, of a daring courage, and at the same time modest, gentle, and kind in his manner. In short, Wolfe is the Nelson of our army.

A few rough notes here of Wolfe's career may be of interest to some who have not studied his life. He was born in 1726, at Westerham, in Kent. He had an excellent education, and obtained his commission as ensign in 1741 in his father's corps, the Marines (his father was General Wolfe, of the Marines). James Wolfe was transferred to Duroure's Regiment (now the Suffolk Regiment), and was acting-adjutant of that regiment at the Battle of Dettingen. He was promoted captain in Barrel's Regiment (the 4th Foot) after Dettingen, missing the battle of Fontenoy, but he was present at Falkirk and Culloden in that distinguished regiment. He was promoted as major to Bligh's Regiment (the famous 20th, of Minden fame) after Culloden, and was present at Laffeldt in 1747.

He greatly distinguished himself in both these actions; at Laffeldt he was thanked personally on the field by the Duke of Cumberland and given his brevet lieutenant-colonelcy, and was promoted full colonel in 1757. He was quartermaster-general of the expedition against Rochefort, commanded by Sir John Mordaunt. Whilst the chiefs of this expedition wasted their time in futile discussions, Wolfe reconnoitred four miles inland, and offered with three ships and 500 men to take the place.

Pitt recognised his value, and gave him the rank of brigadier-general under Amherst in the expedition against Cape Breton, with the result that Wolfe played the chief part in the taking of Louisbourg. He had landed in England in November, 1758, from the capture of Louisbourg, and was at once sent for by Mr. Pitt, who had selected him to carry out his great plan for the conquest of Canada, and he was given the local rank of major-general. Wolfe was only thirty-two years of age, and the three brigadiers selected to serve under him (Monckton, Townshend, and Murray) were also young men; to each of them was given local rank as major-general, as it is worded in the commission signed by the king and Pitt, "in North America only," and dated February 9th, 1759. Monckton and Townshend had served together as

GENERAL WOLFE

aides-de-camp on the Duke of Cumberland's staff in Flanders, and all three of the brigadiers were known as rising officers.

Townshend's *Journal* of the Expedition to Quebec commences as follows:—

> Having had the honour to be appointed to serve in America as Brigadier General in that corps of troops destined against Quebec under the command of Mr. Wolfe, who had a commission of major general in America for this purpose, I embarked on board of the *Neptune*, the admiral's ship, on the 15th February, on board of which also was the general and Colonel Carleton our quartermaster general and Captain Gwyn my major of brigade.
>
> On the 16th February, we sailed from Spithead. The following is a list of the fleet under the command of Admiral Saunders who the day before received his commission as Vice Admiral of the Blue and hoisted his Blue flag at the foretopmast head of the Neptune accordingly:—

Rate.	Ships.	Commanders.	Guns.	Men.
4	Intrepid	Capt. Pratten	60	420
3	Warspite	Bentley	74	600
3	Stirling Castle	Everit	64	480
2	Royal William	Pigot	84	750
2	Neptune	Admiral Hartwell	90	770
3	Shrewsbury	Palliser	74	600
3	Orford	Sprye	70	520
4	Medway	Proby	60	400
3	Dublin	Goosetree	74	600
4	Alcide	Douglas	64	500

Frigates.

Baltimore (bomb)	Capt. Carpenter.
Scorpion (sloop)	„ Cleland.
Cormorant (fireship)	Menat.
Lizard	Doake.
Stromboli (fireship)	Smith.
Vesuvius (fireship)	Chadds.
Pelican (bomb)	Mentford.
Racehorse (bomb)	Richards.

Very bad weather was experienced on the way out across the Atlantic. I see by Townshend's *Journal* the voyage lasted nine weeks to Halifax, and much ice was met with, which delayed matters a good deal:—

> 21st April (Saturday) our course W.N.W., we imagined we made land upon the N.E. quarter but it proved on approach to be one

of those floating islands of ice so frequent in these seas at this season; a little while after we saw another of these islands on the S.W. quarter—and snow came on and being by our reckoning not above 10 or 12 leagues from Cape Breton, which we expected to make every minute—nay some thought they made land at the time, this thick weather came on. The Admiral altered his course from W.N.W. to South ½ East—at which time he dispatched a cutter which had attended us all the voyage, commanded by Captain Douglas, to endeavour to make the land, and get if possible into the harbour of Louisbourg.

The remainder of this day was very dark a great deal of snow and at night a hard gale and such excessive cold that the men were incapable of furling the Foretopsail, so hard was it froze.— Townshend's *Journal*)

Townshend explains in his *Journal* that the principal object of the Government was, by their hasty dispatch of Admiral Saunders's fleet to these waters, to prevent a French fleet and convoy, with supplies and reinforcements, reaching Quebec from one of the French ports. Admiral Durell had already been sent from Halifax to cruise about the mouth of the St. Lawrence, and was effectually blocking means of succour to Quebec by that river. The importance of this measure seemed, if possible, to be increased by the advices which Admiral Saunders received at sea from ships that he met: the report was that the expedition to the West Indies had not been an unqualified success at Guadaloupe, and that the troops composing it were very sickly, so that Wolfe had little hope now of getting reinforcements from those troops which had been promised him by Pitt, as an augmentation of force, that would bring up the strength of the troops destined for Canada equal to what the projectors of the plan had given out.

Admiral Saunders, with his fleet and convoy, reached Halifax on April 30th, and on May 13th the fleet sailed again for Louisbourg, arriving there on May 16th.

The battalions in garrison at Louisbourg on that date were the 22nd Regiment (Whitmore's), the 40th (Hopson's), and the 45th (Warburton's). On May 17th, the Frazer Highlanders arrived from New York. General Monckton, with Amherst's (15th), Anstruthers (58th), and two battalions of the Royal Americans (now 60th Rifles), joined on June 1st, having been delayed a week outside the harbour by extraordinarily dense fogs.

PRESENT STATE OF THE ARMY EMBARKED AT PORTSMOUTH

	General Officers.		Field Officers.			Staff.					Commissioned Officers.			Regimental Staff.					Non-Commissioned Officers.		
	Major-General.	Brigadier-Generals.	Colonels	Lt.-Colonels.	Majors.	Adj.-General.	Quartermaster-General.	Maj.-Brigadiers.	Aides-de-Camp.	Assistant-Quartermaster-Gens.	Captains.	Lieutenants.	Ensigns.	Chaplains.	Adjutants.	Quartermasters.	Surgeons.	Mates.	Sergeants.	Drummers.	Rank and File.
Infantry	1	3	—	12	6	1	1	3	6	2	44	99	53	4	6	6	6	11	227	130	5314
Artillery	—	—	—	—	2	—	—	—	—	—	5	22	—	—	—	—	2	—	9	9	342
Marines	—	—	—	1	1	—	—	—	—	—	5	15	—	—	1	1	1	—	21	16	540
Engineers	—	—	—	1	—	—	—	—	—	—	2	3	5	—	—	—	—	—	—	—	17
Total	1	3	—	14	9	1	1	3	6	2	56	139	58	4	7	7	9	11	257	155	6213

N.B.—Four troops of Burgoyne's Regiment of Light Dragoons.

On June 4th, the whole fleet sailed from Louisbourg for Quebec, just under 9,000 combatants of all ranks.

The transports were distinguished by the following vanes:—

WHITE DIVISION (Brigadier-General Monckton).
1st Brigade—
  Amherst's (15th Foot) . . . Plain white.
  Kennedy's (43rd) . . White, with one red ball.
  Anstruther's (58th) . White, with three red balls.
  Frazer Highlanders (78th) . . White, with two blue balls.

RED DIVISION (Brigadier-General Hon. George Townshend).
2nd Brigade—
  Bragg's (28th) . . . . Plain red (in three ships).
  Lascelles' (47th) . . . . Red, with one white ball.
  Monckton's (2nd battalion Royal
    Americans) . . Red, with three white balls.

BLUE DIVISION (Brigadier-General Murray).
3rd Brigade—
  Otway's (35th) . . Plain blue.
  Webb's (48th) . . . Blue, with one white ball.
  Lawrence's (3rd battalion Royal
    Americans) . . . Blue, with three white balls.

"The Grenadiers of Louisbourg" (made up of the Grenadier companies of the 22nd Foot, 40th, 45th, and of the above-named regiments in the three brigades), half red, half white . . . . . | R | W |

Light Infantry, half blue, half white . . . . | B | W |

Rangers (an American colonial corps of volunteers), red, white, and blue striped.
| R |
| W |
| B |

Artillery, red and blue striped .
| R |
| B |

Draught cattle, *yellow* and a blue stripe in the middle.

Vessels with provisions and no troops, blue and yellow striped.
| B |
| Y |

Navy victuallers, blue and yellow chequered . .
| B | Y | B |
| Y | B | Y |

Sounding-vessels, red and white chequered .

R	W	R
W	R	W

Anchoring-vessels, yellow and blue . . .

Y	B

Vessels to anchor on shoals, all yellow.

Generals' tenders, blue, white, and red. .

B
W
R

To prepare to land.—The signal for the troops is a blue and a yellow chequered flag at the main-top-gallants masthead and a gun.

To land.—A red-and-white chequered flag at the same place and a gun.

Brigadier-General Monckton.

	Lieut.-Colonels.	Majors.
15th (Amherst's)	Brigadier-General Murray .	Irwin.
58th (Anstruther's) .	. Howe . . .	. Agnew.
78th (Frazer's) .	. Frazer . .	. Oliphant.
43rd (Kennedy's) . .	James	Elliot.

Brigadier-General Townshend.

	Lieut.-Colonels.	Majors.
28th (Bragg's) . .	. Walsh . .	. Dalling.
2nd battalion Royal Americans (Monckton's) . .	. commanded by Captain Oswald.	
47th (Lascelles') .	. Hale . .	. Hussey.

Brigadier-General Murray.

	Lieut.-Colonels.	Majors.
35th (Otway's) . . .	. Fletcher .	Morice.
Lawrence's (3rd battalion Royal Americans) .	. Young	. Provost.
48th (Webb's) . .	. Barton .	Ross.

A battalion of Marines.
Grenadiers of Louisbourg, commanded by Lieut.-Colonel Murray.
Rangers, commanded by Major Scott.
Artillery, commanded by Colonel Williamson and Major Godwin.
Engineers, commanded by Major Mackeller.
Miners, commanded by Captain Dernine.
Carpenters, commanded by Colonel Gridley.

We should now turn to the expedition under General Amherst, destined to invade Canada from the south *via* Lake Champlain and Montreal. General Amherst, accompanied by Colonel Roger Townshend, left New York on April 28th, and arrived at Albany on May 3rd, and there busied himself in assembling and organising his army, collecting his boat transport, and getting his raw colonial contingent into form. Brigadier-General Amherst (afterwards Lord Amherst) wrote the following letter to George Townshend, dated New York, April 24th, 1759:—

> Dear Sir
> I had the pleasure on the 13th of this month of receiving your very obliging letter of the 5th of March; your kind assurances of friendship to me, of which I have so often had proofs, make me very happy and I shall try to prove myself deserving of the continuance of it.
> I am in great hopes that this campaign may be attended with such success as will give me an opportunity of meeting you, but I won't flatter myself that you will remain in this part of the world; I should be sorry you did any longer than you like. Your assistance in the service where I am would be a great help, and very agreeable to me and you may be assured I would make it as much so to you as I could.
> Colonel (Roger) Townshend will inform you of everything that passes here, so that I will trouble you no more at present than that I shall gladly seize every occasion that may offer to convince you of the regard and esteem with which I am
>   Dear Sir
>   Your most humble and most obedient Servant
>   Jeff. Amherst.

The following letter from Roger Townshend to Lady Ferrers (wife of George Townshend) is also interesting, as it gives his opinion of General Amherst; and I may mention that Roger Townshend was looked upon in the army as quite one of the most rising men:—

>   Camp at Port Edward,
>   June 7th, 1759.
> Dear Lady Ferrers,
> It is with the greatest pleasure that I can inform you I received a letter from (my brother) George a few days ago dated at Halifax May the 1st, the whole fleet was arrived safe and he was in

perfect health; I have taken care to supply him with fresh provisions of all kinds, and a large quantity of vegetables and roots of all kinds, which are very necessary after a long sea voyage, he will want nothing while he is up the river (St. Lawrence) that the Continent of America affords and he requires to be sent.

Our affairs at present appear very favourable, no accounts as yet of the enemy having received any reinforcements, from Old France, and our fleet under Adml. Durell is certainly so very high up the river that it is impossible for them to receive any this year without a superior fleet which it is impossible for them to fit out. My opinion of Genl. Amherst as an honest good man, and my attachment to him as a soldier I thought would never allow me to wish that I might serve under any other person in America, but the tye of brother and friend united is too powerful and I confess nothing ever gave me more real concern than not being employed on the same expedition.

I shall write to you by every pacquet, may our armys all be successful and Canada reduced this year, George return home in safety to receive the praises due to him from his K(in)g and Country for his truly noble and spirited behaviour in assisting at the reduction of Canada, the consequence of this conquest can be no less than our giving peace to France on any terms we please. My love to (my nephew) George and your little folks, and believe me nobody can have a more real regard, affection and friendship for you and your family than your affectionate brother and real friend.

R. Townshend.

P.S. Since I wrote this the Rt. Governor of New England writes the army and fleet were all well at Louisburg, June the 3rd, and expected to sail up the river on the 12th. Adml. Durell has been successful and sent in four prizes. We have no doubts of success. Our army crosses the lake in this month or early the next. The enemy have got up the river a few merch(an)tmen with provisions and one frigate before the adml. arrived at his station, they are of no consequence.

Amherst sent Major Rogers and 350 men to reconnoitre Ticonderoga, the scene of the previous years defeat to the British troops under Abercromby, and began his advance on June 3rd. The French and their Indian allies continued to raid across the frontier, and practised the same fiendish cruelties which characterised American warfare in 1757, when Braddock's force was massacred. To put a stop to this, Amherst forwarded the following intimation to Montcalm, the Governor of Canada:—

> No scouting party or others in the army are to scalp women or children belonging to the enemy. They are if possible to take them prisoners; but not to injure them on any account. The general being determined, should the enemy continue to murder and scalp women and children, who are the subjects of the King of Great Britain, to revenge by the death of two men of the enemy for every woman or child murdered by them.

Warfare in this part of the world between the English and French was carried on in a revolting, cruel, and bloody manner, but the French were the worst offenders. Scalps were taken even by the *regular* soldiers on both sides, following the example of their Indian allies.

Amherst, with 11,000 men, took Ticonderoga fort on July 23rd, Roger Townshend being killed in action. In Warburton's *Conquest of Canada* his death is thus described:—

> Colonel Townshend, a brave and beloved officer—the Lord Howe of Amherst's army—was struck down by a cannon shot in the trenches and he instantly expired, to the great grief of all who knew him.

A monument was raised to him in Westminster Abbey.

To leave Amherst and to return to Wolfe. It was on June 4th that the fleet conveying his force got under way in Louisbourg harbour and sailed for Quebec, a confident spirit pervading all ranks. The coast of Newfoundland was sighted on June 7th, and the island of Anticosti passed on June 13th.

Some idea can be gathered of the difficulty of navigating the St. Lawrence in sailing-ships from General Townshend's *Diary*. There were French pilots with the expedition, but Admiral Saunders had given the best, De Vitri, to Admiral Durell in the leading squadron, Saunders taking a man named Rabi with him, who proved of little use. Fortunately, Admiral Saunders was a man of great resource and a very able sailor.

> Wind directly contrary, continued tacking and standing all the evening from one place to the other when about 8—five of the men of war upon a tack were nearly running on board each

Place of Arms

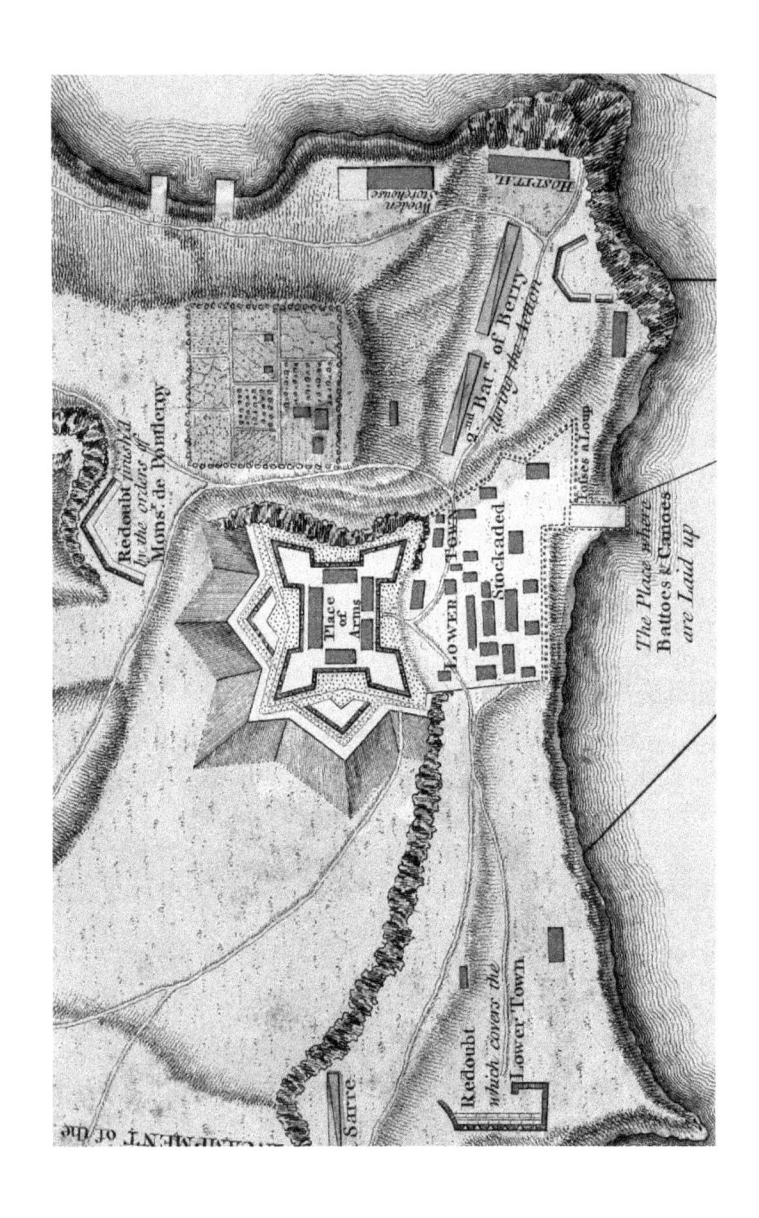

Lower Town Stockaded

Redoubt made by the order of Mons.r de Ponleroy

2.d Bat.n of Berry during the Action

Wooden Storehouse

HOSPITAL

The Place where Battoes & Canoes are Laid up

Redoubt which covers the Lower Town

Sarte

other; the current being very strong, few would answer their helm at first—the *Royal William* of 90 guns and the *Oxford* a 70 gun ship nearly ran down our ship the *Diana* frigate (in which ship Townshend was). In this critical situation, the breeze sprang up, which seconding the ability of the respective commanders of those ships—saved us from that shock, which but a few moments before seemed inevitable. Had the least fog prevailed, or had it been a little later, nothing could have prevented a disaster.

Townshend's *Journal* is full of details. He describes the different French settlements they passed in the voyage up the St. Lawrence. At the settlement of Rimenski, near the island of St. Barnaby (where there was much cultivation and about 300 houses), some seamen in a boat, who had gone in to reconnoitre a stranded French barque on the shore, were fired on. These were the first shots of the campaign, fired on June 18th. That evening Townshend dined on board with the admiral, and learnt there that Admiral Durell had reached Isle au Coudre, and had detached three battleships forward, *viz.* the *Devonshire*, of 70 guns, the *Pembroke*, 60 guns, the *Centurion*, 50 guns, and a frigate.

General Wolfe had received no letters from Colonel Carleton (who was on ahead with Admiral Durell), but from some intercepted French letters it appeared that Monsieur Montcalm commanded at Quebec, that M. Boislebert had left Quebec for Lake Champlain with 100 troops, and that Canada was almost starved, and could make but little resistance unless relieved by succours from France. Townshend also heard some disagreeable news at dinner, to the effect that three French frigates and twenty-six other ships had got into the St. Lawrence five days before Admiral Durell.

On June 19th Wolfe went on ahead in the *Richmond* frigate, to push up the river. In the evening Admiral Saunders made the signal for the transports carrying the Red Division (Townshend's brigade) to proceed upriver under convoy of the *Diana* frigate, Captain Schomberg; they started at three the next morning (June 20th):—

> The river above the Bic is about 7 leagues in breadth; both shores very high—the southern along which we sailed very beautiful, though of a most wild and uncultivated aspect, save where a few straggly French settlements appear—we could now upon this fine river view the whole fleet in three separate divisions upon the river.

On June 21st head winds prevented the progress of the fleet, which

PLAN
de la Ville de
QUEBEC

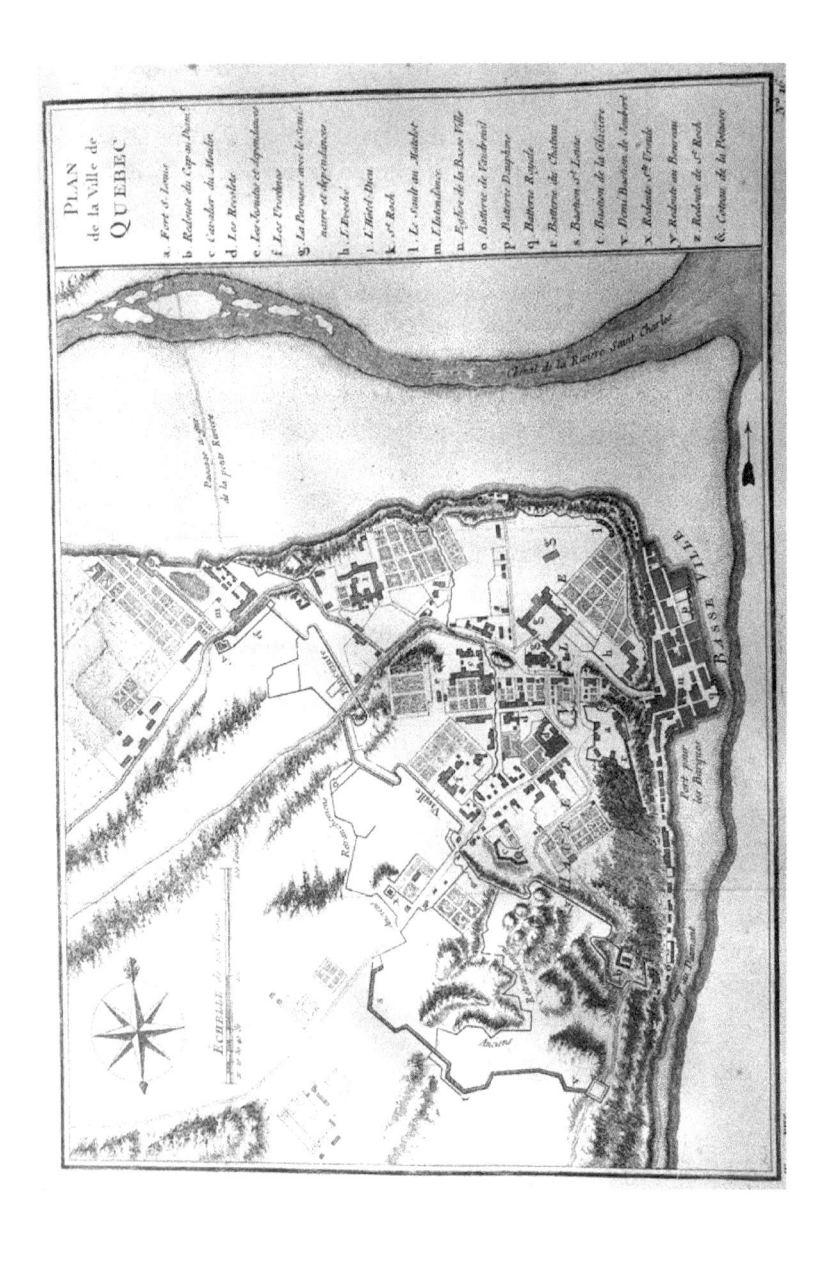

a. Fort St. Louis
b. Redoute du Cap au Diable
c. Cascades du Moulin
d. Les Récolets
e. Les Jésuites et dépendances
f. Les Ursulines
g. Le Séminaire avec le Séminaire et dépendances
h. L'Evêché
i. L'Hôtel Dieu
k. St. Roch
l. Le Coude au Matelot
m. L'Intendance
n. Eglise de la Basse Ville
o. Batterie de Vaudreuil
p. Batterie Dauphine
q. Batterie Royale
r. Batterie du Château
s. Batterie St. Louis
t. Bastion de la Glacière
v. Demi Bastion de Joubert
x. Redoute St. Ursule
y. Redoute au Fourneau
z. Redoute de St. Roch
&. Coteau de la Potence

remained at anchor. Townshend went ashore with Captain Schomberg on the Isle aux Pommes—

> Which though it had at a distance the appearance of a parcel of rocks covered with moss, yet upon our landing we found it very remarkable for the worn state of the rocks which as this island is particularly low and exposed to the currents and waves and is consequently uncommonly battered, its largest rocks peeling away like decayed timber, or honeycombed iron. Upon the highest part of them where the water does not reach, is a very rich vegetation of wild strawberries, cranberries, gooseberries and a sort of grass like rye corn. We found here an Indian wigwam where they had lately dressed their victuals and the Captain of the *Neptune* who we heard since had been there before us, had carried off a very good Indian dress, probably some scouting party had lain there within this day or two.

The worst bit of navigation in the river in the opinion of the pilots at that time was now safely negotiated, after passing the Isle aux Pommes. Every night signal fires could be seen along the heights on shore.

On June 25th, the expedition anchored at the Isle of Orleans, and orders were issued to the force to hold themselves in readiness to disembark. The troops were disembarked early on June 27th on the Isle of Orleans, where there was much cultivation and several villages in which to canton the troops.

General Wolfe, accompanied by Major Mackeller, commanding the Engineers, proceeded to the end of the island opposite Quebec, whence he could get a good view of the fortress and town; he could see the French position extending from the citadel of Quebec as far east as the river and falls of Montmorency—the Montmorency Falls being only about a mile off to Wolfe's right hand (north), as he looked towards Quebec. I attach the original report of Major Mackeller, which describes the French defensive lines perfectly; and the military reader should study this report carefully.

Unfortunately, I cannot find the map which was attached to the report; and after a long search I have come to the conclusion that this map, together with Wolfe's original orders, which I had seen at Raynham some years ago, are lost. I might here mention that I write this account of the expedition to Quebec entirely from the Marquess's Journal of the expedition, which gives many interesting military details.

The great River St. Lawrence ran along the front of the French position extending from Quebec to Montmorency Falls, including the villages of Charlesburg and Beauport. The high bank of the river was liberally garnished with very large breastworks—what we call, on the North-west Frontier in India, *"sungars"*; and Montcalm, who commanded the French, had 12,000 combatants manning Quebec and this position, consisting of regular troops, Canadian militia, and Red Indians.

Major Mackellar's Description of Quebec.

A description of the town of Quebeck in Canada, accompanied with a plan.

The place consits of what they call the High and the Low Town, They are parted from one another by a cliff or precipice of rock which is a natural fortification to about two thirds of the High Town.

Cliff. The cliff begins about a mile up the river and is quite inaccessible where it surrounds the town excepting in the communications undermentioned.

The greatest height of the cliff is a little above and below the redoubt of Cape Diamond, where it must be at least 200 feet high. It falls from thence in several easy breaks to the elbow (*l*) at the north end, where it is about 80 or 90 feet. It falls from this elbow to the westward with a gradual desent to the gateway (11) where it may be about 40 or 50 feet, but about the gateway dies into a quick slope. From this gateway, it runs into the country to the westward and branches into different breaks a little way without the town.

High Town. The High Town from these differences of heights has a considerable declivity from south to north, and still a greater from south east to north west. It has a great deal of vacant ground, and the buildings, a few excepted, are so retired from the edge of the precipice, that it cannot be easily damaged by either shot or shells from shipping. And the precipice upon the east side is so high, that ship guns can scarce have elevation enough to clear it, or if they do, the shot must fly over.

Low Town. The Low Town on the east side is a fair object for both shot and shells from shipping the buildings are in general high and pretty close. This is by much the richest part of the whole, being chiefly taken up with the dwellings warehouses and magazines of the principal merchants which are reckoned of considerable value, and some of them are said to be the king's. This part of the town can be hurt by land battery, only from the hills on the south side of the river, and they are at a distance of 13 or 1400 yards.

The remainder of the Low Town above the dock, and on the north west side consists, only of straggling houses inhabited by poor people, excepting the *intendants* and a few houses near it. In the dock yard, they build 70 gun ships.

Communications. These are the two principal communications between the two towns, one upon the east side marked (10) and the other upon the north west side marked (11).

The former of these marked (10) leads from the publick landing place marked (3) through the Low Town, and leads to the High Town, either by keeping the Bishops Palace (marked *h*) upon the right, which is the main branch of it, or to the 57 gun battery (marked *l*) by leaving the Bishops Palace on the left.

2

This communication has at present no fire upon it, either to flank or scour it, but being narrow, crooked, and steep, may be easily secured.

The communication (marked 11) leads from the country, the *intendants* house &c. through a gateway straight forward into the High Town, or by the first turning upon the left within the gateway to the west end of the battery (*l*) behind the Nunnery Garden. This gateway has something of a flank fire on both sides, but seems to be too much under the fire.

There is a break in the cliff beyond the 8 gun battery (marked 4) where four or five people may pass abreast, it is pretty steep, and may easily be secured.

Between the break and the communication 10 there are two more places where men climb up singly, but they must be very careful, there is likewise a narrow rugged path from the dock yard up to the redoubt of Cape Diamond I think there are none of these communications to be forced, if there is any tolerable resistance made: three of them are liable to be surprised *viz*: 10, 11, and that by the 8 gun battery, but their communication with one another only at low water, and the principal ones 10 and 11, are at half a mile distance.

3

Defences to the Water. The defences to the river or anchoring ground are as follows—*viz*:

		Guns.
From the high Town.		
Battery (*r*)		14
Battery (*l*) consisting in all of 57 Guns, but the Anchoring Ground points only . . .		36
From the low Town.		
Battery (*o*) by some Accounts consists of 16 Guns but by others more to be depended on only of		4
Battery (*q*)		8
Battery (*p*)		12
	Total .	74

Upon occasion there may be more guns mounted towards the anchoring ground in several places, particularly along the wharf of the dock yard.

The other defences to the water on the north west side are as follows *viz*:

Remainder of the Battery (*l*)		21
Battery (4)		8
	Total .	29

The battery (*l*) has room for a great many more guns than there are at present.

4

The use of this defence is to scour the bay or strand along the rivulet of St. Charles. At low water, this bay is dry and all over passable the bottom being a flat rock thinly covered in some places with a little mud sand or gravel.

Defences to ye Land. The defences to the land I can speak of only from the plan and a little imperfect intelligence.

The plan appears to have been taken about the year 1740, and I have not heard that there have any additions to the fortifications since that time.

The inner line which runs quite across from the redoubt of Cape Diamond (*b*) to the Hangman's Redoubt (*w*) is a wall of masonry three or four feet thick, and seems to have designed only against small arms, probably against the incursions of the savages.

This line I saw in several places and have had a little Information about it, and think it can make but little resistance against cannan it has a ditch before some of the faces where the ground seems to obstruct the defence of the opposite flanks.

5

The outward line (*s, t, u*) Seems to be of a more modern construction, and probably part of a design, intended to be cannon proof, and continued across to the bay.

This line stands upon the highest ground without a ditch, and by the information I had, continues no farther than the plan represents it.

The lines marked (old) intrenchments have probably been thrown up, upon first settling the country without the direction of engineers, and seem to have been demolished where they interfered with the designs that were afterwards executed.

The redoubts (*v, w, x*) seem to be of little consequence but must probably be silenced before a besieger comes within them.

The only works within the inner line are the redoubt or citadel (*b*) the cavilier (*c*) and the castle or *château* (*a*).

The two former I can give no account of but was told they were at work upon them when we were there, they must however be of little consequence by their smallness, they neither of them scour any of the streets, they stand very high and probably intended to defend the ground, without the line.

The castle (*a*) likewise called a citadel seems only intended for the defence of the governor general's palace, and is a sort of a court to it, taken up at present with guns mortars and their carriages, there a few small arsenals round it. It is a wall of masonry four or five feet thick and scours only a street or two.

I am perswaded from all the circumstances I could learn that the place must be weak towards the land, and the difficulty they made of our seeing it seems to confirm it.

There is however one circumstance much in its favour which is, that they can have intelligence of a fleets appearing in the gulf and time to bring the whole force of Canada to their assistance before that fleet can probably get up the river.

Attack by Shipping. From some of the foregoing circumstances, I think it will appear that shipping can annoy the Low Town only and can do little or no prejudice to the High Town, but supposing the Low Town destroyed or in possession of the besieger, he is still as far from being master of the High Town as he was before, he can make no lodgement in the former, that he can keep possession of nor take any steps that shall facilitate his getting into the latter, and the ships if within cannon reach, lay under a great disadvantage, as they are exposed to the fire of a considerable battery (*l* of 36 guns) to which they can do no hurt. But if it is thought worthwhile to destroy the Low

Town for its own sake, I should think it most adviseable to do it by shells only and at a distance beyond cannon shot.

Attack by Land. An attack by land is the only method that promises success against the High Town, and in all probability, it could hold out but a few days, against a sufficient force properly appointed.

There is no judging with any certainty where the attacks may be shortest, and easiest carried on, without having seen the ground, which I am told is very uneven and rocky, very thin of soil and the rock extremely bad.

The weakest part of the plan seems to be the half bastion 8 and the bastion to the left of it, but the ground least favourable, and where the ground best *viz*: round the gardens about the bastion (*s*) the works seem to be the strongest, which they must undoubtedly aware of, but the choice of an attack cannot long remain a doubt after the place has been properly reconnoitred.

If the besieger once gets into the town there is nothing of consequence that can afterwards oppose him. The works (*a, b, c,*) are the only things that can, and they have been already described as far as I know about them.

It will be very proper in case of getting in, to take the possession immediately of the buildings round the great square particularly the Jesuits Convent (*l*) and the Parish Church (*g*). The 57 gun battery (*l*) ought to be secured at the same time, and its guns made use of in case of necessity against the above works which will save time and trouble.

Navigation of the River St. Lawrence. Though the navigation of the river ought not to be undertaken without the assistance of a pilot well acquainted with the headlands currents and anchoring places, yet I am far from thinking it to be as difficult and dangerous as the French would have the world believe. In the passage down the river we met only with two difficulties worth mentioning and they are observed by Charlesvoix, and in a chart of the river lately published by Mr. Jefferys.

The first was in the traverse of crossing at the lower end of the Isle of Orleans, where the channell is very narrow and somewhat crooked, and not to be attempted but with enough of daylight and a fair wind, there are directions in Jefferys chart for sailing through it.

The next difficulty was at the Island of Coudres, where there is a whirlpool that forms two different currents. According as it happens to be tide of flood or ebb, these currents carry the vessels inevitably ashore unless they have fair wind enough to stem them.

I remember Charlesvoix mentions several other difficulties in the account of his voyage up the river, particularly some round the Red Island. And contrary to the received opinion, he says there is no harbour in the Island of Anticosti. Though his account is worth perusing, it is not to be supposed compleat as he was no seaman and never made the voyage but once.

The Baron Duskau and his *aide de camp* Monsr. Bernier talked at New York of an invention the French had discovered for infallibly destroying ships going up the river.

At Quebeck we found this invention to be what call (*radeaux a feu*) fire rafts, of which there is a store provided. Tney are loggs of timber tyed together by the ends so as to form a chain, and coated over with the strong composition: They are to be set on fire when the ships are near and floated off from some of the islands down the stream and clinging round the ships bows set them on fire.

Though this invention does not seem to threaten much danger, especially if the boats are out, it is advisable to be prepared against its taking effect.

Landing the Troops. It will be an advantage to land the troops on the town side of the river, which is the north, but I am very doubtful whether their landing within a proper distance of the place, can be covered by the shipping. It is said there is not water enough in the north channel of the Isle of Orleans for vessels of burden and above the island that it is shallow water along the north shore a good way out.

For these reasons, I should think it most adviseable to land upon the island itself and make it a rendezvous. The ships may get a proper anchoring ground either in the south channel or between the island and town, and I think measures may be taken for making a descent or landing from thence in an easier and better manner than from on board.

It will probably make the enemy more doubtful where the landing is intended which may be a very considerable advantage.

I should think it very commodious to keep possession of this island while the troops remain there but to this, the great extent of it may be an objection.

Pat: Mackeller Engr: in Ordy.

Wolfe must have reflected on the enormous task he had before him, as he swept the enemy's position with his telescope; but he was also a student of military history, and must have drawn consolation from the thought that generals who seek by extensive lines to supply the want of numbers or of hardiness in the troops invariably fail.

The same afternoon that the force was disembarked and landed on the Isle of Orleans a tremendous storm came on, and nearly ruined the expedition altogether. In Townshend's *Diary* I find:—

> Landed the 27th June. Bad weather 27th in night—fleet between the Isle of Orleans and the south shore in great distress. Monckton marched his division to Point Levi on the 30th. My brigade marched July 1st to the Point of Orleans.

Wolfe wrote:

> Numbers of boats were lost, all the whaleboats and most of the cutters were stove, some flat bottomed boats destroyed and others damaged.

Several transports were driven ashore, but the better-fitted warships held to their moorings all right. The storm was not of long duration, and the troops settled down in camp for the night. But the excitement of the day was not yet over, for on that night the French made a determined effort to burn our fleet and transports. About midnight a sentry on piquet called the attention of his comrades to some dark objects drifting along the river with the tide towards our fleet. Suddenly these dark objects, which were fireships, burst into flame, and the guns on board them kept up a continuous fire as they went off one by one or in salvoes of artillery.

The piquets on shore retired in confusion and disorder on the camp for no rhyme or reason, and a most discreditable confusion reigned. In the meantime, the blue-jackets on the river were at work to stave off the danger; boats had been promptly lowered from the warships; our seamen, working coolly and courageously, as is their custom, grappled the fireships, and towed them out of the way of our ships.

Next morning Wolfe issued a proclamation to the Canadian people to the following effect:—

> We have a powerful armament. We are sent by the English king to conquer this province, but not to make war upon women and children, the ministers of religion, or industrious peasants. We lament the sufferings which our invasion may inflict upon you, but if you remain neuter we proffer you safety in person and property, and freedom in religion. We are masters of the river; no succour can reach you from France. General Amherst,

with a large army, assails your southern frontier. Your cause is hopeless; your valour useless. Your nation have been guilty of great cruelties to our unprotected settlers; but we seek not revenge; we offer you the sweets of peace amidst the horrors of war. England in her strength will befriend you. France in her weakness leaves you to your fate.

This proclamation seems to have had little or no effect; the Canadian priests used all their endeavours to excite their people against the English invaders, and Montcalm issued counter-proclamations, threatening death to those who refused to serve, and the fury of the Indians those who gave aid to the English. The consequence was that the Canadians threw in their lot with the French, sending in men and supplies, and scalping without mercy all the English stragglers who fell into their hands. Wolfe sent in a letter to ask Montcalm to stop this; but he either could not or would not, for it still continued; and therefore Wolfe was obliged to retaliate, and accordingly the following order was issued to the troops:—

The general strictly forbids the inhuman practice of scalping *except* when the enemy are Indians, or Canadians dressed like Indians.

Wolfe also warned the troops that death would be the punishment for the ill treatment of women, and the severest penalties for plundering; but our troops nevertheless plundered in all directions, looting, one may suppose, being countenanced by the officers; and Townshend severely condemns this in a letter written home at the time.

Admiral Saunders now represented to Wolfe that the ships ought to be taken into the basin, as the last storm was a warning that the south channel, between the Isle of Orleans and the south shore, was not the proper place for the ships; he asked Wolfe to occupy Point Levi, on the south shore opposite Quebec, which was held by the French, the fire from which would otherwise incommode the ships.

Monckton's brigade was detailed for this work. One battalion was sent across in boats from the Isle of Orleans on the night of June 29th. The battalion landed in silence and occupied Beaumont Church, which they put into a state of defence, and awaited attack in the morning. At dawn Monckton left with the remaining three battalions of his brigade, hearing the sounds of musketry as they crossed in the boats. The Canadians had attacked the battalion at the church, but had been driven off and at 10 a.m. Monckton's brigade, in line, covered with skirmishers in front, established itself on the heights of Levi, with only slight opposition.

Having reached the heights, Monckton moved on and attacked the village, which overlooks Quebec, and which was strongly held by the Canadian Militia and Indians. The houses were carried without much difficulty, but the enemy counter-attacked and retook them. Monckton then sent the 78th (the Frazer Highlanders) round to make a turning movement on the village, and led in person the Louisbourg Grenadiers to attack in front; the village was easily taken, but about 1,000 Canadians and Indians got away and managed to cross the river to Quebec.

Wolfe at once threw up his batteries. At this spot Quebec was not a mile distant, and within easy range. The French shelled our working parties, but with little or no effect, and gun after gun was put into position. The batteries of Point Levi were almost completed, and Monckton's brigade was encamped in the works, when Montcalm made a feeble attempt to dislodge the British by attacking with three floating batteries. Admiral Saunders applied the proper remedy by sending the *Trent* frigate to put a stop to the affair; and one broadside, we are told, settled the business.

Wolfe now had batteries established and guns mounted on commanding positions on Point Levi, and considered the position there secure; it was held by Monckton's brigade, but skirmishes in the woods to the south-west of these batteries were of daily occurrence. The general reconnoitred up the south bank, to find a favourable position to bombard Quebec; and accordingly, the grenadiers of the 48th and light companies commenced throwing up earthworks there on July 5th. By means of extremely good work the batteries which were to play on Quebec were soon ready. In the meantime, Townshend with his brigade had entrenched the most western point of the Isle of Orleans, so the fleet was now safe in the basin.

Wolfe now thought he would threaten the eastern end of the French position, which was bounded by the river and falls of Montmorency. Why he did not at the commencement plant himself on the north bank, on the same side as Quebec, and above the city, so as to cut them off from their supplies, which were drawn from Montreal, is a mystery. It will be seen that afterwards, when Wolfe asked his brigadiers to consult as to what was to be done, this plan was at once proposed by them, and was instantly adopted by the general.

To return to Wolfe's plan at Montmorency. He took off the attention of the French by sending in the fleet to bombard the enemy's lines between Quebec and Montmorency Falls, moved Monckton along the south shore upriver, and with Townshend's and Murray's brigades he himself passed over from the Isle of Orleans to the east bank of the Montmorency river (see plan), encamping close to the falls. This was on Sunday, July 8th, and the troops marched from camp at the Point of Orleans at eight o'clock at night.

The flat-bottomed boats to transport the troops across the river to Montmorency had drifted downstream with the current about half-past three in the afternoon of the same day in the full view of the enemy. The *Porcupine* frigate and *Boscawen* sloop had dropped down at twelve in the forenoon. Wolfe gave the command of all the Light Infantry to Colonel Howe (the "Light Infantry" being made up of the light companies of the different regiments), and the Grenadiers, consisting of seven companies from the other brigades and three from Townshend's brigade, to Colonel Carleton.

The strength of Townshend's brigade, as recorded in his note-book, also shows how the Light Infantry and Grenadier companies, in accordance with the custom at that epoch, were detached from their proper battalions, to the detriment, I should say, of the battalions' efficiency:—

Bragg's Grenadiers	67	
Lascelles' Grenadiers	79	
Monckton's Grenadiers (Royal Americans)	97	
	—	243
Bragg's Light Infantry	48	
Lascelles' Light Infantry	72	
Monckton's Light Infantry	40	
	—	160
Bragg's Battalion	356	
Lascelles' Battalion	335	
Monckton's Battalion	393	
	—	1084
Total of the Brigade		1487

Townshend's brigade made the second embarkation, and nearly the entire body passed across the river in the boats at the same time. Upon his landing on the Montmorency shore, he found no one had been sent to show him the road that the other troops, commanded by Wolfe in person, had taken, although the night was intensely dark. However, he found all the baggage of the Grenadiers and Light Infantry left in a long string in the fields near the shore, no orders, no officer even in command of the baggage, and nowhere five men together! As he points out, ten Indians could have massacred the escort one by one and plundered the baggage.

Townshend ordered the whole of the baggage to assemble in one body, and left an officer and twenty men of each regiment to guard this baggage and that of his own brigade, leaving it all in one spot, so that he could push on quicker to the support of the advanced troops. He tried up a road to the right, which, from what he had seen from the Isle of Orleans, he judged would lead up to the commanding ground near the Montmorency Falls.

As soon as he had got the first regiment up the hill he halted it, and sent down a detachment to assist in drawing up the guns. The day was now breaking. In a short time, they got up six 6-pounders, though the road was excessively steep, and such as none but the little country carts could traverse. Upon arrival at headquarters Wolfe hinted to Townshend that he had not pressed on sufficiently fast and that he had been dilatory, though he had only halted to put a proper escort over the baggage, which the general had not done, and to help to get the guns up; he had not even had time to examine several copses they passed through, and there had not been a single sentry or a connecting file on the road to show him the way; and all the officers were expressing their admiration of their men, who, though tired, had got the guns up such heights in so short a time!

Colonel Carleton told Townshend that he had been round the camp and made the best disposition he could with the small force available, that he had placed the right flank on some rocky heights, thickly wooded, and the left flank rested on the Montmorency River. Townshend notes in his *Journal* that in this disposition the troops did not possess the heights, and the right flank was exposed to the attacks from Indians sheltered by the thick woods. Whilst Carleton was in conversation with Townshend, a message came to him to say that General Wolfe had altered the position of the camp, and that the troops were now to encamp with the wooded heights above mentioned in the rear of the left flank of the troops—the front to be towards the Montmorency River, the right flank near the Montmorency Falls. By this disposition Townshend notes:—

> We should have had our front to our friends on the Isle of Orleans—our right flank to the enemy! and a pass under the Falls! and our rear open to the woods and exposed to the incursions of all the savages they chose to pass over the fords on

the Montmorenci River to annoy us. However, the doubt was not long which of their two camps we should prefer—for a number of their savages rushed suddenly down upon us from the rocky woody height (this was the next morning, July 9th), drove a few Rangers that were there down to my quarters for refuge wounded both their officers, and in an instant scalped 13 or 14 of their men and had it not been for Bragg's grenadiers who were in another barn giving to my quarters who attacked the Indians very bravely whilst some inclined round the right to surround them—they had spread confusion everywhere.

Before the grenadiers of Braggs had time to stand to their arms one was wounded at my door and the other close by it. In this situation, we remained till late in the evening, the general having placed the regiment upon that attack in companies with their front to the side the enemy could only attack us. Having no orders to entrench in the evening I thought it necessary not to leave the brigade liable to be attacked in the night and therefore in less than three hours I ran up a very good parapet with re-entering angles which covered the front of the two battalions the general permitted to front the accessible part of the country.

I fortified likewise the front by a parapet round my house a barbette for cannon which raked all the edges of that rocky height whence the Indians could before annoy us, and I may venture to say that I not only made the camp secure but unattackable. Add to this that upon the officer of artillery reporting to me that his guns where General Wolfe had ordered them to be placed, were so far advanced that he must retire them in the night, I ran out a salient angle which enclosed them—part of each face I made a barbette by which these guns raked both angles, right and left, the ground in the front of the two lines of musketry I had made.

We had no alarm this night though several Indians had been seen on this side of the River Montmorenci and not one post of light infantry was charged with the protection of the front of the camp, and the most passable part of that river. The next morning, the general having gone early to rest in the evening, I reported to him what I had done and in the evening, he went round the front and disapproved of it, saying I had indeed made myself secure, for I had made a fortress; that small redoubts were

DEFENCES OF QUEBEC

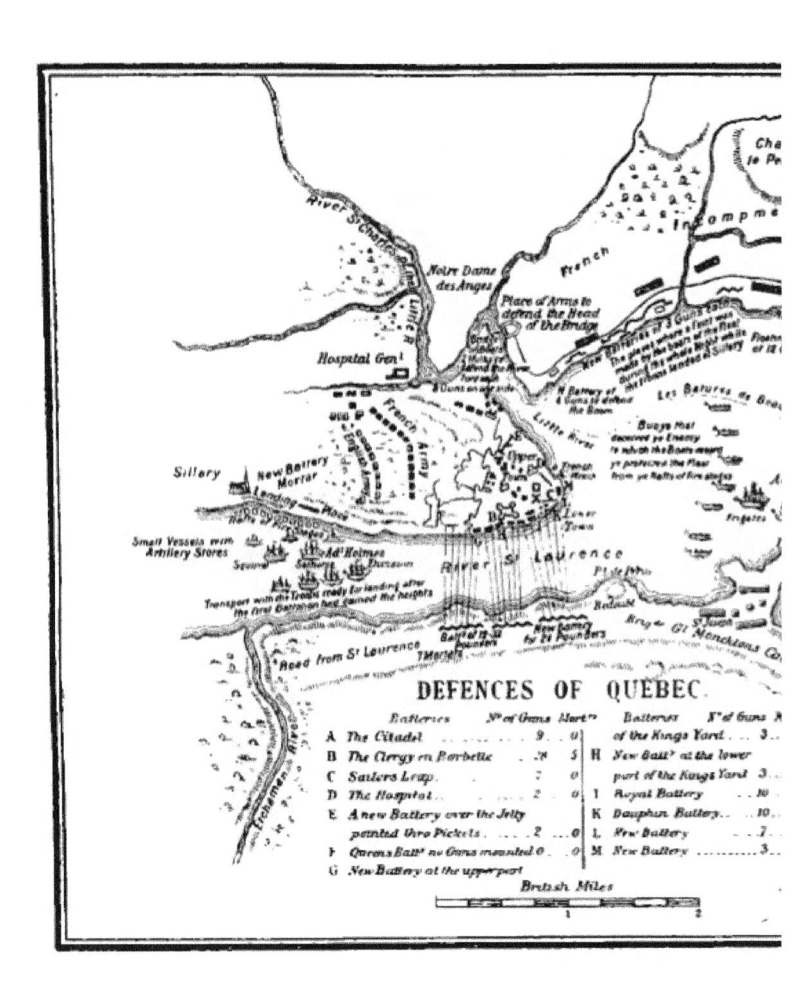

	Batteries	N° of Guns Mort⁶		Batteries	N° of Guns
A	The Citadel	9 0		of the Kings Yard	3
B	The Clergy en Barbette	28 5	H	New Batt⁷ at the lower	
C	Sailors Leap	7 0		part of the Kings Yard	3
D	The Hospital	2 0	I	Royal Battery	10
E	A new Battery over the Jetty		K	Dauphin Battery	10
	pointed thro Pickets	2 0	L	New Battery	7
F	Queens Batt⁷ no Guns mounted	0 0	M	New Battery	3
G	New Battery at the upper part				

British Miles

A PLAN OF THE RIVER ST LAURENCE
from Sillery to the fall of Montmerenci with the observations of the
SIEGE OF QUEBEC
under the Command of Vice Admiral Saunders & Majr General Wolfe.
5th SEPT 1759.
Beauport
French Incampment
Genl Wolfs Camp
The Centurions station for covering the Troops at the Attack
North Channel
Saunders's
Division
Pt of Orleans
Major Hardys Post
Admirals Ship
Transports laid ashore to clean
Part of the Transports at Anchor
Road to Beaumont
Road to St Pierre
Road to St Laurence

better than lines—that the men could not man these lines, nor sally out if they pleased. At the same time that he said this he had one battalion of my brigade and 2 which had arrived that morning (10 July) from the Isle of Orleans encamped upon the descent of the hill with their front to the river St. Lawrence and their rear to the rear of our 1st Line; exposed to the cannon shot of the enemy the first of which went through their tents and raked their encampment from right to left.

Now to prove that had my lines I had made been too extensive (which were only such as covered the front of the companies in line which he himself had drawn up on the sudden incursion of the savages) yet he might have remedied it by bringing up one of these regiments encamped behind in a useless and exposed situation—which regiments in case of an attack must countermarch and take up a contrary front to that he now gave them. With respect to his objection to the making my work like a fortress—I must observe that he must have had an uncommon disposition to find fault with me—for making my work too strong in three hours' time! and I'm sure had anybody considered, that we had an unguarded front, commanding woody heights upon our right, and if the enemy had come in force on commanding ground along our whole front, the ground behind us a descent the whole way to the water side, precipices there and no retreat—would have easily forgiven me for making the brigade as strong as possible in such a situation—and putting it as much as possible in three hours *like a fortress*!

Another objection of the general's was that I could not sally out of my lines. To these lines, or rather to this parapet a little more than a quarter of a mile in front there were three several openings besides the parts I had left *en barbette* for the cannon—about 3 foot high—over which a man with 200 weight on his back might step, and these at the salient angles—the best part to sally from when your enemy is in disorder because you are near him and gain his flanks. These *ouvertures* were left for the cannon *en barbette* which he removed directly.

But what above all shows the futility of his objection and the partiality of his judgment—I need only say what the materials and proportion of this work was so like a fortress. The strongest of the railing of the country fences, 2 of each drove in opposite each other at the distance of about 5 or 6 foot; between these stakes we laid long rails and the intermediate space was filled with earth—as the rails were everywhere at hand—so men could make 20 yards of parapet in this manner in a quarter of an hour. As there was no fosse a soldier could leap over it from the inside in an instant or by pulling up only the stakes on the inside, which is done in an instant, a subdivision may march out in order. Though this was the state of the case yet I was almost reprimanded for the strength and form of my fortification, made the moment after the insecurity of our disposition and outposts had brought the enemy's savages into the very centre of our quarters.

I find a rough sketch in George Townshend's pocket-book, showing the form of his breastworks, in which all modern requirements in the shape of flank fire, etc., are provided for. Breastworks, I need hardly say, should always be thrown up around a camp at night, if a night attack is possible; and the above-quoted incident of Wolfe's finding fault with Townshend for doing what any practical soldier nowadays would do from the first moment shows that Townshend was far more advanced in his views than Wolfe.

To continue the *Journal*:—

On this day before the general removed my cannon, I had observed several officers reconnoitring us from a part of the wood on the other side of the River Montmorenci which enfiladed our camp. Upon which, apprehensive that they would establish some battery there to take advantage of the flank of our position, presented to them, I reported this to the general who treated it lightly. My two pieces of cannon which had obliged the enemy to retire from this place and they had not returned all that evening, were carried down to grace the park of artillery the general chose to ornament his quarters with upon the descent of the hill and our whole right and front left without any. The next day (11th July) I perceived with my glass an officer, with an escort, very much answering the description of Monsieur Montcalm examining our camp from the same spot. I acquainted the general with this who rather laughed at it and at my expectation of any annoyance from that part.

On the 13th July in the morning by break of day Major Morris, field officer of the picquet acquainted me that the French had raised a battery in the wood which enfiladed our camp

Battle of Quebec

and that they had worked as far as to complete the embrasures which were covered at present with fascines. In a short time, the general was out making a disposition for a new encampment, which however would not have been secure from being raked by the enemy's artillery. In this situation of things, I immediately as far as my own brigade extended, examined all the part of the entrenchment which lay parralel to the enemy's battery—which I immediately ordered the regiments to work; and by thickening the parapet and digging a deep ditch behind it, I made pretty near cannon proof, knowing that the regiments were obliged to decamp to their new ground, yet these parts of the work would both cover the brigade in the new camp and protect whatever part of the regiments the general should order to lay advanced on their arms to sustain workmen he had now ordered to begin to work at some batteries.

Whilst I was directing the work, I heard that the general had set out for the Point of Orleans, thence to pass over to the Point of Levi, leaving me the first officer in the camp, not only without orders but also even ignorant of his departure or time of return. Upon this I ran down as fast as I could to the water side—and having desired Mr. Caldwell to stop him till I could come up with him. He received me in a very stately manner, not advancing five steps. I told him that if I had suspected his intentions of going over I had waited on him for his commands which I should be glad to receive and execute to his satisfaction. 'Sir!' says he, very drily, 'the adjutant general has my orders—permit me Sir to ask are your troops to encamp on their new ground, or not to do it until the enemy's battery begins to play?'

Wolfe's plan was now developed to the enemy. He had the bulk of his army threatening the French left (east) of their position; he hoped to find a ford across the Montmorency River some way up-stream, and so force on an action in the open country behind (north) the enemy's lines, and had no doubt in his mind that his better-disciplined troops would make short work of the few French regular troops and numerous Canadian Militia.

But he had entirely underrated the difficulties, and had parcelled up his force with the St. Lawrence between them, (an army should never be parcelled before a concentrated enemy); for Monckton was left across the other side of the river with his brigade at Point Levi, as we have seen. The ford across the Montmorency was three miles up that stream in dense woods; and whenever he tried to reconnoitre, his parties were harassed from the unseen Indians in bush-fighting.

Montcalm was not slow to notice Wolfe's error in frittering up his forces, and at once determined to try to surprise Monckton at Point Levi at night. Fifteen hundred Canadians and Indians were put across the river high up above Quebec, and they came along the bank towards Monckton's camp under cover of the woods, reconnoitred, and settled to attack on the night of July 13th. M. de Charrier, a Canadian, was in command; and having got a reinforcement of 500 more Canadians, he started on July 13th to do a night march and surprise the British camp. The night was very dark, and the British troops, having been on working parties all day, lay in profound repose. The sentries were alert; but unconscious of the danger that lay under the dark shadows of the neighbouring forest, they called out "All's well" as each hour passed away.

The French advanced in two columns, and at first with great steadiness; but the advanced guard, for no reason, suddenly fell into a panic, and rushed back in the dark on the main body, who fired on them, and all was confusion and firing at once. It ended in a general stampede, the French leaving seventy killed and wounded behind.

Wolfe was constantly across the river now at Monckton's camp; and the batteries being ready at Point Levi, the bombardment of Quebec commenced, and was sustained night and day. The batteries at Montmorency Camp, where Townshend commanded, also bombarded the French camp opposite them. The lower town of Quebec was greatly damaged, and on July 16th the shells set fire to the upper town. The flames, fanned by a strong wind, spread with great rapidity, and many buildings were burnt, including the cathedral, with its valuable paintings.

Wolfe returned to Montmorency Camp on July 16th. Four sentries were scalped by the Indians in the night. On the morning of July 17th some Indians attacked a party of Otway's (the 35th) while making fascines, killing five men (three of whose scalps they carried off) and wounding five. About the same time three men of the 3rd battalion Royal Americans deserted; they were Germans, enlisted from a French regiment taken at Louisbourg the year before. General Wolfe ordered the six companies of grenadiers of the line to be at the waterside at 8 a.m. This order was cancelled, and they were ordered to parade with the 35th (Otway's) in the afternoon, when Wolfe put them through several manoeuvres.

A French deserter came into camp in the evening, and was supposed to have given the general good intelligence. On July 18th, the French could be seen, opposite Montmorency Camp, engaged in making new works. General Wolfe went over to Point Levi in the afternoon, leaving orders that Townshend should not fire on the French, for fear of bringing their fire from their batteries on the English camp. About midday, as the boats were going from Montmorency Camp back to the fleet, the enemy sent out their boats and fired on them, our people being obliged to put ashore on the Island of Orleans—our batteries at Montmorency Camp firing several rounds ineffectually on the French boats.

Wolfe continued to hope that Montcalm would come out and fight; and Montcalm, though urged to attack by M. de Levi, refused to do so.

'If thou art a great general, Marius, come down and fight.'
'If thou art a great general, Silo, *make* me come down and fight.'

Wolfe sent a captain with a company of Light Infantry out with the French deserter, in order to make a reconnaissance up the river Montmorency; he lost his way, and was attacked by peasants. The party retired, having lost a man killed, the reconnaissance being a failure.

Colonel Carleton, with three companies of grenadiers and the 3rd battalion Royal Americans, (now the King's Royal Rifles, the old 60th), on board one of the frigates, was sent at midday on July 18th to raid the small town of Point aux Trembles, sixteen miles above Quebec. In Townshend's *Diary* I find he notes that Wolfe seems to direct his attention entirely to the Falls of Montmorency, neglecting the position above the town entirely.

On July 19th Wolfe ordered Townshend to strengthen the outposts at Montmorency Camp, as he was apprehensive of an attack from the French; he also brought up guns from the waterside to cover the front and flanks of the encampment, and gave directions that another redoubt which Colonel Howe had begun in his camp should be completed, and that it should be strengthened with abatis; in short, Wolfe now began to strengthen his camp properly, which Townshend wished to do directly they arrived on the ground on July 8th. The French were working hard also at their breastworks—or "*sungars*"—opposite, and sent out their boats on July 19th to attack our boats, but did no damage.

Wolfe, who had been across the river at Point Levi, returned at two o'clock; and Townshend gave orders for the force at Montmorency Camp to get under arms at their various alarm posts, in case of an attack. The general did not stay more than an hour on the Montmorency side, but left again for Point Levi. Townshend opened fire with guns and howitzers on the French breastworks at the moment of their reliefs approaching, and great confusion was observed amongst the enemy. They received news tonight that the fleet had sailed up past Quebec with no damage at all, only three of the ships being struck by shells from the city batteries; they had burnt some of the French fire-rafts.

I now propose to narrate events from day to day in diary form, to mark the work done in a detailed manner.

July 20th.—Point Levi continued to bombard Quebec steadily. Wolfe sent orders from Point Levi to Townshend for three companies of the grenadiers of Louisbourg and the six other companies of grenadiers to be at the waterside at midnight, in order to go across to the Isle of Orleans before daybreak, without the French noticing any move. The enemy's boats were being manned to come and attack our boats, when Townshend ordered the lower battery at Montmorency Camp to fire on them, four 24-pounders, which not only prevented their coming out, but caused a stampede from the cutters, and parties were observed afterwards burying several men which our artillery fire had killed.

July 21st.—The nine companies of the grenadiers ordered across from Montmorency to the Isle of Orleans last night were safely across by two o'clock in the morning. It rained hard all day, and only with great difficulty were some artillery stores carried to the waterside, and the road mended for guns and howitzers that had to be carried down this night. The enemy were seen beginning to work on their batteries they had before begun on the banks of the river Montmorency, and Townshend opened fire with his artillery, utterly demolishing them. This night some guns and all the howitzers were carried down to the beach and embarked in boats with great secrecy. Townshend puts in his *Diary* that "our lower batteries have so destroyed their floating batteries that they do not attempt to get them out again."

July 22nd.—Townshend received a letter from Wolfe, dated Point Levi, giving him an account of the work of a detachment of the 3rd battalion Royal Americans and the grenadier companies of the 1st

Brigade that he had sent over the north side of the river, under the command of Major Provost. They had taken 200 women, a priest, and some Canadians, and had killed and scalped three Indians; our losses were Major Provost and one of the Highland officers wounded, and also six men wounded. Townshend had also a letter from Admiral Saunders, asking him not to send any more guns over till further orders. Townshend says in the *Diary*, "The general seems to be at a stand which place to make his attack." Wolfe evidently was debating in his mind other plans before finally settling on his disastrous attack from Montmorency, which was to come about very soon.

He sent orders to Townshend on this date to send over Colonel Howe with his Light Infantry to the Island of Orleans in the night, and directed that Anstruther's (58th) should take their ground. Townshend ordered two piquets, a detachment of Light Infantry, a lieutenant, and thirty Rangers, with a working party, to parade before dark, with a design to alarm the French camp. Wolfe came over from Point Levi about 7 p.m.

Townshend marched with the above-mentioned party as soon as it was dark; he sent the Rangers along the Montmorency river bank, whilst he himself accompanied the two piquets, detaching the Light Infantry a mile to his right (east) as a flank guard, to skirt the woods and to sweep round to the north and meet him at a spot indicated. After half an hour's marching firing began on the banks of the river where the Rangers were feeling their way, and a lively fire fight ensued, the officer of the Rangers being badly hit in the thigh and shoulder. Townshend after a short time, having thoroughly aroused the French, slowly withdrew to camp.

July 23rd.—General Wolfe and Brigadier Murray left Montmorency Camp and went across the river. The enemy opened embrasures in a new battery they had thrown up on the waterside. Townshend left camp in the afternoon, going on board the flagship, where he met Wolfe and the other two brigadiers at a consultation. In the evening Wolfe and Murray went back to Montmorency Camp, and Townshend accompanied Monckton back to Point Levi. His visit to Monckton at Point Levi is explained by this quoted letter from Monckton to him, which also shows that Wolfe had not yet decided on his attack from Montmorency Camp:—

Dear George
You have herewith a letter from the general—we are not to

move this day or two— so that if you can be spared from Montmorenci—I shall be glad to see you at Levi.—I think our motion this way must be attended with a decisive success—the admiral intends moving your cannon—which ought to be secret as possible.

I am with much truth
Yours most sincerely
Robt. Monckton.

July 24th.—A new battery of six guns was begun at Point Levi. About 8 a.m. a flag of truce came out from the town with a French officer, who went on board the Admiral's ship and remained there till five in the afternoon. At night, our batteries opened fire on Quebec, again setting the town on fire in three places. Colonel Frazer was sent with 400 of the Frazer Highlanders down the south side of the river on a raid, and Major Dalling with 300 Light Infantry marched to penetrate the woods some distance into the country.

General Wolfe ordered another redoubt and a new battery to be made at Montmorency Camp.

July 25th.—Major Dalling sent into General Monckton's quarters at Point Levi about 300 prisoners, mostly women and children and a priest, and about 200 head of cattle. In the evening, General Townshend went back to Montmorency Camp. Colonel Frazer and his Highlanders returned with six prisoners to Camp Levi, Frazer being wounded.

July 26th.—General Wolfe and Murray started on a reconnaissance up the Montmorency river bank at one o'clock this morning, taking Otway's Regiment (35th) and 350 Light Infantry and Rangers, Bragg's Regiment (28th) being sent out eastward on a raid along the northern shore of the River St. Lawrence. Soon after leaving camp Wolfe sent back the two guns with him—"the horses not being used to draw." Two companies of marines were sent over to Montmorency Camp as a reinforcement from Point Levi. Wolfe and Murray marched up the Montmorency till they reached one of the fords, where the advanced party was suddenly fired on by a party of Indians and Canadians from the opposite bank of the river.

At about 11 a.m. the Canadians and Indians had come across the river, and began to work round our men, a heavy fire being kept up on both sides. Our people eventually drove them across the river again, "although at first the right wing of Otway's regiment was put a little in confusion, so that General Wolfe left them and came back to camp"—from which it would appear that the reconnaissance turned out but little short of a disaster. On Wolfe's arrival in camp he ordered Townshend to turn out the troops. Murray, who had remained with the reconnaissance party, it appears, collected the left wing of Otway's, and made a desperate counterattack on the Canadians and Indians, driving them into the river and killing many in the water. It was found that the enemy had a strong breastwork defending this ford, and that reinforcements had been sent by Montcalm to strengthen their post there.

Murray retired, arriving in camp at four in the afternoon, having lost forty-five killed and wounded. Amongst the killed were Captain Fletcher and Lieutenant Hamilton, Lieutenant Field being mortally wounded, and Captains Mitchelson and Bell wounded, all of the 35th—altogether a very expensive reconnaissance.

July 27th.—Captain Hasen, of Bragg's (28th), who was with a half-company forming an outpost in front of Bragg's battalion along the St. Lawrence, sent into camp at 7 a.m. to say he was being surrounded by about 500 Indians. Townshend ordered off at once a company of Lascelles' (47th), the inlying piquets of Anstruther's (58th) and Royal Americans, under the command of Colonel Hale, of the 47th, and Colonel Howe with his Light Infantry, Townshend accompanying the party. Bragg's Regiment (28th) in the meantime had been attacked, a heavy fire being poured into them from the edge of the wood—"on which the whole regiment stood to their arms and rushed up to the woods, receiving a smart fire all the way without their returning one shot till they got into the woods, they drove the rascals away, took one Canadian prisoner, and observed the tracks of some that had either been wounded or killed and carried off. They left a great many of their trinkets behind them."

Townshend arrived whilst Bragg's were pursuing in the woods and broken up, and he ordered their recall, moving back to camp with the whole party, Bragg's (28th) having lost two killed and six wounded. The prisoners informed Townshend that their party numbered 200 Canadians and Indians, commanded by one Boucherville, a famous partisan leader; there was also a priest with them. Bragg's people drove into camp about 150 horses, cattle, and sheep, but had destroyed no houses, and any loot found to have been taken from churches was ordered by Townshend to be restored again.

July 28th.—"This last night the enemy sent down 80 of their fire floats all made fast together against the fleet but it did no harm." Wolfe sent in a flag of truce to Quebec garrison to say that "if the enemy presume to send down any more fire rafts, they are to be made fast to two particular transports in which are all the Canadian and other prisoners, in order that they may perish by their own base inventions." This stopped the fire-raft nuisance.

Colonel Carleton's expedition up the river to the town of Point aux Trembles, consisting of the three companies of grenadiers and the battalion of Royal Americans, had looted the place, and some letters were found giving us valuable information, throwing light upon the dissensions and bickerings at headquarters in Montcalm's camp, and moreover showing that the besieged were on half-rations. Accordingly, Wolfe started raiding parties to burn and lay waste the country, Bragg's Regiment having been sent on one of these expeditions, as I have described, on July 27th. On the same date, an officer of the Royal Americans was shot in Montmorency Camp from the French breastwork on the opposite side of the Montmorency river, and another soldier was killed also.

A deserter from the French came into camp on July 28th; he was a Pennsylvanian taken at Ohio with Major Grant, and had been obliged to carry arms. He gave much information to Wolfe, said the Canadians were very anxious to get in their harvest, afforded him information about fords up the Montmorency, and Wolfe was very much pleased with the intelligence he had gained.

July 29th.—On this day in Townshend's *Diary* I find, "The general intends to make an attack on one of the enemy's detached redoubts at the water side with the grenadiers tomorrow." This was to be Wolfe's famous attempt to pierce Montcalm's lines at the Montmorency River, which resulted in a grave disaster. He had not enough men to send up the Montmorency in order to strike at Montcalm's entrenched camp from the north, so he had now made up his mind to attack the French in their entrenchments on their left (eastern) flank near the Montmorency Falls. He had been some five weeks before Quebec, the summer was nearly past, and he had used a good deal of ammunition. Action was necessary—in short, Wolfe felt that time was slipping away, and that he must justify his selection by Pitt.

His plan of battle was as follows:—

Monckton's brigade was to be brought over in the boats of the fleet from Point Levi at night, and to be mustered off the north-west point of the Isle of Orleans at daybreak; this brigade would land about a mile west of the mouth of Montmorency River, where the French had an isolated redoubt on a narrow strip of beach. The *Centurion*, with Admiral Saunders on board, and two armed transports were to stand in as close as the depth of water permitted, and cover the landing of Monckton's brigade. Townshend, with 2,000 men from the camp at Montmorency, was to ford that river at the mouth below the falls, and march along the beach to support Wolfe in his advance up the heights, on which were the French entrenchments. The transports were to go as close in shore as possible, and even ground if necessary. Wolfe was to be on board one of the two transports, and at the proper moment would land with Monckton's troops.

At 10 a.m., on July 31st, Monckton's brigade —consisting of the 15th (Amherst's), the 78th Highlanders, thirteen companies of the Louisbourg Grenadiers (the picked battalion which was the flower of Wolfe's force), and 200 of the Royal Americans—was ready in the boats lying off the Isle of Orleans, waiting for the signal to dash in and land. At 11 a.m. the two armed transports stood in and grounded close to the redoubt, and at the same time the *Centurion* line-of-battle ship, of sixty-four guns, with Saunders on board, hove to opposite the fort, all three ships opening fire at the same time. This was the signal for the batteries opposite Quebec to bombard the town, and Townshend's forty guns at Montmorency Camp opened a heavy fire on the French breastworks opposite. The boats transporting Monckton's brigade began to row in towards the shore about 2 p.m.

Townshend had ordered his two brigades to store all their baggage and tents within the second line, and then to fall in under arms, to be ready to march, on General Wolfe making the signal or sending him orders. Colonel Howe, in order to make a feint, had orders to march with the 58th and the Light Infantry up the bank of the Montmorency River, and to march back again on his receiving orders to join the rest of Townshend's and Murray's brigades. General Townshend gave him orders to retire when he had drawn up the three battalions of Bragg's (28th), Otway's (35th), and Lascelles' (47th)—Anstruther's (58th) forming up in rear, Townshend being on the right and Murray on the left.

At four o'clock Wolfe sent orders to Townshend to advance, and accordingly the two brigades were beginning to cross the ford at the mouth of the Montmorency River as the grenadiers reached the shore in their boats. Why Wolfe had wasted so much time in waiting about is not explained. He had bombarded the French redoubt and breastworks for the greater part of the day, and the receding tide had warned him there was not much time to lose. Wolfe himself had been on one of the two grounded transports; and as soon as he had hoisted the red flag, the signal to land, on his transport, he had shoved off in a boat and joined the boats of Monckton's brigade, who were pulling in hard for the beach under a heavy fire from the French guns. One or two boats were sunk by this fire, and there was a little delay in finding an opening through some reefs close in shore, but the troops were soon jumping out of the boats into the water and forming up on the beach—the French evacuating the isolated redoubt on the beach and taking to the heights.

The grenadiers were the first on shore, where they formed and began to advance, before receiving Wolfe's orders to move, in a tumultuous disorder, in no formation whatever, running across the fields and swarming up the heights crowned by the breastworks. Monckton's remaining regiments, the 15th and 78th, were forming up in admirable order on the shore, and Townshend was now nearly across the ford at the mouth of the river with his force. It is said that Wolfe tried to recall the grenadiers, but in vain.

The result was as might be expected: the battalion, in great disorder and blown, straggled up the steep heights, to be met by a biting fire of musketry and grape; and by the time the dishevelled battalion got close to the enemy's breastworks the men were huddled together, hesitating under their heavy losses, and then shortly came down again in a disorderly flight.

It was now pouring with rain, which rendered the priming of their muskets wet, and so useless. A regular bolt took place back to the redoubt, and even here the men could not be rallied, for the redoubt was commanded from the heights at point-blank musket-shot range, and men were being hit right and left. It must have been a nice picture for Wolfe, looking on with the rest of Monckton's brigade, passive spectators at this exhibition of the famous "Grenadiers of Louisbourg," his picked corps, so called because he had formed the battalion at that place out of all the grenadier companies of regiments in the Louisbourg expedition, and the grenadier company contained the picked men of a battalion.

They had lost thirty-three officers and about 400 men killed and wounded; the redcoats dotted the terrain, some quite close up to the

CLIMBING THE HEIGHTS OF ABRAHAM

breastworks of the French; and the Indians were seen to come down the hill and scalp and finish off the wounded, while our troops were looking on. Some of the 78th Highlanders were eventually sent up, and they chased these cowardly fiends away at once.

I cannot understand, in this attack, why, when Wolfe saw the grenadiers go on, followed by two companies of the Royal Americans, who had been ordered to support them, he did not make the best of a bad business, and push on Amherst's (15th) and the Frazer Highlanders (78th)—the remainder of Monckton's brigade—in support. Townshend, with his column in excellent order, had crossed the ford, and was marching along the beach; and as soon as he got about 200 yards from where Wolfe was, he sent an officer to him for orders, but received a reply that he was to retreat in as good order as possible back over the ford again, after he had covered the embarkation of the remains of the grenadiers and Royal Americans. Townshend covered the retreat, and then recrossed the Montmorency River in admirable order under a heavy artillery fire. Our casualties were 420 men and thirty officers killed and wounded, mostly grenadiers.

The confidence of the troops in Wolfe was much shaken by this disaster. For nothing in war is so bad as failure and defeat. One naturally would ask, How came it that the battalion officers of the grenadiers allowed the men to thus get out of hand? In my opinion, the officers must have led the men, and the battalion commander must himself have advanced. I read in Warburton and in Bradley's *Life of Wolfe* that "the men of the grenadiers advanced in spite of the orders and imprecations of the officers"; but this I do not believe, nor do I think that any officer who has been under a heavy fire when attacking with men will believe it. The men invariably look to their officers to lead them: in short, the officers *must* lead to make the men advance under a heavy fire.

I feel convinced that the cause of this disaster, as in so many other cases, was the burning thirst for battle on the part of the troops, officers and men alike, such as one sees in men who, never having been on active service before, are impatient to find themselves engaged. Townshend gained much credit in this unfortunate affair for the skilful way in which he covered the retreat.

Wolfe published the following order to his troops:—

The check which the grenadiers met with will, it is hoped, be a lesson to them for the time to come. Such impetuous, irregular, and unsoldierlike proceedings destroy all order, and put it out of the general's power to execute his plan. The grenadiers could not suppose that they alone could beat the French Army, therefore it was necessary the corps under Brigadiers Townshend and Monckton should have time to join them and the attack might be general. The very first fire of the enemy was sufficient to have repulsed men who had lost all sense of order and military discipline. Amherst's (15th) and the Highland Regiment by the soldierlike and cool manner in which they formed, would undoubtedly have beaten back the whole Canadian Army, if they had ventured to attack in time. The loss however is very inconsiderable and may be easily repaired when a favourable opportunity offers, if the men will show a proper attention to their officers.

Yet in this attack luck was wanting. The storm of rain which fell just as the grenadiers rushed forward to attack the breastworks on the heights rendered the steep ascent so slippery as to make it almost impossible to stand up. Why Wolfe combined a land-and-sea attack together is not plain. It would surely have been better had Monckton's brigade joined Townshend's, and all crossed the ford together. The defeat preyed on Wolfe's mind terribly; he fretted and worried, and ended by going down with fever.

The two stranded transports had been set on fire by the order of Admiral Saunders; but it was done in too great a hurry, as the guns and two brass field-pieces which had been put on board them were left there.

August 1st.—This day a deserter came in who had left the enemy's camp two days before; he said that many deserted, but they fell into the hands of the Indians, who scalped them all; he himself nearly underwent the same fate. The lower batteries at Montmorency fired several rounds at the enemy who were going on board the wrecks of the two burnt transports and carrying the shot and other things ashore.

August 2nd.—The French were busy repairing the breastworks and traverses which had suffered from the artillery bombardment. Wolfe went across to Point Levi in the morning, and a letter came in under a flag of truce from Captain Ochterlony, of the 2nd battalion Royal Americans, who had been mortally wounded and taken prisoner in the attack on the heights on July 31st.

Three days after the unfortunate affair at Montmorency Wolfe sent

Murray with 1,200 men up the river on an expedition. His force consisted of the 15th (Amherst's), three companies of Royal Americans (60th), and two companies of marines.

Raiding parties were sent out from Montmorency Camp daily, different battalions in turn, whilst our guns continuously pounded the French breastworks on the opposite side of the Montmorency River, which were industriously repaired by the French.

Murray embarked on Admiral Holmes's ships above Quebec; his boats, going up, had caused great alarm to the French; and the expedition sailed up-river, Montcalm sending 1,500 men under Bougainville to follow them along the north bank. Murray found every point along the river guarded; twice he tried to land, and twice he was repulsed. The French ships up the river sent their stores and ammunition on shore, and so, being lightened, managed to warp up creeks into shallow water. Murray, however, occupied the village of Duchambault, and got some valuable letters there. From these letters Wolfe learnt that Amherst had occupied Crown Point on Lake Champlain, and that Johnson had captured Niagara.

Quebec was bombarded harder than ever. The lower town was by now in ruins, and nightly fires occurred. Far and wide farms and villages were burnt by our raiding parties, and all live stock was brought into our camp; as Townshend wrote home to his wife, it was "a scene of skirmishing and devastation; it is war of the worst shape."

By the middle of August, we had 1,000 men in hospital. Wolfe himself was sick and in bed in his quarters—a farmhouse in Montmorency; his high spirit kept his determination unshaken, but he must have had a great anxiety on his mind, as the dreaded Canadian winter was close at hand.

The *Journal* from August 1st on is a repetition of raiding parties to visit the different villages; the enemy were perpetually at work making traverses and additions to their entrenchments and breastworks, and our artillery constantly bombarding them.

August 8th.—This morning an Indian swam over the ford below the falls with the intention as we supposed to scalp a sentry, but the sentry saw him and ran up to him presenting his piece to his breast. The Indian went down on his knees threw away his knife and delivered himself up, he was a very savage looking brute and naked—he seemed very apprehensive that we intended to put him to death. Although there were several in the camp that spoke Indian language we could not get him to understand anything. Most nights we hear the Indians holloaing in the woods all about us.—Braggs and the Lt. Infantry ordered to march tomorrow morning on a foraging party.— Braggs returned this afternoon they saw some peasants who fired on them out of a house and wounded five men.—2 marines were found scalpt in the woods this morning.

August 11th.—This morning at 6 o'clock as the working party of 300 men went out to cut fascines, on their coming to the skirts of the wood and going to post their covering parties they discovered people among the trees. The commanding officer of the party posted his men in order to prevent his being flanked, before he had done this they gave him a smart fire from the woods, on hearing firing the picquets and Lt. Infantry were ordered out to assist him but as usual the enemy had retreated through the woods. They had killed and wounded of ours 33 men and we only killed of them one poor miserable Canadian.

Wolfe received a letter from Brigadier Murray on this date, sending the letters he had found, and giving an account of his fighting; he had lost 100 killed and wounded, Major Irwin Maitland and Captain Delaur being amongst the wounded. Captain Goreham, who had gone to St. Paul's with a detachment of Rangers, sent a report of his having taken and burnt that settlement; he had lost seven men wounded.

Wolfe sent off at ten o'clock this night on two men-of-war and three transports a detachment of 200 of Kennedy's (43rd), under Major Elliot. Murray had reported 4,000 French and Canadians to be upriver.

General Wolfe gave it out in orders on this date that if any soldier chose to go out in the woods and lay in ambush for the Indians and bring in a scalp, he should have five guineas' reward.

Seven marines deserted to the enemy from Point Levi.

I find in the *Journal* that parties often went out at night to lay in wait for Indians, in order to get Wolfe's reward:—

> There has been parties every night in ambush for the Indians since the order was given out but has met with no success. Last night a volunteer and 18 men went out with that design, 200 Canadians and Indians discovered them and surrounded them in a house which he defended till he managed to send word to camp.

Wolfe ordered the piquets to march below the hill until they came to the house, and sent the Light Infantry on to the rising ground above them, with an intention, if possible, to surround and take them. They managed to save the defenders of the house, but failed to take the party of Canadians and Indians. There was an Indian wounded, when our piquets came up, who could not get away; one of the sergeants knocked him on the head with his piece, and the Light Infantry came up and scalped him. In this affair, we had eight killed and wounded. The Indians used to send sheep out of the woods in front of our camp, to entice the English soldiers to come near.

General Murray returned from upriver on August 26th; and on that date, I find in the *Journal* an incident mentioned of a sergeant of the 35th (Otway's) deserting to the enemy; he was not seen by the piquets till he was halfway across the ford below the falls; a heavy fire was then opened on him, but he managed to escape.

On August 28th Townshend and Murray went across together to Point Levi to see Monckton, who accompanied them on board the admiral's ship, where they stayed till the evening. On August 29th, the three brigadiers again met on board the admiral's ship for another consultation, and stayed there all night. The subject of their consultation is very evident from the letters I quote in the following pages.

On August 30th Townshend and Murray left the admiral at midday, and came across to Montmorency Camp. The next day Monckton and Admiral Saunders came across to Montmorency, and the three brigadiers and the admiral held a consultation with General Wolfe. Wolfe had dictated a letter to the brigadiers, asking them to consult for the public safety, and suggested a plan of attacking again on the Beauport side, where he had made his former disastrous attempt. The brigadiers rejected his plan, and substituted another—that of transferring operations to above Quebec, as by effecting a lodgement on the north shore above Quebec the garrison would be cut off from the source of its supplies, *viz.* Montreal; and let it be noted that the brigadiers said it was perfectly easy to obtain a lodgement on the north shore.

Wolfe instantly adopted their plan. I here produce the two original letters—*viz.* that of Wolfe to the brigadiers, and their reply—which I do not believe can have been published before; this documentary evidence directly contradicts Lord Mahon, and proves that he was wrong when he went out of his way in his *History* to say:

The honour of that first thought belongs to Wolfe alone.

To the Brigadiers, from General Wolfe.

Headquarters Montmorency, Augst. 1759.

That the public service may not suffer by the general's indisposition, he begs the brigadiers will be so good to meet, and consult together for the public utility and advantage, and to consider of the best method for attacking the enemy.

If the French Army is attacked and defeated, the general concludes the town would immediately surrender, because he does not find they have any provisions in the place.

The general is of opinion the army should be attacked in preference to the place, because of the difficulties of penetrating from the Lower to the Upper Town, in which attempt neither the guns of the shipping, or of our own batteries could be of much use

There appears to be three methods of attacking this army.

1st. In dry weather, a large detachment may march in a day and a night so as to arrive at Beauport (fording the Montmorency 8 or 9 miles up) before day in the morning.—It is likely they could be discovered upon their march on both sides the river. If such detachment penetrating to their intrenchment and the rest of the troops are ready, the consequence is plain.

2dly. If the troops encamped here passed the ford with the falling water and in the night march on directly towards the point of Beauport, the Light Infantry have a good chance to get up the woody hill, trying different places and moving quick to the right would soon discover proper places for the rest. The upper redoubts must be attacked and kept by a company of grenadiers—Brigadier Monckton must be ready off the point of Beauport to land when our people have got up the hill, for which signals may be appointed.

3dly. All the chosen troops of the army attack at the Beauport at low water—a division across the ford an hour before the other attack.

N.B. For the 1st it is enough if the water begins to fall a little before daylight or about it, for the other two it would be best to have it low water, about half an hour before day. The general thinks the country should be ruined and destroyed, as much as can be done, consistent with a more capital operation.

N. There are guides in the army for the detachment in question.

To Genl. Wolfe, from the Brigadiers.
Answer to the paper of the other side.

The natural strength of the enemy's situation between the River St. Charles and the Montmorency, now improved by all the art of their engineers, makes the defeat of the French Army, if attacked there, very doubtful. The advantage their easy communication on shore has over our attacks from boats, and the ford of the Montmorency, is evident from late experience, and it cannot be denied that part of the army which is proposed to march through the woods nine miles up the Montmorency to surprise their army, is exposed to certain discovery and consequently to the continual disadvantage of a wood fight.—But allowing we got footing on the Beauport side, the M. de Montcalm will certainly still have it in his power to dispute the passage of the St. Charles, till the place is supplied with two months provisions (the utmost you can lye before it) from the ships and magazines above, from which it appears they draw their subsistence.

We therefore are of opinion that the most probable method of striking an effectual blow is by bringing the troops to the south shore and directing our operations above the town. When we have established ourselves on the north shore, of which there is very little doubt, the M. de Montcalm must fight us upon our terms, we are betwixt him and his provisions and betwixt him and the French Army opposing General Amhurst. If he gives us battle and we defeat him, Quebec must be ours, and which is more, all Canada must submit to His Majesty's arms; a different case from any advantage we can hope for at Beauport, and should the enemy pass the St. Charles with force sufficient to oppose this operation, we can still with more ease and probability of success execute your third proposition (in our opinion the most eligible of the three you have made) or any other attempt on the Beauport shore, necessarily weakened by the detachments made to oppose us before the town.

With respect to the expediency of making an immediate attack, or the postponing it to be able the more effectually to prevent the harvest and destroy the colony; or with a view of facilitating the operations or our armies now advancing into the heart of the country, we cannot take upon us to advise, although we cannot but be convinced that a decisive affair to our disadvantage must enable the enemy to make head against the army under the command of General Amhurst already far advanced by the diversion this army has made on this side.

Plan of Operations in Consequence of the Above Answer.
By the Brigadiers.

It is proposed to move the ordnance and troops from the Montmorency in three days, beginning with the heavy artillery. Tomorrow night the stores to be carried to the water side directly to gain time.

The troops to be transported to the Isle of Orleans; some corps may go from hence tomorrow night that they may assist in putting the works at the point of Orleans in a good state of defence. The sick to be transported the day after to-morrow by which time provisions must be made for them in the hospitals. 600 men of the marines and Hardy's Corps for the defence of Orleans. 600 for Point Levy and 1000 for the batteries.

The army to encamp on the other side of the Etchemin. As many transports, as will contain two months provisions to get up the first opportunity. The boats of the fleet will disembark 2500 men, the remainder of the troops, or any part of them, to be sent on board of the ships which are to be stationed so as to be ready to land the men as immediately as possible to sustain the first corps that disembark from the boats. There can be no difficulty to effectuate a landing in the night without the least loss, it may be done anywhere for an extent of four leagues *viz*. from the height of St. John to Cap Rouge River.

Two attempts may be made, either of which succeeding is sufficient. Allowing the transports cannot get up in a few days the enterprise need not for that reason be delayed a moment, we have a sufficient number of carts to make a depot at the camp of the Etchemin, and we have a further resource from our boats which at all times we know, without interruption can pass and repass the town. Another method of effecting the landing on the north shore, two thousand men to embark at the point of levy in the boats at low water the middle of the night; by break of day they will have passed the town, have arrived and disembarked at a proper place for the purpose half a league above the River Cap Rouge.

The same night the troops to move up to the camp of the Etchemin already mentioned. Previous to this it will be right to fill the ships already above the town with as many troops as they will contain; that may be done from Gorhams post in three nights, without giving the smallest jealousy, by the boats already above, but for this purpose the ships already above must fall down to a proper station. The ships already above the town will contain for the requisite time, 2000 men; consequently 4000 men may in one tide be landed without the least jealousy given to the enemy, and the remainder may be brought over with any number of artillery, the next from the Etchemin Camp. (Here some pages are missing from the manuscript.—C. V. F. T.) .... no doubt but that we are able to fight and to beat the French Army, in which I know you will give your best assistance.

I have the honour &c.

Jam. Wolfe.

Sutherland 8½ Oclock
12 Septembr 1759.

In Warburton's *Conquest of Canada*, vol. ii., this incident of the consultation of Wolfe's brigadiers is thus described:—

> The brigadiers assembled in consequence of this communication, and after having maturely deliberated, agreed in recommending the remarkable plan which Wolfe unreservedly adopted.
> The merit of this daring and skilful proposition belongs to Colonel George Townshend, although long disputed or withheld by jealousy or political hostility. This able officer had left every happiness that domestic life could bestow, and every gratification which fortune and position could procure, to face the hardships and seek the honours of his country's service. When the Ministry's determination to prepare the expedition against Quebec became known, he successfully exerted his powerful interest to obtain employment, and was appointed to the third post of seniority in Wolfe's army.

Wolfe having adopted the suggestion of the brigadiers, evacuated the camp at Montmorency on August 29th, with a view to the new plan's being carried out. It is an old and a sound saying that a council of war never fights, but here is a case of an exception. On August 29th, all the troops were brought across to Point Levi Camp and to the Isle of Orleans.

On September 2nd Wolfe sent home a dispatch of his operations up to date, and on September 3rd his plans for putting his force across the St. Lawrence on to the north bank were completed. I quote the following letter of George Townshend's to his wife, Lady Ferrers, dated at Camp Levi, September 6th, in which he mentions news of the death of his brother Roger at Ticonderoga, and gives his opinion on Wolfe's generalship:—

Camp Levi, September 6th 1759.

My dearest Charlotte,

I hope Mr. Perceval will arrive safe and bring you these two letters from me. The happiness of writing to you is beyond all I know. My concern for your sufferings, my affection for you and your dear little ones, convince me how unfit I am for this scene, which another month, thank God, will give a conclusion to. The captive women and children which I see every day brought in here, often tell me what I am and who belong to me, but above all, the malencholly news I received the day before yesterday upon my arrival here from the cursed camp of Montmorenci of my poor brother's death has reproved me for not consulting my own nature more, when I asked you to (let me) return to the army.

It had then pleaded for you, when you did not plead for yourself, and I had not been now in a sceene of ambition, confusion and misery; and you oppressed as I know you must be, with terrours and affliction. I dare say poor Lady Townshend too now starts at every knock at the door. Let us look up with hopes my Charlotte to the Disposer of all things and trust he will in his Mercy and Goodness do all for the best. I have wrote a line to poor Lady Townshend to comfort her by convincing her of my own health and safety. One month more will put an end to our troubles. I never served so disagreeable a campaign as this. Our unequal force has reduced our operations to a scene of skirmishing cruelty and devastation. It is war of the worst shape. A sceene I ought not to be in, for the future believe me my dear Charlotte I will seek the reverse of it.

Genl. Wolfs Health is but very bad. His generalship in my poor opinion—is not a bit better, this only between us. He never consulted any of us till the latter end of August, so that we have nothing to answer for I hope as to the success of this campaign, which from the disposition the French have made of their force must chiefly fall to Genl. Amhurst and Genl. Johnson.

God bless you my most dear wife, my blessing to my children, my good George in particular, and thank him for his letters. I have constantly thanked God for the success in the innoculation, a most comfortable circumstance for you. Mr. Barker has been slightly wounded. Mr. Gay quite recovered and joined us. Our campaign is just over. I shall come back to Admiral Saunders' ship and in two months shall again belong to those I never ought to have left.—*Adieu*—Your most affecte. husband and faithful friend.

Geo. Townshend.

September 1st—Wolfe began to evacuate his camp at Montmorency, in view of the new plan of operations, in order to transfer the whole to Point Levi. Townshend was ordered to make his dispositions for covering the embarkation of the other troops. The outlying detachments at Château Rêch and Angille Gardien, consisting of Grenadiers of Louisbourg and Frazer Highlanders, were recalled, burning all the houses and damaging the country as much as possible on their way in. The 2nd battalion Royal Americans and the three companies of Grenadiers of Louisbourg and the detachment of Frazer Highlanders were sent over to the Isle of Orleans before dawn on the morning of the 1st, and all the troops were transported across to Point Levi this night. Sick, tents, and baggage were carried down to the waterside on September 2nd. Townshend at midnight had occupied four houses on the right with Bragg's Regiment; Lascelles' and Otway's were posted in redoubts on the left, and he kept Anstruther's in reserve. They remained in perfect silence, every man at his post.

The signal for Townshend's troops to retire was the burning of a barn in front of his quarters, and then he commenced retiring from the right. Everything went off without a hitch, except that Townshend had to wait two hours after the barn was burnt, as the boats were not ready for him, the other troops having taken so long to embark. The enemy did not attack, which they might easily have done with advantage; but Monckton with his brigade had made a demonstration, as if he intended to land and attack Beauport from Point Levi, some frigates standing in with his boats, thereby causing the enemy to believe that a repetition of the attack at Montmorency was in contemplation; and this demonstration was completely successful, for the enemy quite expected the attack on Beauport, and so remained inactive and allowed Wolfe to carry out his evacuation of Montmorency unmolested.

Townshend's brigade had to remain three hours in the boats until the tide made enough for them to pass the enemy's batteries at a longer range. All the way up the river to Point Levi the enemy's batteries kept up a heavy but ineffectual cannonade on them. They had orders to encamp at Point St. Pierre; but as soon as their tents were up the batteries from Quebec opened fire, sending their shells into the camp; so, they were obliged to move the camp higher up.

September 4th.—A messenger arrived from General Amherst at Crown Point; he had come by way of the Kennebeck River, and confirmed the news obtained by Murray from prisoners he had taken above the town and the intercepted letters, by which Wolfe learnt of the occupation of Crown Point by Amherst and of Johnson's victory at Niagara.

Orders were issued to commanding officers of battalions today to have their men in readiness to move at a moment's notice from Point Levi Camp; battalions were only to leave small parties to look after the regimental baggage; the men's tents and the small amount of baggage required by officers were to be taken by boats, passing the town of Quebec in the night, and to be put on board the warships now above Quebec. General Murray was to march this night with Bragg's, Anstruther's, and the Light Infantry; but his march was counter-ordered the same evening.

September 5th.—The boats with the baggage passed the town all right in the night, unnoticed by the enemy: the French were observed, though, to move two regular battalions *above* the town. At 2 p.m. General Murray, with Bragg's, Anstruther's, Otway's, Lascelles', and the Light Infantry of the army, crossed the Etchemin river, there to be embarked on board the ships. Generals Monckton and Townshend were ordered to follow with the rest of the army the next morning.

September 6th.—Generals Monckton and Townshend marched at 2 p.m. with Amherst's Regiment, Kennedy's, and the Frazer Highlanders. They crossed the Etchemin River, and a little above lay our ships, with the troops that had gone up with Murray and the two battalions of Royal Americans on board. The boats embarked the troops, and the ships were excessively crowded. Wolfe came from Point Levi an hour later, escorted by 100 Frazer Highlanders.

September 7th.—The ships in the night went up the river and anchored off Cap Rouge, where is a large bay about three miles in breadth, an excellent place for landing; but the enemy had placed, at the mouth of the river of the same name that falls into the bay, six or eight floating batteries; also large numbers of Canadians and some regulars had taken post there and thrown up breastworks, and a large body of cavalry could be seen.

General Wolfe and the three brigadiers met on board the *Sutherland* in the forenoon, when the army was freshly distributed into three brigades, and an order for forming a line of battle was given out,—the 1st and 3rd Brigades were to form the first line, under Generals Monckton and Murray, the 2nd Brigade to form the second line, under General Townshend. The troops were also ordered to be in readiness to land this night. General Wolfe went out in his barge reconnoitring. The three brigadiers went up in the *Hunter* man-of-war to reconnoitre the coast as far as Point aux Trembles.

September 8th.—It rained hard all day. Another large transport and four sloops came past Quebec and joined the fleet above that town. The troops were ordered to be in readiness to land at 4 a.m. the next morning; but it was given out that, if the weather continued bad, a signal would be made for the troops not to land. Wolfe was out in his barge all day reconnoitring *down* the river, and the *Hunter* man-of-war and a transport were ordered up-river to Point aux Trembles, to make a feint of landing there.

September 9th.—As it continued raining very hard, the landing was put off. The *Seahorse* was sent down halfway between the fleet and Point Levi, to keep the communication open. Wolfe ordered Monckton and Murray to land some of their men on the south shore in the afternoon, to the number of 150 men from each ship, the troops being greatly crowded on board. They landed at seven in the evening at the church of St. Nicholas without opposition. It had continued raining all day.

September 10th.—Wolfe, Townshend, Monckton, and Admiral Holmes, with Major Mackeller, the C.R.E., went down the river reconnoitring, to find a good landing-place. A narrow path was discovered winding up the side of a steep precipice from the water's edge, about three miles above Quebec, where the precipitous banks form a cove—now called Wolfe's Cove, but at that time called Le Foullon. At the top of the path they saw some tents, and from the number Wolfe judged that there must be 100 men posted at the top of the cliff. This path ran up to the Heights of Abraham. Wolfe's plan was now made—

viz. to get his army secretly at night up on to the Plains of Abraham, and to fight on that ground. The plan was a bold one; but how often in war do such plans succeed best!—very often the extreme audacity of a plan is its own safety.

September 11th.—Monckton and Murray were ordered to have the men they had landed, to stretch their legs, on board the next morning at 5 a.m. Orders were issued for the whole army to be ready to attack the enemy. They were to get into the boats of the fleet at 9 p.m. the next night.

The following letter was written by Wolfe to the Secretary of State on September 9th, in which Wolfe appears to be anxious to prepare the public mind in England for a failure; he seems to have had gloomy views as regards the success of the expedition.

Copy of letter from Major-General Wolfe to the Secretary of State, dated on board the *Sutherland*, at anchor off Cap Rouge, September 9th, 1759:—

My Lord,
If the Marquis de Montcalm had shut himself up in the town of Quebec, it would have been long since in our possession, because the defences are inconsiderable and our artillery very formidable, but he has a numerous body of armed men (I cannot call it an army) and the strongest country, perhaps, in the world, to rest the defence of the town and colony upon. The ten battalions, and the Grenadiers of Louisbourg are a chosen body of troops, and able to fight the united force of Canada upon even terms. Our field artillery, brought into use, would terrify the militia and the savages; and our battalions are in every respect superior to those commanded by the *marquis*, who acts a circumspect, prudent part, and entirely defensive; except in one extraordinary instance, he sent sixteen hundred men over the river to attack our batteries upon the Point of Levy, defended by four battalions.

Bad intelligence, no doubt, of our strength, induced him to this measure; however, the detachment judged better than their general, and retired. They dispute the water with the boats of the fleet, by the means of floating batteries, suited to the nature of the river, and innumerable *battoes*. They have a great artillery upon the ramparts towards the sea, and so placed, that shipping cannot affect it.

I meant to attack the left of their entrenchments, favoured by our artillery, the 31st July. A multitude of traverses prevented, in some measure, its effect, which was nevertheless very considerable, accidents hindered the attack, and the enemy's care to strengthen that post has made it since too hazardous. The town is totally demolished, and the country in a great measure ruined particularly the lower Canada. Our fleet blocks up the river, both above and below the town, but can give no manner of assistance in an attack upon the Canadian Army. We have continual skirmishes; old people seventy years of age, and boys of fifteen, fire at our detachments, and kill or wound our men from the edges of the woods. Every man able to bear arms, both above and below Quebec, is in the camp of Beauport.

The old men, women and children are retired into the woods. The Canadians are extremely dissatisfied; but, curbed by the force of their government, and terrified by the savages that are posted round about them, they are obliged to keep together, to work and to man the intrenchments. Upwards of twenty sail of ships got in before our squadron and brought succours of all sorts; which were exceedingly wanted in the colony. The sailors of these ships help to work the guns, and others conduct the floating batteries; their ships are lightened and carried up the river out of our reach, at least out of the reach of the men of war. These ships serve a double purpose; they are magazines for their provisions and at the same time cut off all communication between General Amhurst's army and the corps under my command, so that we are not able to make any detachment to attack Montreal, or favour the junction, or by attacking the fort of Chambly or Bourlemaqui's corps behind, open the generals way into Canada; all which might have been easily done with the floating batteries carrying each a gun, and twenty flat bottomed boats, if there had been no ships in the river.

Our poor soldiery have worked without ceasing and without murmuring; and as often as the enemy have attempted upon us, they have been repulsed by the valour of the men. A woody country so well known to the enemy, and an enemy so vigilant and hardy, as the Indians and Canadians are, make entrenchments everywhere necessary, and by this precaution we have saved a number of lives, for scarce a night passes that they are not close in upon our posts watching an opportunity to surprise and murder. There is very little quarter given on either side.

We have seven hours and sometimes (above the town after rain) near eight hours of the most violent ebb tide that can be imagined, which loses us an infinite deal of time in every operation on the water; and the stream is so strong, particularly here, that the ships often drag their anchors by the mere force of the current. The bottom is a bed of rock; so that a ship, unless it hooks a rugged rock, holds by the weight only of the anchor. Doubtless if the equinoctial gale has any force a number of ships must necessarily run ashore and be lost.

The day after the troops landed upon the isle of Orleans, a violent storm had nigh ruined the expedition altogether. Numbers of boats were lost; all the whale boats and most of the cutters were stove; some flat-bottomed boats destroyed and others damaged. We never had half as many of the latter as are necessary for this extraordinary and very important service. The enemy is able to fight us upon the water, whenever we are out of reach of the cannon of the fleet.

The extreme heat of the weather in August and a good deal of fatigue threw me into a fever, but that the business might go on, I begged the generals to consider amongst themselves what was fittest to be done. Their sentiments were unanimous that (as the easterly winds begin to blow and ships can pass the town in the night with provisions and artillery, &c.) we should endeavour by conveying a considerable corps into the upper river, to draw them from their inaccessible situation, and bring them to an action. I agreed to the proposal; and we are now here, with about three thousand six hundred men waiting an opportunity to attack them when and wherever they can best be got at. The weather has been extremely unfavourable for a day or two, so that we have been inactive. I am so far recovered as to do business; but my constitution is entirely ruined; without the consolation of having done any considerable service to the State; or without any prospect of it. I have the honour to be, with great respect, My Lord,

    Your Lordships most obedient
        and most humble servant,

                              Jam. Wolfe.

(Correspondence of Chatham.)

This painfully interesting letter, in which Wolfe laments the ruin of his constitution, without having done any considerable service to the State, was written on September 9th, only four days before his death, reached England on October 14th, and three days after, in the midst of the gloom and despair of the public caused by this letter, an express arrived saying that Quebec was taken.

★★★★★★

A letter of Walpole's to Sir Horace Mann, who was then British Envoy to the Court of Tuscany, gives some idea of the effect of Wolfe's letter on the Government:—

> In short you must not be surprised that we have failed at Quebec as we certainly shall. You may say, if you please, in the style of modern politics, that your Court never supposed it could be taken: the attempt was really made to draw off the Russians from the King of Prussia, and leave him at liberty to attack Daun. Two days ago, came letters from Wolfe despairing, as much as heroes can despair. The town is well victualled; Amherst is not arrived, and 15000 men encamped defend it. We have lost many men by the enemy, and some by our friends—that is we now call our 9000 only 7000. How this little army will get away from a much larger, and in this season, and in that country I don't guess—Yes I do.

★★★★★★

Extracts from General Orders by Wolfe to the troops on September 11th:—

> The troops on shore except the Lt. Infantry and the Americans are to be upon the beach tomorrow morning at five o'clock in readiness to embark; the Light Infantry and Americans will re-embark at, or about 8 o'clock. The detachment of artillery to be put on board the armed sloop this day. The Army to hold themselves in readiness to land and attack the enemy.
>
> The troops must go into the boats about nine tomorrow night, or when it is pretty near high water . . . and as there will be a necessity for remaining some part of the night in the boats the officers will provide accordingly. When the boats are to drop away from the *Sutherland* she will show two lights in the maintop-mast shrouds, one over the other. The men to be quite silent, and, when they are about to land, must not, upon any

account fire out of the boats.

The plans were of course kept secret; a deserter might have ruined all. A man from the Royal Americans *did* desert on the morning of September 12th, but he could tell nothing, for he went off before orders had been issued to the men; on the other hand, one of the French regulars deserted at the same time to us, and gave a very good account to Wolfe of the state of affairs in Montcalm's camp. He said that the main force of the French Army was still below Quebec in its old position. The General (Montcalm) would not believe that the British intended to attack anywhere but on the Montmorency side. The Canadians were dissatisfied and alarmed at the fall of Niagara, and in great stress for provisions. M. de Levi, with a large detachment, had left for Montreal to stop Amherst; and M. de Bougainville, with 1,500 men, was watching the motions of the British ships above Quebec. Ammunition was running short, no supplies were coming in, and provisions were very scanty.

Although the spirits of the French had been raised over our disaster at Montmorency, when the Canadian peasant militia had fought steadily behind breastworks, still, the misdirected valour of our grenadiers had greatly impressed Montcalm, and the garrison was now getting depressed at the obstinacy and tenacity of the British. One thing cheered them, and that was the approach of the dreaded Canadian winter.

Montcalm wrote in a letter:

Unless Wolfe lands above the town, and forces me to a battle, I am safe.

And on the night of September 12th, while he watched the bogus preparations of our ships below the town—for Admiral Saunders, with the main squadron, was below Quebec—Wolfe's troops were floating silently and rapidly down-stream towards the appointed landing-place in the shadow of the cliffs, unseen and unchallenged.

Wolfe issued his last orders to the army from on board the man-of-war *Sutherland* in the evening of September 12th:—

The enemy's force is now divided, great scarcity of provisions is now in their camp, and universal discontent among the Canadians; which gives us reason to think that General Amherst is advancing into the colony; a vigorous blow struck by the army at this juncture may determine the fate of Canada—the troops will land where the French seem least to expect it. The first body that gets on shore is to march directly to the enemy—the battalions must form on the upper ground with expedition and be ready to charge whatever presents itself—the officers and men will remember what is expected from them, and what a determined body of soldiers, inured to war, is capable of doing, against five weak French battalions, mingled with a disorderly peasantry.

In accordance with the plan, the line-of-battle ships which were *below* Quebec moved this evening towards the Beauport shore, anchoring as near the enemy's lines as the depth of water would allow; the boats were lowered, filled with seamen and marines, and drawn up in order, so as to make the enemy believe that we intended to effect a landing between Beauport and the mouth of the St. Charles.

Wolfe's force had embarked in the boats about 9 p.m. on the night of September 12th. It was a starlit but moonless night. The boats were laden with the troops sitting between the seamen at their oars. At sundown Admiral Saunders began to bombard Quebec from below the town, keeping up the deception of a landing at Beauport, and at the same time the guns at Point Levi started their usual bombardment. At one o'clock the tide was ebbing; Wolfe left the *Sutherland* and got into his boat, the brigadiers being already at their stations; two lanterns showed from the maintop-mast shrouds, one above the other—the appointed signal; and the whole flotilla began to glide down the stream, the seamen hardly dipping their oars.

I now propose to give an account of the night and the action from a *Rough Notes of the Siege of Quebec*, found amongst Townshend's papers. I find in these notes a circumstance which nearly ruined the plan of scaling the cliffs, illustrative of the uncertainty of war and night operations in particular. To quote Napier:—

> When Sylla after all his victories styled himself a lucky rather than a great general, he discovered his profound knowledge of the military art. Experience taught him that the speed of one legion, the inactivity of another, the obstinacy, the ignorance or the treachery of a subordinate officer, was sufficient to mar the best concerted plan—that the intervention of a shower of rain, an unexpected ditch or any apparently trivial accident might determine the fate of a whole army.—Napier

September 13th.—The troops landed below the place intended owing to the rapidity of the tide.

Just before we were ordered to land, Captain Smith a very active and intelligent officer of the Light Troops, informed the brigadiers that the naval officer who was to conduct the first detachment down the river, assured him that if he proceeded down by the South side of the river the current was so strong that they should be carried beyond the place of attack and probably below the batteries and the town, and thereupon the brigadiers (there not being time to report and receive General Wolfe's directions thereon) authorised him to carry them down the North side of the river and fortunately it was followed, for even then the boats could only land before daybreak considerably below the place of attack (l'ance Guardien) and Col. Howe (now Sir William) found he was below it, and Major Delauney a very active and enterprising officer who had a command in the light corps, saying the place was higher up the river, and the colonel knowing the consequence of the enemy perceiving at daylight our situation and being reinforced, he ordered that officer to attack where proposed and very gallantly himself scrambled up the rocky height in his front by which he turning to his left he attacked and drove the enemy from their position and most happily facilitated the success of the former up a narrow precipice with an abattis and a battery just over it which was firing on them.

Just at daybreak another most fortunate circumstance contributed to the success of this critical operation, when the first corps for disembarkation was passing down the North side of the river and the French sentries on the banks challenged our boats, Captain Fraser who had been in the Dutch Service and spoke French answered—*'la France et vive le Roy'*—on which the French sentinels ran along the shore in the dark crying—*laisser les passer ils sont nos gens avec les provisions*—which they had expected for some time to come from Montreal.

As soon as the boats carrying the first body of troops under Monckton and Murray were emptied, they were sent back for the second detachment under Townshend, who at once disembarked his men also, and followed up the path on to the heights above, where they joined the first lot of troops on the ground where General Wolfe was

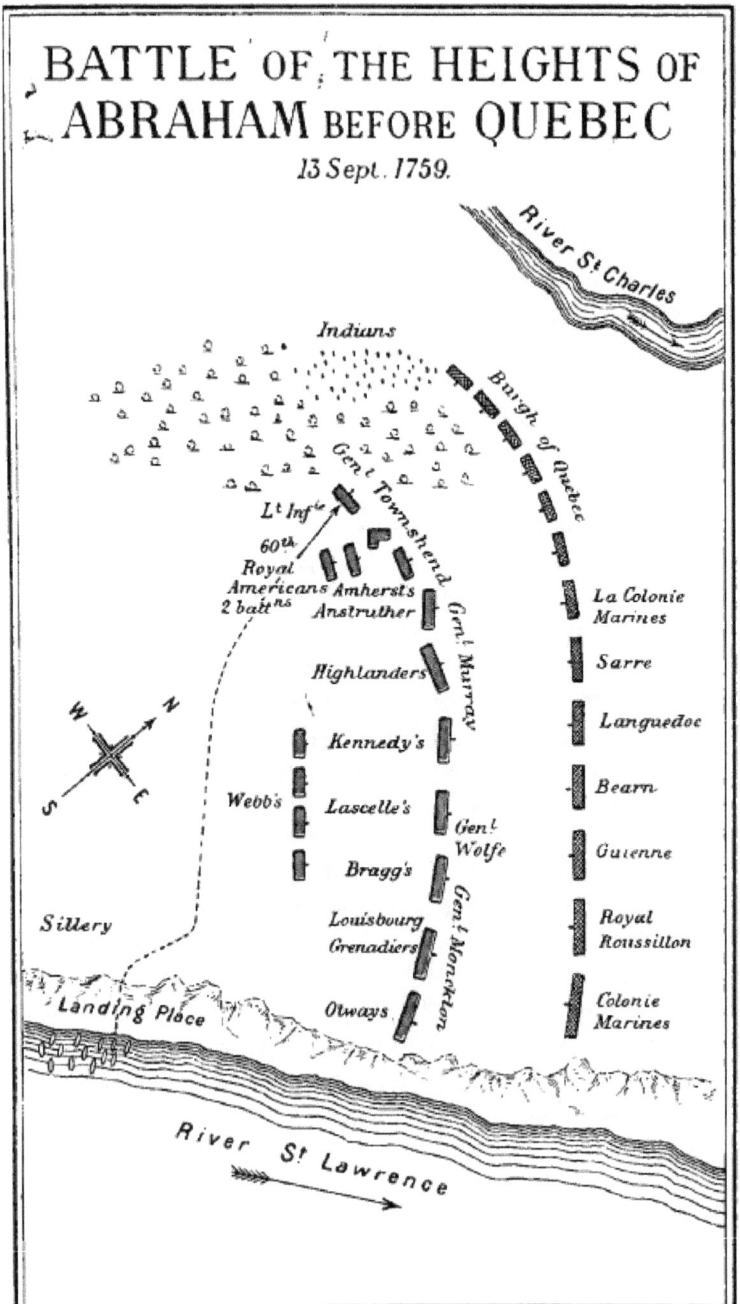
BATTLE OF THE HEIGHTS OF ABRAHAM BEFORE QUEBEC
13 Sept. 1759.
River St Charles
Indians
Burgh of Quebec
Genl Townshend
Lt Infie
60th Royal Americans 2 battns
Amhersts
Anstruther
Highlanders
Genl Murray
Kennedy's
Webb's
Lascelle's
Bragg's
Genl Wolfe
Louisbourg Grenadiers
Genl Monckton
Otways
La Colonie Marines
Sarre
Languedoc
Bearn
Guienne
Royal Roussillon
Colonie Marines
W
N
S
E
Sillery
Landing Place
River St Lawrence

forming up his force; and when day broke the whole of Wolfe's available force was formed up in line ready for action on the tableland above the cove. They were only able to get one gun up the precipice, and that required superhuman toil to do it. Montcalm by this time had received news that the British troops were on the Plains of Abraham.

All night long he had waited to oppose the expected landing from Admiral Saunders's ships, which had bombarded all night, and whose guns had increased their fire towards morning, the ships warping in as close to shore as the depth of water permitted, as if to cover a landing of troops. At daybreak Montcalm heard distant musketry beyond Quebec, and soon a horseman came galloping in to say that the British troops were advancing towards the town over the Plains of Abraham. As fast as Montcalm could muster his battalions he sent them across the river St. Charles over the bridge, to take up their ground for battle west of Quebec.

Our troops had moved forward rapidly to occupy the rising ground, which was done without opposition. Otway's (the 35th) held the right of our line, resting on the precipice about three-quarters of a mile from the ramparts of the town. Next came the Grenadiers of Louisbourg; the 28th (Bragg's) prolonged the line to Lascelles' (47th); then Kennedy's (43rd), the Highlanders (78th), and Anstruther's (58th).

Monckton commanded the right of the line, and Murray the left. (It will be seen, by reference to a list of the brigades at the commencement of this chapter, that the brigades were now all mixed up—a most pernicious habit, it being most essential to the fighting power of a brigade to keep it under the same commander whom the men know.) Townshend had command of the second line, consisting of Amherst's (15th), which rested their right flank on the precipice above the river, and the two battalions of the Royal Americans (60th). Webb's (the 48th), under Colonel Burton, formed the reserve, drawn up in line, with large intervals between their sections. The rear and left flank were covered by Colonel Howe with Light Infantry troops.

It was about 6 a.m. when parties of the enemy began to appear under the ramparts of Quebec. An hour later they showed in large numbers, and opened fire with two field-pieces, causing some annoyance. Canadian and Indian skirmishers began to annoy us from some small plantations in our front; however, they were speedily cleared out by Colonel Howe and some light troops. The whole line then received orders to lie down and wait.

Civilian writers have wondered why Montcalm should have come out and fought in the open, doing what he must have known was the longed-for desire of Wolfe for so many days. Montcalm, they say, could have remained in the town behind the ramparts, but he deliberately came out and pitted his few regulars and numerous untrained Canadian Militia against the veteran British regular battalions! The real reason of Montcalm's coming out to fight in the open was that Wolfe had now cut him off from his supplies, and was holding the Heights of Abraham, which dominate the town of Quebec; and the place was not tenable against an army in possession of the heights.

At 8 a.m. the French columns began to appear, ascending the hill from the St. Charles River to the Plains of Abraham, and our one gun opened fire, causing them to alter their direction. The enemy finally formed up in three columns to the north-west of the town, sheltered from our gun.

At 9 a.m. Montcalm formed into battle order, and threatened to outflank Wolfe's left flank, whereupon Wolfe sent Townshend on the left with Amherst's battalion (15th), which Townshend formed what was then called *en potence*, but now termed "thrown back" (see plan attached).

In Townshend's dispatch to Pitt will be seen the disposition of the French troops, as near as he could judge. On the right of the French were the La Sarre and Languedoc regular regiments and a battalion of French marines, a total of about 1,600 combatants; also, a militia battalion of 400 combatants. On the left of the French were the Royal Roussillon regiment and a battalion of French marines; total, 1,300 combatants. There were about 2,300 Canadian levies in support. Total, about 7,520, including Indians.

Wolfe's field state on the morning of September 13th showed 4,828 combatants of all ranks. Townshend writes:

> Montcalm began the attack. A swarm of Canadian and Indian skirmishers pressed our left flank where Townshend commanded, the brunt of the attack falling upon Colonel Howe and his Light Infantry. He was very hardly pressed, but held on to the houses and a coppice with great tenacity. In the notes, I see mentioned the gallant conduct of a Captain ——— (the name left blank), who had quitted a house which protected the front of General Townshend's position by mistake, but on finding out his error he dashed back again—attacked them with bayonets and put all to the sword within the house.

Townshend then ordered up the 15th (Amherst's), and was soon after reinforced by the two battalions of the 60th, or Royal Americans; and the steady countenance of this brigade turned the tide at this point of the battle.

Meanwhile, things had not gone so well in the right and centre of our line. Swarms of skirmishers drove in our Light Infantry, which Wolfe had posted in our front, and they fell back in disorder, causing confusion. The French columns continued their advance, and Wolfe hurried along the line, restoring order and exhorting the men not to fire without orders. The French came on with loud shouts, and opened a heavy fire. Our men fell fast, but not a shot was returned, showing what splendid discipline these battalions must have had. The 35th and the Grenadiers of Louisbourg, we are told, lost very heavily; Wolfe was slightly wounded in the wrist; and still our splendid infantry, notwithstanding their losses, stood manfully, not returning the fire, the French advancing and shouting. Townshend says our men reserved their fire till within forty yards. Wolfe then passed the order to fire, and volleys were poured in all along our line, completely shattering the French columns, which staggered, having lost heavily, and then broke and gave way.

The battle reads exactly like one of the Peninsular battles, Wolfe using exactly the same tactics as Wellington did. The French came on in *columns* firing, and our troops awaited them in *line*, a first line and a second line in reserve. When these columns came within close range, our troops in line simply shattered their heads with volleys.

This is exactly what Wolfe did then. Directly the French columns wavered and staggered under the deadly fire of the British, he at once passed the order to advance with the bayonet, and our line moved forward in beautiful order; but soon our men broke into a run with cheers, and the French gave way on all sides. Wolfe had placed himself at the head of Bragg's (the 28th) and the Louisbourg Grenadiers as they advanced. He was hit a second time in the body. He did not fall, but tried to stagger on; but was almost immediately shot through the right breast, and fell mortally wounded. General Monckton was severely wounded at the same moment whilst at the head of Lascelles' Regiment (the 47th), and Wolfe's *aide-de-camp* went off to find Townshend, who at once came from the left flank and assumed command.

The advance of the English battalions was irresistible. The 35th (Royal Sussex), then called Otway's Foot; the 28th (Bragg's Regiment), the famous "Slashers"; the 47th (Lascelles'); and the Louisbourg

Grenadiers carried all before them at the point of the bayonet, cheering wildly, and roused to that pitch of enthusiasm which compels victory. Townshend says that the 78th Highlanders, supported by the 58th (Anstruther's), completed the rout of the French, and was loud in his praise of the Highlanders; the magnificent order of the 43rd (Kennedy's) in their advance rivalled the glorious deeds of that splendid regiment in the Peninsular War fifty years after, the 43rd forming part of the famous Light Division, which was to Wellington what the 10th Legion was to Caesar.

But to return to the moment when Townshend assumed command. The rapid advance and pursuit had naturally thrown our line into great disorder; the 47th and 58th were brought to a stand by the French artillery fire as they approached the ramparts of the town; and Townshend writes that, "finding a part of the troops in great disorder I formed them as soon as possible." He had only just got the dishevelled line into tolerable order when Bougainville's troops were seen in *our rear*, coming from Cap Rouge.

The military reader will understand at once from this that Townshend had been called on to command at a most critical juncture of the battle. The commander-in-chief was killed, the second in command severely wounded, the troops in disorder and checked in their advance, and a fresh force of the enemy sighted in our rear coming on to attack! I can imagine a no more difficult situation, and nothing more highly calculated to test the ability of a commander in the field; moreover, Townshend could not have known also the strength of the fresh force of the enemy. No writer, in any of the accounts I have read, has ever grasped the difficulty of Townshend's position in such a case.

If Bougainville had at once attacked boldly, he would have in all probability defeated our troops, disordered and *strained* by the battle just fought. Townshend would then have been blamed; the world would have said that it was owing to Wolfe's death and Townshend's being in command, and so forth; no allowance would have been made for the critical juncture and the difficulties of a general being suddenly put into a position of command in such a situation, and at the same time a situation not of one's own *making*. However, Townshend at once showed himself a *cool*, prompt, and energetic leader, the three best qualities a general can possess. He at once re-formed his battalions into line, opened fire with two field-pieces (captured from the French), and sent forward the 48th (Webb's) in line, this regiment having been in reserve during the battle, and therefore fresh and *keen on fighting*; the 35th also were brought into line with the 48th to hold the approaching column of Bougainville in check.

The confident bearing of these two regiments had the desired effect, for the French were seen to halt, and then to retire to the thick woods in their rear. Townshend was not going to risk the fruits of the victory in following up Bougainville in the woods and swamps, and began entrenching at once, directly the action was over, and widening the road up the cliff to get the naval guns up.

★★★★★★

A year after this General Murray, who was left at Quebec as governor, with the same battalions which had formed Wolfe's force, moved out of Quebec on the approach of De Levi with a French force, and attacked the French at this very place in the woods and swamps; the consequence was, Murray was severely defeated, losing very heavily, but managed to retreat into Quebec; the garrison and Quebec were only saved by the timely arrival of a British fleet, and De Levi hastily retreated. (See Appendix to this chapter.)

★★★★★★

The next morning he commenced establishing batteries to bombard the town and cut off all communication of the garrison with the surrounding country. Bougainville had retired to Cap Rouge. Wolfe died in the hour of victory—like Nelson, like Sir John Moore, and like Abercrombie; his last moments were like Nelson's; and the words of Napier applied to Moore should be applied to Wolfe:

If glory be a distinction, for such a man death is not a leveller!

The day after the battle Townshend issued the following General Orders:—

General Orders.
14th September 1759. Plains of Abraham.
Parole—Wolfe. Countersign—England.

The remaining general officers fit to act take the earliest opportunity to express the praise which is due to the conduct and bravery of the troops; and the victory, which attended it, sufficiently proves the superiority which this army has over any number of such troops as they engaged yesterday. They wish that the person who lately commanded them had survived so glorious a day, and had this day been able to give the troops their just encomiums. The fatigues which the troops will be obliged to undergo, to reap the advantage of this victory, will be supported with a true spirit, as this seems to be the period which will determine, in all probability, our American labours.

Late on the evening of September 14th Montcalm died of his wound, and was succeeded in the command by M. de Ramsay, the Governor of Quebec.

Townshend, on the day succeeding the battle and up till the day of capitulation, worked hard in pushing on the works against the city. By the evening of September 17th, he had no less than 118 guns mounted in the batteries and ready to open fire, and the whole fleet was in the basin waiting the order to bombard the town. The enemy had tried in vain to delay proceedings by keeping up a constant fire with every available gun, but the annoyance they caused was slight.

On September 17th, at midday, an officer arrived with a flag of truce from the French lines, bearing proposals of surrender from De Ramsay, the Governor of Quebec, and he was conducted in the pouring rain to Townshend's tent. Townshend sent back the officer with the answer that he would give them four hours in which to surrender, failing which he would take the town by assault.

In the early morning on September 18th Quebec surrendered. The keys of the city were delivered up to Townshend, who marched in with the Grenadiers of Louisbourg, preceded by a detachment of artillery and one gun, with the British flag hoisted on a staff on the gun-carriage.

Townshend wrote:

> We compute our loss at about 500 killed and wounded; theirs about 2,000.

The following is Townshend's dispatch to Mr. Pitt, the Secretary for State, which left for England on September 22nd. I believe this letter has never been published in a book before.

> From Brigadier, the Hon. George Townshend
> to the Right Hon. Mr. Secretary Pitt.
> Camp before Quebec,
> September 20th, 1759.
>
> Sir,—
> I have the honour to acquaint you with the Success of His Majesty's Arms on the 13th inst., in an action with the French on the heights to the westward of this town.

It being determined to carry the operations above the town, the posts at Point Levi and l'Isle d'Orléans being secured General Wolfe marched with the remainder of his forces from Point Levi, the 5th and 6th, and embarked them in transports which had passed the town for that purpose.

On the 7th 8th and 9th a movement of the ships was made up the river by Admiral Holmes, in order to amuse the enemy, now posted along the North shore. The transports being extremely crowded, and the weather very bad, the general thought proper to cantoon half his troops on the South shore, where they were refreshed and re-embarked upon the 12th at 1 in the morning. The Light Infantry commanded by Col. Howe, the regiments of Bragg's Kennedy's Lascelles', and Anstruther's, with a detachment of Highlanders and the Royal American Grenadiers, the whole being immediately under the command of Brigadiers Monckton and Murray were put into the flat bottomed boats, and after some movements of the ships, made by Admiral Holmes, to draw the attention of the enemy up the river, the boats fell down with the tide, and landed on the north shore, within a league of Cape Diamond, an hour before daybreak.

The rapidity of the tide of ebb hurried the boats a little below the intended place of attack, which obliged the light infantry to scramble up a woody precipice in order to secure the landing of the troops, and to dislodge a captains post, which defended a small entrenched road, where the troops were to move up.

After some firing, the light infantry gained the top of the precipice and dispersed the Captain's post, by which means the troops, with very little loss, from a few Canadians and Indians in the wood, got up, and immediately formed. The boats as they emptied, were sent back for the second disembarkation, which I immediately made.

Brig. Murray, being detached with Anstruther's battalion, to attack a 4 gun battery on the left, was recalled by the General, who now saw the French army crossing the River St. Charles. General Wolfe thereupon began to form his line of battle having his right covered by the Louisbourg Grenadiers on an eminence behind which was Otway's, on the left of the Grenadiers were Bragg's Kennedy's, Lascelles', Highlanders and Anstruther's the right of this body was commanded by Brig. Monckton, and the left by Brig. Murray; his rear and left were protected by Col. Howe's light infantry who was returned from the 4 gun battery, which he had found abandoned and the cannon spiked up. Webb's was formed as a reserve in the centre with large intervals between their subdivisions, and Lawrence's soon after detached to preserve our communication with our boats. General Montcalm having collected the whole of his force from the Beauport side, and advancing, showed his intention to flank our left, where I was immediately ordered with Gen. Amherst's battalion, which I formed *en potence*.

My numbers were soon after increased by the arrival of the two battalions of Royal Americans; the enemy lined the bushes in their front with 1500 Indians and Canadians, and I have reason to think most of their best marksmen, who kept up a brisk, though irregular fire upon our whole line, who bore it with the greatest patience and good order, reserving their fire for the main body, now advancing. This fire of the enemy was however checked by our posts in the front, which protected the forming our own line. The right of the French line was composed of half the troops of the colony; the battalions La Sarre, Languedoc, with some Canadians and Indians. Their centre column was formed by the battalions of Bearn and Guienne, and their left was composed of the other half of the troops of the colony, with the battalion of Royal Roussillon.

Such was as near as I guess their line of battle. The French brought up two small pieces or artillery against us, and we had been able to bring up but one gun, which being extremely well served galled their column exceedingly. My attention to the left will not permit me to be very exact with regard to every circumstance which passed in the centre, much less to the right, but it is most certain that the attack of the enemy was very brisk and animated on that side. Our troops nevertheless reserved their fire until well within 40 yards, which was so well continued that the enemy everywhere gave way.

It was then our general fell at the head of Bragg's, and the Louisbourg Grenadiers, advancing to charge their bayonettes about the same time Brig. Gen. Monckton received his wound at the head of Lascelles. On their side fell the French General Mr. de Montcalm, and his second in command since dead of his wound on board our fleet. The enemy in their confusion flung themselves into a thick copse wood in their rear and seemed preparing to make a stand. It was at this time that each corps seemed in a manner to exert itself with a view to its own peculiar character. The Grenadiers, Bragg's and Lascelles, drove on the enemy with their bayonettes. Brig. Murray briskly advancing upon the enemy the troops under his command completed the rout on this side; when the Highlanders supported by Anstruther's took to their broadswords, and drove part into the town, and part over the River St. Charles.

The action on our left and rear of our left was not so severe. The houses into which the Light Infantry were thrown were well defended, being supported by Colonel Howe, who, taking post with two companies behind a small copse and frequently sallying upon the enemy who attacked them, drove them often into heaps against the front of which body I advanced fresh platoons of Amherst's regiment which prevented their right wing from executing their first intention.

One of the Royal American battalions being detached to a post which secured our rear, and the other being sent to fill up the space which the battalions advanced with Brig. Murray had vacated, I remained with Amherst's to support these posts, and to keep the enemy's right in check. The efforts of the enemy on this side could never break in upon this disposition, and the hopes of a great body of Indians and Canadians who waited impatiently to have fallen on our rear in case of a defeat, were entirely frustrated.

This, Sir, was the situation of things, when I was told in the action, that I commanded: I immediately repaired to the centre, and finding that the pursuit had put part of the troops in great disorder, I formed them as soon as possible. Scarce was that effected when M. de Bougainville, with about 2,000 men, the corps from Cap Rouge and that neighbourhood appeared in our rear. I advanced two pieces of light artillery, and two Battalions towards him, but upon two or three shots he retired.

You will, I flatter myself, agree Sir, that it was not my business to risk the fruits of so glorious a day and to abandon so commanding a situation to give a fresh enemy battle upon his own terms and in the midst of woods and swamps where he was posted. I have been employed from the day of action to that of the capitulation in redoubting our camp against any insult, in making a road up the precipice for our cannon, in getting up the artillery, preparing the batteries, and cutting off the communications of the garrison with the country. The 17th a flag of truce came out with proposals of capitulation about noon before we had any battery erected, I sent the officer who had come out back to the town, allowing them four hours to capitulate or no further treaty. He returned with terms of capitulation, which with the admiral were considered, agreed to, and signed on both sides eight o'clock in the morning the 18th instant.

The terms you find we granted, will, I flatter myself, be approved of by His Majesty, considering the enemy assembling in our rear, the inclemency of the season which would scarcely admit of our bringing a gun up the precipice, the critical situation of our fleet from the Aequinoctial gales calling for our immediate attention, add to this the entering the town in a defensible state, against any attack which might otherwise be attempted against it in the winter. This I hope will be deemed sufficient considerations for granting them the terms I have the honour to enclose you.

I herewith send you a list of the killed and wounded and the list of French prisoners as perfect as I have yet been able to obtain it. I believe their loss that day might amount to 1500, they have at least now 500 wounded in their Hospital General. Another list of the Artillery and Stores in the town as well as those fallen into our hands at Beauport in consequence of the victory. The inhabitants bring in their arms very fast and cheerfully take the oath of alleigance to His Majesty.

By the latest intelligence from deserters M. de Levi now commands their army. He is returned some say with troops from the Montreal side, they are collecting their scattered forces at Cape Rouge, his left extending by different posts as near us as Old Loretto six miles from our camp. Their regular battalions are now reduced to 150 men each and are in great want of provisions.

I should be wanting in paying my due respects to the admirals of the naval service if I neglected this occasion to acknowledge how much we are indebted for our success to the constant assistance and support we have received, and to the perfect harmony and immediate correspondence which has prevailed throughout our operations, in the uncommon difficulties which the nature of this country in particular presents to military operations of a great extent, and which no army can in itself solely supply the immense labour in transportation of artillery stores, and provisions, the long watchings and attendance in boats, the drawing up our artillery, even in the heat of the action, it is my duty, short as my command has been, to acknowledge for that time, how great a share the navy has had in this successful campaign.

I have the honour etc. etc.

Geo. Townshend.

No. LXXI.

Articles of Capitulation demanded by M. de Ramsay, the King's Lieutenant, commanding the high and low towns of Quebec, chief of the Military Order of St. Louis, to his Excellency the General of the Troops of his Britannic Majesty.

The capitulation demanded on the part of the enemy and granted by their Excellencies, Admiral Saunders and General Townshend, &c. &c, is in manner and form as hereafter expressed:—

1. M. de Ramsay demands the honours of war for his garrison, and that it shall be sent back to the army in safety, and by the shortest route, with arms, baggage, six pieces of brass cannon, two mortars or howitzers and twelve rounds for each of them.—The garrison of the town, composed of land forces, marines and sailors, shall march out with their arms and baggage, drums beating, matches lighted, with two pieces of French cannon and twelve rounds for each piece; and shall be embarked as conveniently as possible, to be sent to the first port in France.

2. That the inhabitants shall be preserved in the possession of their houses, goods, effects, and privileges.—Granted, upon their laying down their arms.

3. That the inhabitants shall not be accountable for having carried arms in the defence of the town, forasmuch as they were compelled to do it, and that the inhabitants of the colonies, of both crowns, equally serve as militia.—Granted.

4. That the effects of the absent officers and citizens shall

not be touched.—Granted.

5. That the inhabitants shall not be removed, nor obliged to quit their houses, until their condition shall be settled by their Britannic and most Christian Majesties.—Granted.

6. That the exercise of the Catholic, Apostolic, and Roman religion shall be maintained, and that, safe-guards shall be granted to the houses of the clergy and to the mountaineers, particularly to his lordship the Bishop of Quebec, who, animated with zeal for religion, and charity for the people of his diocese, desires to reside in it constantly, to exercise freely, and with that decency which his character, and the sacred offices of the Roman religion require, his episcopal authority in the town of Quebec, whenever he shall think proper, until the possession of Canada shall be decided by a treaty between their Britannic and most Christian Majesties.—The free exercise of the Roman religion is granted, likewise safeguards to all religious persons, as well as to the bishop, who shall be at liberty to come and exercise, freely and with decency, the functions of his office whenever he thinks proper, until the possession of Canada shall have been decided between their Britannic and most Christian Majesties.

7. That the artillery and warlike stores shall be faithfully given up, and that an inventory of them shall be made out.—Granted.

8. That the sick and wounded, the commissaries, chaplains, physicians, surgeons, apothecaries, and other people employed in the service of the hospitals, shall be treated conformably to the cartel of the 6th of February, 1759, settled between their Britannic and most Christian Majesties.—Granted.

9. That before delivering up the gate and the entrance of the town to the English troops, their general will be pleased to send some soldiers to be posted as safe-guards upon the churches, convents and principal habitations.—Granted.

10. That the King's lieutenant commanding in Quebec

shall be permitted to send information to the Marquis de Vaudreuil, governor general, of the reduction of the place, as also that the general may send advice thereof to the French Ministry.— Granted.

11. That the present capitulation shall be executed according to its form and tenor, without being subject to non-execution under pretence of reprisals, or for the non-execution of any preceding capitulation.—Granted.

Duplicates hereof, taken and executed by and between us, at the camp before Quebec, this 18th day of September, 1759.

Charles Saunders.
George Townshend.
De Ramsay.

Wolfe's body was embalmed and sent to England, the remains being escorted by the troops in solemn state to the beach. One can hardly imagine a more impressive sight than this must have been. Wolfe was deeply loved by the troops, and their sorrow was great. There, stands a small and simple monument on the Plains of Abraham, on which the date and the following words only are engraved:—

Here Wolfe died Victorious.

On October 18th Admiral Saunders and the fleet weighed anchor and dropped down to Isle aux Coudres, sailing for Halifax and England. Townshend was on board the admiral's ship, proceeding direct to London; Monckton, recovering from his wound, returned to New York; Murray was left as Military Governor of Quebec, Wolfe's original force, with the exception of the Grenadiers of Louisbourg, being left as garrison. The total combatants now amounted to 7,300, the bad cases of wounded and sick having been sent home to England.

I find the following letters amongst Townshend's papers which are of interest:—

Admiral Saunders to Brigadier the Honourable
George Townshend.

On Board the *Stirling Castle*,
September 13th, 1759.

Dear Sir

The loss of our friend General Wolfe gives me the greatest concern which in some measure is taken off by the great victory of

today; as I have not heard how you are situated, I have sent all the 24 pounders with the ammunition that I had boats for, till those are cleared that are now above. I heartily wish you farther success, and should be glad to know what I can do to promote it. I have had the dispatches General Wolfe sent me to go with the great ships. They are not gone, and I shall keep them till I have yours. I beg my best compliments of General Murray and that you will believe me most sincerely
    Yours

                                        Chas. Saunders.

    General Townshend to ———. (Unaddressed.)
                                    Camp before Quebec,
                                    September 25th, 1759.
Dear Sir—The method of sending this will I hope sufficiently excuse the shortness of the relation. It being determined to carry the operations above the town, the Corps at Montmorency passed over to Point Levi. The Posts of Isle Orleans and of Point Levi being secured, the General embarked the troops in transports on the 5th and 6th; after some movements up the river to amuse the enemy, we landed on the 13th and surprised a French post on the N. shore, within 3 miles of the Town. Our troops to about 3500 met Monr. de Montcalm's Army from the Beauport side upon the Heights before the town. He began the attack, was repulsed twice.

The firmness with which our troops bore the Tirallerie of all their Indians Canadians etc. for a considerable time, preserving their fire for their Regulars; and the home attack which they made upon the latter with their bayonets, when they came down to the charge, decided the day. The Highlanders seconded by Anstruther's pursued them to the gates of the Town with their broadswords. We had but 2 pieces of cannon up and but one played for a considerable time.

We took five besides a great quantity of artillery and stores which fell into our hands, on the Beauport side—as well as in the Town which surrendered, before we had a battery ready, on the 18th instant in the morning. We lost poor General Wolfe who fell in the warmest part of the engagement. Genl. Monckton was wounded near the same place and about the same time. Monr. de Montcalm and the second in command were also killed. Their regulars suffered extremely—we have a great many of their officers prisoners. We compute our loss at about 500 killed and wounded; theirs about 2000. The remains of their army is assembling, and cantooned about St. Augustine. Monr. de Levi Commands. Monr. de Boucainville had a separate corps of 1500 men who came upon our Rear just as the action was over, attacked one of our posts, and suffered a good deal.

I write this to you by order of Genl. Monckton, who though wounded in the breast, is in so fine a way as to be able to do all business but write—I have the honour to be with the most grateful respect—Dear Sir—Your most faithful and affectionate
              Geo. Townshend.

On September 26th, 1759, Townshend wrote to General Amherst, dating his letter at the "Camp before Quebec":—

Dear Sir

Having General Monckton's commands to write you a relation of the action of the 13th, which decided the fate of this town and I hope will contribute not a little to the total reduction of Canada; I have the honour to send you a copy (I believe pretty exact) of my account of that victory to the Secretary of State. Were I really to attempt to point out the most striking cause of this successful stroke I must attribute it to the admirable and determined firmness of every British soldier in the field that day; conducted by the manifest ability of the officers at their respective posts.

Victory or no quarter was I may affirm in every man's face that day; the ground we scrambled up in the morning, the motions of the enemy to surround us, the time of tide and the Heights which command the boats taught us this lesson, and thank God, the whole army made a proper application. General Monckton who is so well recovered as to command us, will I conclude write to you upon the intelligence he has of the situation of the remains of the French Army and how far things may admit or not of any further movement on our side. This is not my province. He proposes to leave Genl. Murray commander at Quebec.

I cannot consequently whenever the army becomes a garrison be of any use here, and may embrace the leave to return to England you so long ago bestowed upon me. I am sorry the advancement will not allow me to pay my respects to you in America, but shall only say that I shall be one of the very many who shall think himself happy to serve under your command. We heard this day by a deserter, you had taken Montreal. I hope t'is true. *Voila donc* Monr. de Levi *investié*.

I hear I have got Barrington's regiment. Alas! what a Bouquet this had been a year or two hence for poor Roger. I assure you I return thoroughly wounded from America. I loved him sincerely. My respects to all who do me the Honour to remember me and forgive me dear Sir for not sending you the relation of the action in my own handwriting. I had made a thousand blots. I hope to pay you my respects upon more momentous occassions.

    I am with the most sincere respect—
        Your most faithful and obedient servant
                        Geo. Townshend.

P.S. There were two field pieces and not only one up in the action.

The following letter from General Murray to General Townshend, received by the latter on board ship just before sailing from Quebec for England, indicates the opinion the brigadiers held of Wolfe's generalship:—

                              October 5th, 1759.
Sir

I this moment had the honour of yours. The shaving trunk I think myself obliged to you for and I enclose an order for the re-establishment of it. I doubt not of its being presented a few weeks after your arrival in England. As I am sure you are desirous to serve your country it certainly will avail itself of your inclinations and nobody can wish you greater success in everything you undertake than I do.

I remember we did joke about the chairs. I am of your opinion that they are too heavy for the field. I thank you however for the offer. I send the map you mention and wish I had anything more worth your acceptance. I have a few embroider' d birch curiosities which Lady Ferrers would like perhaps, and you may not have met with any like them. You will oblige me if you will accept of them. As I am to stay here you know I can easily get others for my female friends in England.

I shall look for the letter you mention, take a copy of it and deposite the original with you. Since so black a lie was propagated I think myself very happy that you will be on the spot to contradict whatever ignorance or faction may suggest.

I have no copy of the paper I sent by you to General Wolfe concerning his scheme of landing between Point au Tremble and St. August in, but the public orders are a sufficient proof of his intention to do it, and likewise of the suddenness of the thought of landing when we did. Indeed his orders throughout the campaign show little stability, stratagem or fixed resolution; I wish his friends had not been so much our enemies, his memory would probably have been dearer to his country than now it can be. We are acting on the defensive, you have the execution of the plan and I am well persuaded you will manage it with as much tenderness to the memory of the poor general as the nature of things will admit of.

I find I am not to have the honour of a visit from you so I must take the opportunity of wishing you a good voyage and a happy meeting with your friends.

    I am—Sir

        Your most obedient humble servant

                Ja. Murray.

The following two letters from Monckton to Townshend are also of interest:—

    To the Honble. Brigadier Genl. Townshend.

                Camp at Point Levi
                Sepbr. ye 16th 1759.

Dear Townshend—

As notwithstanding my wound, I am so well as to sit up—And never in better health; I have wrote a short letter to Mr. Pitt referring him to yours for the particulars of that day—As I was obliged to quit the field just as the French gave way—Col. Hale for whom I have a great esteem; for many pressing reasons, would be glad to be the barer of this good news—And I should bee glad he did—If therefore you have no objection to it—be pleased to tell him he may—You will greatly oblige one who is very deserving of any favour that can be done him—Cap. Bell is collecting the publick papers—I shall send you such as may be necessary for you—I hope you keep your health—And that

everything goes on as you could wish—Pay my compliments to Murray and believe me
>Yours most sincerely
>>Robt. Monckton.

Hussey, who is Major to the 47th, may be very well spared from the Light Infantry.

>To the Honble. Brigadier Genl. Townshend.
>>Medway Sepbr. ye 18th.

My Dear Townshend

You are one of the last men in the world that could give me offence—And I do most sincerely assure you that I never said anything either *pro* or *con*, except that I did suppose I should see the capitualation before it was signed, and that, to Adl. Saunders, and Col. Carleton, the latter of whom was of that opinion—Ever since the 14th I have been as well as ever I was in my life—And as there are many things, which in the present state I am in—No one can properly transact but myself—I hope you will not impute my coming to town tomorrow, to any other than that, thee real cause; and the benefit of the air—The admiral was with me this morning, and we purposed to meet you tomorrow, to settle what was to be done—In regard to your going home, you will just choose your own time—But I should be glad that it was not very soon—As there are many things to be done—Which I am convinced you will be good enough to assist me in—

I hope My Dear Townshend, that malicious tongues will not be suffered—to hurt me in your opinion—As I do most faithfully assure you that I am, as much as ever
>Yours most sincerely
>>Robt. Monckton.

P. S.—I could never think of sending you the parole—Or that you should wait on me—

I enclose you Mr. Amherst Letter.

Wolfe's last dispatch had thrown all England into gloom; the news of the victory, the glorious conclusion of the greatest year England had ever seen, sent the nation mad with joy; but the nation mourned at the same time, as it afterwards mourned for Nelson at Trafalgar. New England rejoiced also with the mother country at the overthrow of the French, who had threatened their very existence in North

America; yet twenty years after, when George Townshend was Viceroy of Ireland, New England was allied with; the French, fighting against their own blood!

The battle on the Heights of Abraham was politically one of the greatest battles in modern history. It gave Canada to England, and established the supremacy of the Anglo-Saxon race in North America. Wolfe and his handful of British soldiers settled one of the greatest political questions that have ever moved the human race.

The Adjutant-General, Sir Richard Lyttelton, K.C.B., writing to Pitt in a letter dated October 18th, 1759, says:—

> The loss of Wolfe is indeed ever to be lamented, but Providence gives not the cup of joy unmixed, and were it not for a little ingredient of bitterness it would be too intoxicating. Townshend still remains and many a gallant officer animated by your spirit and by you brought forward into action.

I take the following extracts from the papers of the time:—

> The King has been pleased to appoint Brigadier Townshend—Colonel 28th (Bragg decd.)—*Gentleman's Magazine*, vol. xxix., p. 498, October 9th, 1759.
>
> *Nov. 23.* Some of the ships from Quebec have arrived at Plymouth and some at Spithead; the Lords of the Admiralty began to be in pain for Admiral Saunders when they received a letter of excuse from him dated in the chops of the Channel acquainting them, that as he had heard the Brest Squadron were sailed, he hoped he should be pardoned for going to join Admiral Hawke without orders. In this noble enterprise, he is joined by General Townshend—*Annual Register*, vol. ii., p. 128.

In Townshend's *Diary* I find:—

> Returned from Quebec and declined being landed but proceeded with Admiral Saunders to join Sir Edward Hawke in the bay.
>
> 18th November we lay becalmed in the chops of the Channel and about 12 in the morning met with the Juno frigate who acquainted Admiral Saunders that the Brest fleet had sailed out of Toulon 21 or 22 ships of the line—Admiral Hawke about 20. Upon this the admiral ordered the transports then about a day's sail from Portsmouth to make the best of their way and himself with the *Vanguard* of 64 guns and the *Devonshire* of 64 made

the best of his way to the bay to join Sir Edward Hawke. He asked me if I'd go on board a merchantman with the 2 French pilots he sent in a boat, or go on with him. I preferred the latter having first wrote to Mr. Pitt. Soon after this that forenoon the wind came fair for Portsmouth and at the same time enabled us to start down the Channel making all possible sail for the bay.

Admiral Saunders was too late for the battle, which was a glorious victory for Hawke, and Saunders returned to Portsmouth.

January 23rd, 1760.—"Vice Admiral Saunders, Rear Admiral Holmes and Brigadier General Townshend, having come to the House of Commons, Mr. Speaker acquainted them that the House had unanimously resolved that the thanks of the House be given to the admirals and generals employed in the glorious and successful expedition against Quebec, and Mr. Speaker gave the said members the thanks of the House accordingly.

Appendix

Various writers have mentioned the existence of an anonymous public letter bringing accusations against George Townshend, and a letter in reply is also vaguely mentioned, which Mr. Parkman, the author of *Montcalm and Wolfe*, terms "angry but not conclusive!" In answer to this and to establish the proof, I publish both letters in full—both the famous accusation and the reply. Let the reader judge; the absurdity of the accusing letter needs no comment from me.

Townshend attributed the authorship of the "Letter to an Honourable Brigadier General" to Lord Albemarle, and accordingly challenged Albemarle to a duel; people interfered, and the duel was stopped. Some say that "Junius" wrote the letter, and others Mr. Charles Lee. As regards the "Refutation," I must say I think it absurd not only to drag in Prince Ferdinand of Brunswick, but to compare that great leader to Lord George Sackville, who, after all said and done, was tried by a court-martial composed of British officers and found unfit to serve His Majesty; and I prefer to take the view of the court-martial

Writers on the Quebec Expedition all seem to attack Townshend; like sheep following each other through a gap, they repeat the same histories.

Bradley, in his *Life of Wolfe*, says that "Townshend had some talents and much bravery, but was of a queer disposition and inclined to presume somewhat on his social rank and powerful connections."

Mr. Parkman, in his *Montcalm and Wolfe*, says that "though his perverse and envious disposition made him a difficult colleague Townshend had both talents and energy," but goes on to say that "Townshend went home to parade his laurels and claim more than his share of the honours of victory."

Townshend never claimed his rightful share, much less more than his share. On the contrary, I find, after a careful search into his life, that he was modest; and I also find, from his note-books and so forth, that he was a diligent student of the art of war, and studied far more than ninety-nine officers out of a hundred nowadays in the army—though in justice it must be said that the regimental officer has so much to do in these days that he has little time for study, a fact which the general public are evidently ignorant of when they demand more work for the regimental officer.

The military reader judges of the talents of a general by his conduct in the field, and in my opinion Townshend's action on the day of the Battle of the Heights of Abraham, when he was suddenly called to the command at a most critical juncture, stamps him as a first-class leader, as also does his action in compelling the French garrison of Quebec to surrender.

Warburton, in his famous *Conquest of Canada*, clearly gives the credit of the daring plan of scaling the cliff to George Townshend, and Warburton stands out far ahead of any historian of that campaign.

I have often wondered why, in other accounts, the authors scatter about in pepper-pot fashion assertions that Townshend was a "cold proud aristocrat," "presumed on his social rank and powerful connections," "contemptuous, sullen," and so forth, and similar gallery clap-trap, as if Townshend's great crime was that he belonged to the aristocracy. I do not see that the fact of being "born of poor but honest parents" ever yet—except on the stage of a transpontine theatre—conferred special virtues over those of another born in a higher rank of social life.

There was absolutely no "parading of laurels" on the return of Townshend and Admiral Saunders to England. They simply received the thanks of the Houses of Parliament, and it must be remembered that the expedition had added the whole of Canada to the British Empire! A campaign like that, which reflected more honour and more *advantage* on England than had happened in the whole century! What would have been the reward of these officers for such a campaign in the present day—in this age of hysterical newspaper accounts of battles, where the imagination is so often drawn upon for facts.

Finally, I see that the author of *Montcalm and Wolfe* quotes Walpole as his authority for his views on Townshend! —it being well known the two were great enemies. "Who will vouch for the voucher?" as Agesilaus would ask, when any one was strongly recommended—or otherwise—to him.

The following account of the battle is taken from the *Annual Reg-*

ister, a paper of the time, and as it is of interest I attach it:—

(*Sept. 13th.*) Montcalm when he heard that the English had ascended the hill, and were formed on the high ground, at the back of the town, scarcely credited the intelligence, and still believed it to be a feint to induce him to abandon that strong post which had been the object of all the real attempts that had been made since the beginning of the campaign. But he was soon and fatally for him undeceived. He saw clearly that the English and army were in such a situation that the upper and lower town might be attacked in concert, and that nothing but a battle could possibly save it. Accordingly, he determined to give them battle, and quitted Beauport, passed the River St. Charles, and formed his troops opposite to ours.

He filled the bushes that were in his front with detachments of Indians and Canadians and his best marksmen, to the number of about 1500. His regular forces formed his left, his right was composed of the troops of the colony, supported by two battalions of Regulars. The rest of the Indians and Canadians extended on that side and attempted to out-flank the left of the English, which was formed to prevent the design in a manner which the military men called 'Potence,' that is in a body which presents two faces to the enemy. Here Brig. Gen. Townshend commanded six regiments, and the Louisbourg Grenadiers were disposed in a line to the right of this body extending to the river.

A regiment was drawn up behind the right for the reserve. It formed in eight sub-divisions with large intervals. The Light Infantry, under Colonel Howe, protected the rear and the left. The disposition on both sides began with spirit. The English troops were exhorted to reserve their fire: and they bore that of the enemies' Light troops in front, which was galling although irregular, with the utmost patience and good order, waiting for the main body of the enemy which advanced fast upon them. At 40 yards distance, our troops gave their fire, which took place in its full extent, and made a terrible havoc amongst the French. It was supported with such vivacity as it was begun, and the enemy everywhere yielded to it.

But just in the moment when fortunately, the field began to declare itself Gen. Wolfe, in whose whole life everything seemed included, fell; General Monkton, the next to him in command, fell immediately after, and both were conveyed out of the line. The command now devolved upon General Townshend. It was at a very critical time. For though the enemy began to fall back and were much broken the loss of the two generals was a very discouraging circumstance, and it required great temper and great exertions to support the advantages that had been gained and to push them to their proper extent.

General Townshend showed himself equal to so arduous a duty. The truce preserved their spirit and each corps seemed to exert itself with a view to his peculiar character. The Grenadiers with their bayonets, the Highlanders with their broadswords, and the rest of the forces with a steady and continued fire drove the enemy in great disorder from every post and completed their defeat.

I attach a couple of letters which are of interest, one being from Montcalm, and the other from De Ramsay, the Governor of Quebec, who commanded the garrison on the death of Montcalm,

>Monr. De Ramsay's Letter to me concerning the Prisoners:—
>(The originals are obscure in places.—C.V. F. T.)

>*Quebec Le 14 7bre 1759*

Monsieur

M. Bernier Comm^{dre} des guerres m'a remis la lettre que votre Excellence ecrit à M^r Le Mis Laquelle Je lui ai fait passer. Il m'a aussi rendu compte des arrangemens qu'elle avoit daigné prendre pour l'execution du cartel entre les troupees de Sa Majesté trés Chretienne et Celles de Sa Majesté britannique.

Je donnerai les ordres les plus formels pour qu'on observe de notre coté   Mr Bernier m'a rendu compte. En mon particulier je serai toujours   de reconnoissance des   genereux que Votre Excellence voudra temoigner à nos blessés et nos prisonniers, Je la prie d'etre persuadé de l'estime et de la consideration respectueuse. Avec la quelle J'ay l'honneur d'etre,

>*Monsieur*
>>*Votre tres humble & trés*
>>>*Obeissant serviteur*

>>>>*De Ramsay.*

From Mr. De Montcalm: —

Monsieur

Obligé de Ceder Quebec à vos armes. J'ay l'honneur de demander à votre Excellence ses bontés pour nos malades et blessés et de lui demander l'execution du traité d'echange qu'a eté convenû entre Sa Majesté trés Chretienne et Sa Majesté Britannique. Je la prie d'etre persuadé de la haute estime et de la respectueuse consideration. Avec la quelle J'ay L'honneur d'etre,
  Monsieur
     Votre trés humble & trés
       Obeissant serviteur
          Montcalm.

 The following letter from General Murray, written from Quebec on April 30th, 1760, is interesting, as it describes his own defeat by M. de Levi, and gives an idea of how near the French were to retaking Quebec. The letter proves that Quebec was untenable once an enemy got possession of the Heights of Abraham. I attach a letter also from Mr. Désbruyêres, at Quebec, to George Townshend, giving him an account of General Murray's defeat, and of the arrival of the English fleet, raising the siege:—

         Quebec, 30th April 1760
The intelligence I had the honour to communicate to you by St. Montressor of the enemys designs proves true.
The 17th of this month I was informed that they had everything in readyness to fall down the river, with 8 frigates the moment it was clear of ice, and it did not break up here sooner than the 23rd—consequently as the country was covered with snow and the earth impenetrable, it was impossible to attempt entrenching myself on the Heights of Abraham, which I formerly told you was my plan of defence. Before the 25th and even then, as will no doubt appear by the journal of the engineer in chief, It was hardly posible to drive the first pickets, The thaw having reached no further than 9 metres from the surface, As the river was clear above and as I had reason to think the enemy would take the first opportunity of making themselves masters of the embouchure of the River Cap Rouge as the most convenient place of disembarking their artillery and stores and for securing their retreat
I took possession of that post the 18th Apl. with the L. I. commanded by Mr. Dalling, which obliged them to land their army

20 miles higher up and to risk a battle without artillery after a march of 30 miles.

At 3 o'clock in the morning of the 27th instant I knew they had marched from the Point au Tremble with an intention to take post at St. Foix and so cut off our communication with Major Dalling and the post I had established at Loretto. I instantly with Amhersts Regt. the Grs. & picquets of the army, commanded by Col: Burton Marched and took post so advantagously as to fustrate their scheme, and to withdraw all their posts with the loss of 2 men only; They had begun to form from the defile they were obliged to pass, but thought proper to retire on reconnoitring our disposition and receiving some shot from the 2 field pieces I had with me.

About four that afternoon I marched back to town without the loss of a man though the enemys regulars did everything in their power to harrass our rear.

As the place is not fortifyd and commanded everywhere towards the land my garison which was now melted down to 3000 fighting men by the most invetrate scurvy, were day mouldring away, and it was now imposible for me to entrench myself on the heights of Abraham, though fascines and every other requisite material had been provided long ago, I could not hestitate a moment about giving the enemy battle.

As everyone knows the place is not tenable agt. an army in possession of the heights I therefore this night gave the necessary orders and by 7 o'clock next morning marched with all the force I could muster, and formed the little army on the heights in the following order. Amhersts, Anstruthers, 2 Battn. Rl. Ams., and Webbs composed the right brigade under the commd. of Col. Fraser. Otways and the 3d Battn. R. A. were formed as a *Corps de Reserve*. Major Dallings Corps of L. I. covered the r: flank and Captn. Hezzens Company of Rangers with 100 Volrs. under the command of Captain D. MDonald a brave and experienced offr. covered the left. The battns. had each two field pieces.

Whilst the line was forming I reconnoitred the enemy, and perceived they had begune to throw up some redoubts, though the greatest part of their army was on their march, I thought this was the lucky moment and marched in the outmost order to attack them before they had formed. We immediately beat them from the works they had begune, and Major Dalling who cannot be too much commended forced their corps of grs. from a house they had occuppyed to cover their left, here he and several of his men were wounded; his men however pursued ye fugitives to their 2nd Line which soon checked our Light Infantry who dispersed along ye front of our right wing and prevented Col. Burton from taking ye advantage of ye first impression they had made on ye enemies left flank

They had imediately orders to clear ye front and regain ye right flank, but in attempting this; they were charged threwn into confusion, retired to ye rear and could never be brought up during ye action; I no sooner perceived this disorder, than I sent to Majr. Morris who comanded Otways Regiment in ye 2nd Line; to wheel to ye right and support our right flank; this soon recovered everything there, but ye left a little after began to retire though they had early made themselves masters of ye 2 redoubts; I orderd Kennedy's Regiment and ye 3rd Battalion to sustain them, but they were too late.—The disorder of ye left soon comunicated to ye right and ye whole retired under ye musquetry of our block houses—abandoning their cannon to ye enemy.

As we have been unfortunate I am sensible I may be blamed universally at home; but I appeal to every officer in ye field; if anything was wanting in ye disposition or my endeavours to animate the men during ye whole affair. The superiority of these troops had acquired over ye enemy ever since ye last campaign together with ye fine field train we were furnished with, might have tempted me with an Action, supposing I had Not been thoroughly Convinced of ye necessity of it.

We lost in ye battle about one third of our army, and have certain intelligence that ye enemy had no less than 10,000 men in ye field. They have already compleated their first parraled; but I am in hopes We shall not be reduced to extreamities till ye arrival of ye fleet—which we expect daily in that event I shall retreat with what I can to ye Island of Orleans and wait ye arrival of reinforcements unless I can do better. Had we been masters of ye river in which it is evident ships may safely winter they never would have made the attempt.

I must do ye justice to Col. Barton in particular and to ye officers in general that they have done everything that could be expected of them and to reward them as far as in my power as well as from ye necessity of such a measure I ventured to appoint to ye vacancies officers to act till your pleasure is known. I shall take care to do ye utmost and hope you'll think proper to confirm them.

I send this by Capt. Mackartny as his ship can be of no further service in ye river at present and that it prefer you should know what is passed on this side.

Strength of ye Garrison 2400 Men.

	Comd. Officers.	Non-Comissd.	Privates.
Killed	26	21	232
Wounded	89	39	685
Prisoners	13	2	
Missing	2		

Dear General,

It was not potable for me to give you by my last note of the 29th of April more than a short hint that we had been beat in the field and were bettered in the town. I shall now give you *en gros* the occurences of last winter, as far as my abilities & my present situation in the army have permitted me to observe.

As soon as the business of getting in the arms of the French people, and taking the oath of allegiance of those who were either willing to remain quiet, or to impose upon us by that hypocritical piece of submission was over, some steps were taken to set a price on the meat and other commodities that were to be brought to market, but no proper measures being really taken to settle a market none of the inhabitants submitted to the regulations proposed, and everybody who had it in his power was glad at any rate to procure what he could scarcity and most extravagant prices were ye consequence of this.

Next supplying the garrison with wood was considered, wood cutters were sent in different places, and hand sleighs made for each regiment to bring in their wood, to secure these operations two posts were taken in December, one at St Foy the other at old Loretto. they effectually covered our wood parties and none were insulted during the whole winter, however the fatigue our soldiers underwent and the want of vegetables and other refreshments brought on the scurvy etc. and weakened our garrison very early. The cold though very intense did not

RETURN OF THE NUMBER OF OFFICERS AND MEN THAT MARCHED INTO THE FIELD, AND THE NUMBER KILLED AND WOUNDED, APRIL 28TH, 1760

Regiments.	\multicolumn{14}{c	}{Strength in the Field.}													
	Colonel	Lieut.-Colonels	Majors	Captains	Lieutenants	Ensigns	Chaplain	Adjutants	Quartermasters	Surgeons	Mates	Sergeants	Drummers	Rank and File	Colonel	Lieut.-Colonels	Majors	Captains	Lieutenants	Ensigns	Sergeants	Drummers	Rank and File	Colonel	Lieut.-Colonels	Majors	Captains	Lieutenants	Ensigns	Sergeants	Drummers	Rank and File
								\multicolumn{6}{c	}{}		\multicolumn{9}{c	}{Killed.}	\multicolumn{9}{c	}{Wounded.}
Amherst's	...	1	1	1	14	8	...	...	...	...	...	25	12	325	...	...	...	...	2	1	4	...	21	...	...	...	1	6	5	9	...	82
Bragg's	...	1	...	3	6	7	...	...	...	1	...	18	11	274	...	...	...	...	...	...	1	...	14	...	1	...	2	2	2	4	...	100
Otway's	...	...	1	6	9	7	...	1	1	1	1	21	11	285	...	...	...	...	...	...	1	...	12	...	...	...	...	...	...	3	...	43
Kennedy's	...	1	...	6	4	7	...	...	...	...	...	17	8	169	...	...	...	...	1	...	1	...	5	...	...	...	1	1	1	3	...	16
Lascelles'	...	...	1	2	11	5	...	1	...	1	...	30	14	264	...	...	...	...	...	1	1	...	10	...	...	...	...	3	...	...	...	43
Webb's	...	1	...	5	12	5	...	...	...	1	...	29	14	307	...	...	...	...	1	1	1	1	22	...	...	...	1	4	2	3	...	63
Anstruther's	...	...	1	5	9	3	...	1	1	1	1	18	6	277	...	...	...	...	...	...	...	...	7	...	...	...	...	...	...	...	...	45
Monckton's	...	1	...	4	9	5	...	1	1	1	...	16	6	191	...	...	...	...	...	...	...	...	1	...	...	...	...	...	...	...	...	9
Lawrence's	...	1	...	4	9	5	...	1	1	1	1	23	6	232	...	...	...	1	...	...	...	...	9	...	...	1	...	1	2	3	...	32
Frazer's	...	1	1	4	18	10	...	1	1	1	1	30	14	370	...	...	...	...	1	...	3	1	51	...	...	...	4	12	5	10	...	119
Rangers	...	...	...	6	1	...	...	...	...	...	...	4	...	78	...	...	...	...	...	...	...	...	2	...	...	...	1	...	...	1	...	9
Light Infantry	...	1	1	4	13	10	...	...	...	...	...	27	11	339	...	...	...	1	1	...	8	...	78	...	...	1	1	5	5	7	1	124
Total	...	6	5	45	115	72	...	5	3	6	4	258	107	3111	...	...	...	1	4	3	19	2	232	...	2	1	14	34	23	39	6	685

N.B.—1 Colonel, 4 Captains, 4 Lieutenants, 4 Ensigns, prisoners, not included.
1 Major, 2 Second Lieutenants, 1 Lieutenant Fireworker, wounded, belonging to the Train.
1 Lieutenant-Fireworker, prisoner. Chief Engineer, wounded."

cause so much damage as was apprehended considering the numerous guards that were always kept up during the whole winter.

Several reports of the French Army approaching towards us, though groundless, kept us very alert the fortifications were repaired in some important places and a chain of block houses were built advanced of the ditch of the town from Cap Diamond to the escarpement of St Roch's suburb, this you see, Sir, would guard the town against a surprise and give time to man the ramparts: they were all for musquetry, except a large one with 3 cannons built where the mill opposite to your house in St. Louis suburb stood.

Some time in December Mr. Cannon, with the munitionaire's frigates and some merchants' ships to the number of eight came down and passed the town spight of our artillery.

Another line of deffense within the ramparts was thought of from the cittadel to Amherst's barracks and made of casks filled with snow, a battery was made at ye old cittadel and another at the mill behind Governor Murray's house, & all lanes and paths in the lower towns were shut up.

In the month of February a party of 2, or 500 hundred French came to Point Levy to take post and prevent any provisions coming over to town, it has been known since that they were intended as the van of ye French Army if they had kept their ground there, they had hardly been there four and twenty hours when we received intelligence of it and in consequence of that Major Dalling with 500 light infantry and 200 men as piquets with small field pieces went across the river upon the ice to dislodge them, 'twas thought that the French would dispute the landing and annoy us before we could effectuate it. Happily, they took no advantage of their situation and run away without making any resistance. We immediately took post in the church till a couple of block houses were built to prevent the French coming there any more, before these forts were finisht the enemy to the amount of 800 returned to repossess themselves of that spot and were repulsed with great ease, and no loss, five battaillons marched out of the garrison upon the ice for that purpose.

In March, the French having advanced some of their posts as far as St. Augustin, parties were sent to reconoitre and harass them and at different times about a hundred of their soldiers were taken, our constant successes and the facility with which we obtained them naturaly would create in us contempt for ye enemy and raise our confidence.

In April, some notice were given of the French preparing themselves for some expedition, 'twas thought then that no place being so proper to land their stores and artillery as Cap Rouge, a post there would be very necessary notwithstanding its distance, and the difficulty of supporting it. The Light Infantry marched there and had orders to fortify themselves. Meanwhile the ice bridge broke, the post at Loretto was called in, and the inhabitants were drove out of Quebec.

Our Light Infantry were hardly settled in their post when a man picked up on a cake of ice during ye night of the 26th and 27th brought certain intelligence that the French were in motion to come by ye way of Loretto and St. Foy to cutt off our Cap rouge post; their frigates with all manner of stores &c. and were come down to St. Augustin and ready to advance as soon as the Cap Rouge affair was decided, this providential notice gave us just time to march out ye piquets of the garrison and the grenadiers some battaillons followed and it gave us an opportunity to bring in ye Light Infantry after some popping shots.

The French pursued their advantage, and appeared ye 28th early on the height where the Light Infantry encamped after ye 13th of 7^{ber} last, skirting ye wood. General Murray marched out his garrison consisting of about 3,000 men, most part with tools to possess the Heights of Abraham and there to entrench themselves, the number of the French appearing but small their brigades being then sheltered by the woods we received orders to quitt ye eminence and advance into ye plain, where we drew in two lines 7 bataillions in ye 1st and three in ye second having 150 yards distance from each other and both lines two deep and large intervalls between the regiments, our Light Infantry on ye right and some volunteers on the left. The French soon appeared to be divided into three brigades, one of Regulars, another of La Colonie, and the third of Canadians, a fourth of regulars also was as yet in the woods behind, Indians on their right wing where there was most wood, they all seemed to be pretty deep.

Our light infantry at first had some advantage and drove some grenadier companies, but they were soon supported and rallied, meanwhile our whole line advanced and the left being rather too near ye wood suffered much and were forced to yield, at the same time the light infantry being repulsed on ye right, while the line on that wing were engaged the French were seen to try to out flank both wings of our army, upon which a retreat becoming necessary it was ordered and made in ye best order then possible, some vain efforts were made to rally on the Heights of Abraham, and we marched into town after having left our artillery behind and all the tools we carried out with us. Our loss is reckoned to have amounted to about 1200 killed wounded and taken amongst which above one hundred officers.

Col. Young was taken, Col. Walsh, and Col. Fraser wounded, Major Hussey killed, Majors Dalling, Mackeller, and Godwin wounded. &c. &c. &c. the struggle lasted above an hour, the French are said to have lost above 2000 in all, a great number of officers included, they were reported to be twelve thousand men in the field.

The 29th in the morning the French appeared upon the heights of Abraham having already opened their trenches at about 600 yards distance from ye saliant Angle of La Glacieres Bastion.

The diligence and indefatigable labour of the soldiers, in filling ye parapet, cutting embrazures in every curtain, raising banquettes for musquetry, mounting cannons upon the ramparts, seconded by the slow and regular approaches of the French, soon put the town in a very good posture of deffense. The French did not open their Batteries consisting of 13 cannons and 2 mortars in 3 different places mostly against Cap Diamond and la Glaciere till the 11th instant, two days before this, ye arrival of the *Lowestoft* from England, with ye news of a squadron following him, raised the spirits of the garrison in proportion as it depressed that of the French.

We had some reasons to think that Mr. De Levy ye French General, considering the slowness of his approaches, had meant nothing else by his coming so near us but to take post, and hold himself in readiness to make the most of what succours might be sent from Europe, and indeed as soon as Commodore Swanton in the *Vanguard* and ye *Diana* appeared in the bason which was ye 15th at night the French prepared to raise ye siege.

Their frigates and other small crafts which anchored at ye foulon were early in the morning of ye 16th chased by our frigates and drove ashore, the French Army abandoned their trenches in the night of ye 16th and 17th leaving 14 pieces of artillery behind, and 6 mortars with most all their stores, and great part of their baggage, ye Light Infantry and ye Grenadiers went after them almost as far as Cap Rouge without being able to come up with them, our frigates are now stationed at Cap Rouge, and every face in the garrison is brightened up to a degree *a peine reconnoissable, entre nous soit dit nous sommes heureux d'en avoir été quittes pour la peur.* Ye 18th my Lord Colwill and ye Hallifax Squadron arrived in the bason.

This all I have been able to observe, some other people will I hope give you some of the particular anecdotes of the garrison relating to ye civil and private government, which will certainly divert you. I am not equal to ye task and will conclude with wishing you joy upon your new regiment the news made the whole corps happy, and no wonder.

I beg leave to recomend myself to the honour of your protection, and humbly to offer those sentiments of respect with which I shall for ever be

 Dear General

   Your most devoted and

     obliged humble Servant

         J. Désbruyêres.

Quebec ye 19th May 1760.

P.S. We have as yet no news from Genl. Amherst. Gay has been indisposed most all ye winter, and is now recovering. Mr. Barker was wounded in the thigh ye 28th last month and is in a good way.

Mr. Des Barres letter and plan will correct the errors I may have committed in my letter in regard to the operations since the 26th.

        Le 11 8bre 1759.

Monsieur

J'apprends que vous etes sur le point de vous embarquer. comme je sais qu'il est presque impossible de trouver des volailles à Quebec, je vous prie d'accepter le peu que je vous envoye. Il ne faut pas pour l'honneur

d'un aussi bon pays que celui ci, que vous disiez en Europe qu'on ny pouvoir trouver de poules, il seroit dengereux d'en degouter les autres.
"J'ai l'honneur de vous remercier de l'argent que vous avez eü la bonté de me preter. Je crains d'avoir eté indiscret en vous en faisant la demande: si ce n'eut eté la necessité pressante de nos blessés, je ne l'aurois pas hazardé, si ma reconnoissance peut etre quelque chose, je l'aurai toujours la plus grande; je vous prie d'en etre persuadé ainsi que des sentiments avec les quels
J'ai l'honneur d'etre
Monsieur
Votre tres humble et tres
Obeissant Serviteur
De Bougainville.
Prouvez je vous prie a mes gens et a ma voiture un passeport pour qu'ils sortent sur le champ de la ville.

The following letter is from General Murray, Military Governor of Quebec for some time, to Townshend when he was Viceroy of Ireland, dated still at Quebec in 1770:—

Beauport 28th August 1770.

My Lord

I wish to avoid being troublesome, and, for that reason, I have refused, at least a hundred solicitations, to write to your Excellency since you have had the command in Ireland; Most people think the generals who served at Quebec in the year 1759 should be upon a friendly footing, and as my inclinations have a strong propensity to that opinion, and am very conscious of having done nothing to prevent it, I with pleasure, and confidence embrace the opportunity my relation Lieut. Mackenzie of the Royal gives me of beging a favour of your Lordship; This gentleman is second son of the late unhappy Earl of Cromartie, he has served twelve years with reputation as a soldier, and with esteem as a gentleman, in short he is a young man, of a most amiable character, for whose behaviour and principles I stand answerable to your Lordship, and to all the world: Lieut Col. Grahame of the Royal Hilanders desires leave to sell out of the army for the support of his family.

His conspicuous merit and distinguished services will, beyond a doubt, induce your Excellency to make an exception to a rule, which, though in general a good one, would in his case be cruel, and to allow him to sell a commission which he has dearly purchased at the expense of toil, constitution, and grey hairs; The major and eldest capt., both unexceptionable men, I understand, are desirous to purchase, but as there is not a subaltern in the regiment who can buy the company, I shall not only esteem it a very high favour and obligation, but a very particular honour done me, if your Excellency will recommend my kinsman for the purchase of the company: By this request your Lordship sees how sollicitous I am to renew, and keep up the ancient friendship which subsisted betwixt us; I think it should still exist, for I am certain that nobody can be with more warmth, and zeal,

    My Lord,

           Your Excellencys most obliged, and

                Most obedient humble servt.,

                        Jas. Murray.

His Excellency Lord Townshend.

Vellinghausen

February 17th, 1761. Major-General Townshend set out for the army in Germany.

Such was the notice in the *Gentleman's Magazine*. He had had about a year's leave after returning from Quebec, and was now given command of the 2nd Brigade in the field force in Germany under the Marquess of Granby, who commanded the British contingent sent to aid the army of Prince Ferdinand of Brunswick, fighting now against the French in Westphalia. Considerable reinforcements of the line had left England for Germany in the spring of 1760, and the second battalions of the Foot Guards (3,000) were sent in July, embarking at Gravesend. The total British force under the Marquess of Granby on the field state was 32,000 combatants.

The composition of the army corps was as follows:—

LIEUT.-GENERAL THE HONBLE. HENRY CONWAY'S CORPS.

Infantry
- 1st Brigade (Brigadier-General Cæsar).
  - Grenadiers of the Foot Guards.
  - 2nd battalion 1st Foot Guards.
  - „   „   Coldstream Guards.
  - „   „   3rd Foot Guards.

Infantry
- 2nd Brigade (Brigadier-General the Honble. George Townshend).
  - 8th, King's (Barrington's).
  - 25th Foot.
  - 50th „ (Carr's).
  - 20th „ (Kingsley's).

Cavalry Brigade (Brigadier-General Douglas).
- 1st Dragoons (Bland's), 3 squadrons.
- Howard's Dragoons, 2 squadrons.
- 5th Dragoon Guards (Waldegrave's), 2 squadrons.

LIEUT.-GENERAL SIR CHARLES HOWARD'S CORPS.

Infantry
- *1st Brigade* (Lord Frederick Cavendish).
  - 11th Foot (Bockland's).
  - 33rd „ (Griffin's).
  - 51st „ (Brudenel's).
  - 23rd Royal Welsh Fusiliers.

Cavalry Brigade (Brigadier-General the Earl of Pembroke).
- The Blues, 2 squadrons.
- 7th Dragoon Guards (Honeywood's), 2 squadrons.
- Carabiniers (6th Dragoons Guards), 2 squadrons.

LIEUT.-GENERAL MARQUESS OF GRANBY'S CORPS.

Infantry
- *1st Brigade* (Brigadier-General Beckwith).
  - Waldegrave's Foot.
  - Maxwell's „
  - Campbell's „
  - Keith's „
- *2nd Brigade* (Brigadier-General Waldegrave).
  - 5th Foot (Hodgson's).
  - 24th „ (Cornwallis's).
  - 37th „ (Stuart's).
  - 12th „ (Napier's).

Cavalry Brigade.
- Scots Greys, 2 squadrons.
- 11th Light Dragoons (Ancrum's), 2 squadrons.
- 7th „ „ (Mostyn's), 2 squadrons.

Besides Artillery.

When Townshend reached the army, it was in winter quarters, his own brigade being at Paderborn with Conway's corps. It is interesting to note that Gerard Lake, who was afterwards to win fame as Lord Lake of Laswaree, was present, serving his first campaign as a subaltern in the Grenadier Guards in General Caesar's brigade of Guards.

All the four battalions in Townshend's brigade were distinguished regiments,—the famous 20th (the East Devon), then known as Kingsley's Regiment, changed in the present day to the Lancashire Fusiliers; its name had been made by Wolfe, who commanded it after Culloden, and the regiment had made itself famous at the Battle of Minden, in the same country where Townshend was now campaigning, two years before; it was in the 20th (then Bligh's) that Townshend had got his company after Fontenoy; since those days the 20th has always maintained its glorious reputation: the 50th (Carr's), destined to make a great name in the Peninsula in Rowland Hill's division: the 8th or King's, which began to be famous with Blenheim: and the 25th King's

Hamm

R. Ase

Vellinghauser

Sud Dunckern

Kir

Scheidingen

Wambeln

Hilbeck

Budberg Werle

VELLINGHAUSEN
15th 16th July 1761.
The attack of 16th July.

Sporcke

Hersfeld

To Lippstadt

chdunckern

Hultrup

Nordel

R. Ase

Soest

Own Scottish Borderers, a regiment which has ever been second to none. Townshend wrote in a letter:

> I think myself happy in having corps and field officers of such reputation, in this brigade.

It was indeed a brigade to be proud of.

In the earlier part of the campaign in 1760 Prince Ferdinand of Brunswick had held the French in check, who, under the command of the Duc de Broglie and Soubise, had tried to penetrate into Hanover. Prince Ferdinand had especially handled them severely at Warburg on July 31st, 1760, where the French had lost 1,500 men and ten guns. The British troops had upheld their good name, and were always placed in the post of honour; consequently, they suffered very severe losses, but in return were invariably lavishly praised by Prince Ferdinand in his dispatches.

The French were in possession of Cassel and Gottingen. In March the allied army advanced, the French retiring before them to Hesse-Cassel; 7,000 Prussians reinforced the allied army, and the enemy were driven from Langensalza. The French retired to Fulda, and then to Frankfort-on-Main, their magazines established about the country being nearly all destroyed. Prince Ferdinand then laid siege to Cassel with the German troops, whilst the British force was posted as a corps of observation.

Townshend's brigade was detached from the main body, as I gather from the following letters of his, dated in May from Soist, Weidenbruck, and Hamm. I quote these in full, as they are of interest to a soldier, giving some idea of the training of our officers in those days. It will be seen that Townshend is always asking for entrenching tools (in the present-day entrenching tools have become of equal importance with ammunition).

In the way of military precautions our force in Germany in 1761 was certainly as far advanced as the arrangements of today (I speak with regard to reconnaissance, outposts, advanced and rear guards, etc.), perhaps even more so, when one reflects on the number of times our troops have been taken by surprise in South Africa. Ferdinand of Brunswick, it must be remembered, was an apt pupil and lieutenant of Frederick the Great, who held always that it was pardonable for an officer to be defeated, but that there is no pardon for the officer who is surprised.

To Lt. General Conway at Soist (*par Estafette*).

Weidenbruck 23 May 1761.

I had the honour of receiving your commands dated 21 May, and those of the 22nd, last night by Estafette. I am sorry I could not send you the report of the brigade sooner. I waited for that from the Kings Regiment (which was sent to Soist by mistake) as soon as I received it, I forwarded the whole returns with all expedition. I should be very unhappy if in this or any other article the execution of your orders in this brigade appeared to be dilatory or neglected, for I can assure you Sir, no one is more ambitious of executing to your satisfaction than myself. I observe by your orders of the 21st that I am directed to report what forage I find in this neighbourhood and endeavour to form what depot or magazines I can for the troops under my command, and to take care the deliverys are regular and according to the effective horses.

Upon my arrival here I found a Jew who had forage, he had furnisht the 24th at this place, I accordingly foraged the whole Brigade from him until further orders. He applied to me for an order to demand horses from the magistrates to bring up more. Upon reading your orders, and having then none to forage elsewhere I thought myself authorised to give such orders upon the country, he first shewing me authority from Colonel Peirson to establish magazines. Be pleased to favour me with your directions whether I am to continue this order to this Jew, or withdraw it? whether I am to order the brigade to continue to forage here, or to forage at the places as directed in your last order of the 22.

I have reconnoitred some of the roads and communications of the cantonments, they are very bad and almost impracticable since these rains. I shall take care that the commanding officers of the Brigade inform themselves minutely concerning them, and you shall very soon have an exact description of the state and distances of the whole. As I was out reconnoitring the roads the greatest part of yesterday, I have not yet been able to fix upon the signals, but I shall do that immediately and report them to you. Have you any particular directions to give me for the conduct of my brigade in case of any alarm or emergency? am I to give such orders as may appear to me the most proper upon a view of their position.

BATTLE OF VILLINGHAUSEN

I was at Stromberg yesterday, it is 2 leagues from hence to the S.P. the roads impracticable to artillery and baggage; it is situated upon a considerable height, it is so woody that they can see no signal I make from hence; it is an open village. 3 companys of the kings are there. It is 2 stone from Waterloo the other quarters, very bad roads and 2½ stone from Leisborne. The roads forwards to Hamm are bad. Buken is the next town towards Hamm is 2½ leagues from Stromberg. Hamm is 4½ leagues from thence. I am going round the other cantonments today.

I should have been glad to have saved you the trouble of reading this long letter by waiting on you, but that I remain here to execute your orders concerning the discipline and economy of the several regiments be punctually executed. I think myself happy in having corps and field officers of such reputation, in this brigade.

Some of them complain to me that their Independant draughts (not reviewed I believe by Lord Frederick Cavendish) are unfit for service. Would you please I should look them over and report them? Carr's, (50th Regiment), has 2 waggon loads of stores they dont want; what do you please to order I should do with such stores as only embarrass the regiments, and where would you have them sent. Where are we to send for Pioneers implements. We can get none here.

    I have the honour to be etc.

Geo. Townshend.

P.S.: The men quartered in this town have good rooms; it has an old rampart round it, but no parapet, a ditch fordable in several places, 4 gates with draw bridges. I have ordered post guards, and the brigades to be drawn up at retreat beating. It is the best post the companys at Stromberg could fall back upon in case of an alarm as it is as near as any of their own quarters. This is 2 stone from Retburg.

The roads between these two last places not so bad as they are forwards. I beg leave to enclose a letter about a deserter from Major Boisragon. There are 2 companys of Independants just arrived here. I shall divide them and send them off to the regiments. I'm sorry to send so foul a letter, but write in very great haste.

From Majr. Genl. Townshend to Lt. Genl. Howard.
Weidenbruck 24 May 1761.

Dear Sir

I am very sorry that the returns of the brigade should not give satisfaction. I have ordered them to be explained by the commanding officers of the several regiments with all possible dispatch, and you and General Conway will I hope be so good as to consider, that as I am so lately appointed to this brigade, they were the first returns that ever came to my hands, and consequently that the great difference between these and the preceding could not strike me; this I only begg leave to observe in excuse, for what may appear otherwise great inattention on my part; give me leave to assure you on this occasion that I am too well convinced how essential it is for everyone to be active on his station, for to desire to give my superiors any unnecessary trouble; the very distant situation of some of the quarters of this cantonment and the extreme bad and inundated state of the roads has prevented (I believe) in a great measure the speedy execution of orders.

When the orders come here they pass through quarters to which they must return from thence answers and Reports must come back here, before we send a more general report; however, be assured that every method will be taken to expedite every order and Service commanded.

The orderly officer was sent as my Major of Brigade assures me without loss of time and such was the state of roads that he was obliged to swim his horse thrice, and I was much in the same situation on reconnoitring the country according to Genl. Conway's orders of which I send him a description as far as I had gone. Please to tell him that tomorrow morning I will reconnoitre as far as Hamm myself. I was yesterday evening at Langenbrück, the roads are very indifferent, and if I have not Pioneers tools, I fear on a forced march any way we must leave our baggage and perhaps artillery behind. The enclosed report of the artillery offrs. (left by mistake yesterday on my table) increases my apprehensions on this article.

If I had pioneers tools I am sure I could do a great deal. There might be very good roads made here every way, by new roads and now and then felling a few willow trees, and laying them over with fascines; where otherwise in the present roads, baggage and cannon will be all laid fast—and I would observe moreover that the Boors have ditched up all the old march routes, which are good and might be restored in a few minutes, if we had proper instruments.

I have not yet got the return of the officers of the brigade capable to serve as engineers or of artificers. I hope to send you that, this evening or tomorrow forenoon, and an exact account of the country towards Hamm. I expect the offrs. of the different regiments are all this day reconnoitring the country communicating to their several cantonments and further as directed by Genl. Conway's letter.

The Independants, arrived here, were 185, they were divided for the oldest brigades 62 to the 3rd 61, they were seven deserters sent this day to Soist and five not taken, drawn for by the 12 battns. of infantry, I gave the offrs. commanding them proper march routes one to Soist through Lepstadt, the other to turn off from thence to Erwille with orders to halt discretionarly as they found quarters.

I do not recollect anything Sir that I have omitted mentioning to you that has not be said to Genl. Conway sooner if I had been desirous of reporting the Independant Companys then arriving.

 I have the honour to be
  Dr. Sir etc.

      Geo. Townshend.

  To Lt. General Conway.

      Ham, 26th May, 1761.

Dear Sir,

I have taken the first opportunity to endeavour to send you a description of this part of the country, according to your orders, by an Estafette which Major Stockhausen is sending to you; it is in my power to transmit an immediate (though imperfect account) of what I have reconnoitred. The roads from Weidenbruck to Stromberg are much mended within these few days, yet require assistance; the distance from thence to Beckham is three leagues, the roads better, after one league good marching in general by subdivisions; there is a commanding height called Mackenberg on the left, a good post, from whence you command the country to the N.W. and the course of the Lippe to the west lower than Ham. The country round Beckham is more open, and the roads pretty good to the Lippe, where is a good post, at a chateau called Hourcharen a league and one half from Ham. Here is a bridge over the Lippe and two other *châteaux*.

The meadows are wide and the commanding heights are at a considerable distance from the river, that height called Heiungberg is the most commanding. The bottom from this to the Chateau before mentioned is bad and from thence to this place is a league and a half, the roads sandy though good.

The fortifications very contemptible, you will excuse my not being more particular a great way to get home, I must go some part of it this night, when I receive the general report of the brigade tomorrow, I shall draw out the best state I can of the roads, the distances and calculations necessary for marching. In the interim, I flatter myself you will be pleased to accept of this imperfect state of it, as a proof of my desires to obey your commands on all occasions.

    I am, Dear Sir,
        Yours, etc.,

                          Geo. Townshend.

                Weidenbruck, May 30th 1761.

Dear Sir,

I have the honour of transmitting to you a report of the brigade under my command as cantoned, with the distances of the several quarters from hence, their bearings from the church of this place and some observations on the posts. I remained the night of the 26th at Ham that I might have an opportunity of making some remarks next day on the country to the right of the Lippe, nearer the river than that part described in my letter from Ham.

The distance from that place to Dabourg is a league and one half; the roads good; from thence to Nutrop a league and from thence to Lippebourg one league and a half, the roads practicable for carriages. There is a ford near Lippebourg which is passable for men and horses, when the river is not swelled by the falling rains. The distance from Lippebourg to Hersfield is two leagues, the roads good for one English mile and the rest very bad and heavy, the village open, there is a castle called Hofstadt opposite to it.

From Hersfield to Leisburn the distance is two leagues the roads pretty good, but as this last mentioned place is one of our quarters described in the report, I shall not now trouble you on that subject. The country in general is strong and much wood in it, and such (in my judgment) that cavalry should have difficulty to act in. The Lippe is fordable in many places from Ham to Lippestadt. Want of time has prevented my reconnoitring any part of the country on the left of the Lippe as directed by your letter. If that is thought necessary I shall take the first opportunity of doing it, as I shall at all times be ready to execute your orders according to the best of my abilities.

I forward reports and returns with all the expedition of the situation of the several quarters can admit of, and if unforeseen accidents occasion any delay, I hope the adj. genl. shall take the trouble to write to my Major of Brigade before mention is made of it in public orders, I shall give further directions about sending immediately these returns called for by the order of the 24th.

I am, Sir, etc.,

Geo. Townshend.

Early in the month of July, 1761, Prince Ferdinand of Brunswick, obliged to raise the siege of Cassel, had taken position behind the Salzbach, with his left wing resting on the south bank of the Lippe, to the east of Hamm, near the small villages of Vellinghausen and Hohenover, and he there determined to await the attack of De Broglie and Soubise, who had formed a junction in the same month. The French numbered about 160,000 combatants, against Prince Ferdinand's 95,000; but, happily for the allies, De Broglie and Soubise were jealous of one another, with the usual friction and misunderstandings common in an army among generals of equal rank.

I quote several orders from George Townshend's order-book of the 2nd Brigade, as they give a very clear idea of what the discipline and training in the army were like in those days. These orders show that all military precautions were taken as regards advanced guards, outposts, etc., that the expenditure of ammunition in action was properly controlled, and that the baggage arrangements were excellent. When in touch with the enemy, the army had to be dressed and ready to march at 3 am. I have *The Regulations for the Prussian Infantry by Frederick the Great* which belonged to the old *marquess*, and I find that everything in this campaign was carried out according to the regulations of that great soldier; they are excellent, and very little improved on today. (*Frederick the Great on Warfare: Battlefield Tactics of the Seven Year's War & Military Instruction to the Officers of His Army* by Frederick II, King of Prussia is also available in book form and kindle from Leonaur).

When in touch with the enemy, every soldier had to have sixty rounds in his pouches; this was a standing order. It is true the orders are somewhat long and repeat themselves, but I am not sure that they are the worse for that, and I feel certain that they will be of interest to military readers. The order-book I have of this campaign is entitled "*Orderly Book of the 2nd Brigade of British Infantry, under the orders of Major General The Honourable George Townshend,*" dating from June 26th, 1761, Soist, to November 2nd, 1761. (This order-book is kept in the handwriting of a non-commissioned officer, and many of the names of persons and places are spelt wrong.—C.V. F.T.)

With the exception of the few letters I publish of George Townshend's in this campaign, I have not got a single letter to write from, so I draw largely on the order-book. I cannot find any private letters of Townshend's relating to this campaign, except those written to his wife, which are not of a nature interesting to readers of military history.

Camp at Soist 27th June 1761.

Parole . . .

Countersign . . .

For the day tomorrow Lieut: Genl. Conway

Major Generals	Cavalry	. .	Col. Gold
	Infantry	.	Lord Pembroke
Picquets this night	British Guards	.	Lt. Col. Clark
	British Infantry	.	Lt. Col. Dallop
	Hanoverian	.	Major Hallnel
	Brunswick	.	Major Hardwick
	Hesse	.	Lt. Col. Harwine
	Cavalry	. .	Lieut. Col. Last
Majors of Brigade	Webber		
	Courtenay		

The army is hereby ordered to remain assembled together and every soldier to keep in camp. Those regiments that are in want of forage must endeavour to procure it as near camp as possible. At 6 in the evening the army will strike their tents and pack up the baggage and the regiments shall form up on their parades, the infantry will ground their arms and stay by them; the cavalry to remain with their horses. As soon as the regiments are formed on their parades, each soldier is to be served with 60 cartridges of ammunition; the wagons may be left behind.

The following officers are appointed to assist Lieut. Col. Pitt in the superintendence of Forage, Infantry Lt. Col. Rolt 11 Regt.; Quartermaster Hardy of *ditto*. Cavalry Major Sandford Carabiniers. Captain Whitmore Inniskillings. Lieut. Walker of Blands; Lieutenant Abercrombie of Howard's; the assistant quartermasters are also to be under Lieut. Col. Pitt's orders on this duty.

After Orders 4 o'clock.

H.S.H. the Duke orders that the picquets of the army both cavalry and infantry are to assemble precisely at 4 o'clock this afternoon in the front of the 3rd regiment of British Guards together with the field officers of the picquets; likewise the generals of the day will assemble at the same place, from whom the field officers of the picquet will receive orders for their destination. Four light 6 pounders to be furnished from the British Park of Artillery to be at the same rendezvous.

The order given this morning for the tents to be struck at 6 o'clock this evening is countermanded and they are not to be struck till further orders.

After Orders 7 at night.

The regimts. to send to Mr. Rheden at Soist to know how many days bread he can supply them with, to make up 8 days bread with that they have already with them, they are to receive as much as will complete them for 8 days, if there is sufficient, and report directly to the major of brigade to what time they are supplied.

The regimts. likewise are to report if they have made up cartridges to complete to 60 rounds per man, and what number they have made besides to furnish the complement wanting for their respective tumbrils.

After Orders half past 8 at night.

The disposition of the march of the army from the camp at Soist, the army will march by the left in 6 collumns by subdivisions exactly at 12 o'clock this night, 6 collumns Coldstreams Regimt., at the head 3rd Regimt., first Regimt. Grenadiers of the Guards, Griffins, Bocklands, Waldegraves, Howards, Blands, Lieut. Genl. Conway will command this collumn. Each under the orders of a field officer will form the advance guard respectively; the collumns will march well closed and no carriages no batt. horses to be suffered within the collumns excepting the field pieces and ammunition waggon to each cannon, the batt. horses are to follow their collumns according to the order of march; after them, the other ammunition waggons, then the chaise of bread waggons, the chaplain and surgeons waggon, and lastly the suttlers waggon, the whole in order of march in their respective regiments.

Every genl. officer leading a collumn will appoint an officer to regulate the march of the baggage. The baggage belonging to Lord Granby's Corps will remain upon the present ground till the first collumn have past by it, when it will fall in the rear.

The officers to be particularly attentive to their platoons and divisions.

A regimental court martial to be held after coming to the ground in each regimt., to try and punish on the spot all such men as shall, unnecessarily stay behind on the march.

The baggage and carriages of the 6 collumns the (*vizt.*) The infirmary and bread waggons and batt horses are all to remain in the rear of the camp of their respective regiments till the troops of the whole column are past, as soon as Blands Regiment of Dragoon Guards are past, the baggage of the general officers the (*vizt.*) Lieut. Genl. Conway, Major Genl. Caesar Lord Frederick Cavendish and Major Genl. Douglass to follow that regiment then the baggage of Coldstream Regt. of Guards followed by that of the other regiments of this collumn in the same order the regimts. marched after Coldstream the 3rd Regimt. of Guards, then first Grenadiers, Griffins, Bocklands, Waldegraves, Howards and Blands, any driver or conductor breaking into this order, will be punished on the spot.

H.S.H. orders that half after 11 o'clock a cannon shall be fired which is to serve as a signal for the tents to be struck and for the whole army to form in order of battle, a second cannon that will be fired at 12 upon which the army will march off according to the disposition above given at the signal of the first cannon that the picquets of each collumn will assemble at the head of their respective collumns, the empty bread waggons to be left behind at the bakery at Soist, to bring up bread for their respective regts.

A subaltern per brigade to put the baggage in march according to the above order, who is then to join the regiment.

Camp at Worlea 28th June 1761.

Parole ...
Countersign ...
For the day tomorrow Lieut. Genl. Mostyn

Major Generals	{ Cavalry	Lieut. Col. Walmoden
	Infantry	Lieut. Col. Keeple
Picquets	British Guards	Lt. Col. Thomas
	British Infantry	Major Howe
	Hannoverian	Lt. Col. Holton
	Brunswick	Major Rabbille
	Hesse	Major Broom
	Cavalry	Major Stewart
Majors of Brigade	Hall	
	Lawless	

The soldiers are not to absent themselves from or quit the camp and are to hold themselves in constant readiness to march.

The regiments to forrage tomorrow morning according to the disposition of the order which win be given out to them for that purpose by Lieut. Col. Pitt.

The regiments are to provide themselves with bread to the 4th July inclusive, and for the future they must endeavour to keep bread up to the same time, when they send for it to Lippstadt they are to pass the Lippe at Overstadt, and are not to go through Soust, the Guards to continue making up cartridges till the ammunition is compleated.

When the regiments want wood it is to be a standing order that no man is to be suffered to go out for it without officers to attend them.

Camp at Laudereu 29th June 1761.

Parole ...
Countersign ...
For the day tomorrow Lieut. General Scheill

Major Generals	{ Cavalry	Flugall
	Infantry	
Picquets	British Guards	Colonel Forbes
	British Infantry	Lieut. Col. Well
	Hannoverian	Major Coraygan
	Brunswick	Lieut. Col. Demar
	Hesse	Major Buttler
	Cavalry	Lieut. Col. Johnston
Majors of Brigade	Evellin	
	Courteny	

The new picquet of the whole Infantry, will march immediately, the British and Hessian will be (assembled at the head of the Hessian Infy. of the first line, the Brunswicks and Hannoverians at the head of the Hannoverian guards, Lieut. Col. Keppel has already reed. H.S.H. orders and instructions for posting them. As soon as the said picquet of the collumns of this morning will rejoin their regiments.

At one o'clock tomorrow morning the whole camp to be dresst and accoutered the cavalry saddled and the artillery park as well as the regiments field pieces to be harnest.

All the empty bread waggons to be sent immediately to Lippstadt for bread, a subaltern officer to be appointed to attend them, who is to be as expeditious as possible to bring them back.

Morning Orders the 30th June 1761.

The cavalry may unsaddle and the men be at liberty to go on with the usual camp business, but no man must be suffered to straggle from camp, and the whole to be kept in readiness to march at the shortest notice.

The British to forrage immediately as near the camp as possible, the forragers of the infantry will assemble in the rear of the brigade of Guards the whole will receive their instructions from Lieut. Colonel Pitt.

Camp at Kamalau 5th July 1761.

Parole ...
Countersign ...
For the day tomorrow Lieut. Genl. Howard

Major Generals	{ Cavalry .	.	Col. Walden
	{ Infantry	.	Genl. Townshend
Picquets .	{ British Guards		Lt. Col. Steele
	{ „ Line .	.	Lt. Col. Wells
	{ Hannoverian		Major Hardenburg
	{ Brunswick	.	Major Wardorph
	{ Hesse		Major Black
	{ Cavalry	.	Major Kelliott
Majors of Brigade	{ Hall		
	{ Courteny		

The collumns may return to their former ground from which they marched this morning and the new infantry picquets will march immediately with one field piece per battalion, and be posted in the front of the camp. The major genls. of the day for the Infantry will see they are properly posted.

The New Grand Guard to be posted immediately and the cavy. picquets are to march at 8 this evening. The Major Genl. of the day of the cavalry will post them so as to sustain the infantry picquets.

The park of artillery are to return to the encampment they occupied last night.

Camp at Hohenover 15th July 1761.

Parole ...
Countersign ...
For the day tomorrow Lieut. Gen. Conway.

Major Generals	{ Cavalry	Ohaiml
	Infantry	Boke
Picquets	{ British Guards	Lt. Col. Scott
	Line	Lt. Col. Graham

As long as the army remains in this position a field officer is to be ordered for the picquets of each of the four divisions, of which it is composed. The commanding officers of each Division, are to order one cavalry captain for the picquets of the cavalry attached to it, with the usual number of men and squadron in the village of Illingzen and the house late General Conway's quarters.

H.S.H. ordered to be posted yesterday in the afternoon a captain and a 100 men from the Prince of Anhalt's division with orders to keep up a communication with Genl. Howard's Division upon his right and the Prince of Anhalt's division upon his left, as also to push his posts forwards, in order to gain the earliest intelligence of any movements of the enemy towards them. This detachment to be relieved at 5 this afternoon by Lieut. Genl. Howard's division.

One captain and 100 infantry from the Prince of Anhalt's division is posted at the bridge of Curtamuhl which is also to be relieved at 5 this afternoon, by the same division, a captain and 100 infantry to be posted likewise at 5 this afternoon at the Nawmuhl, which are to be furnished by Lieut Genl. Watgenaw's division, which division has also posted an officer and 40 at the *château* called Madenau, and an officer and 50 at the Schwainmuhl. All these posts during the army continuance in its present position are to be relieved every 24 hours, that the men may be kept more alert whilst on duty,

H.S.H. orders that every officer who is posted with a detachment in any redoubt fleches or other fortified posts is to maintain and defend himself in it to the utmost, and not to abandon or retire from it, till he sees there is no possibility of keeping it any longer or that he receives orders to quit it from his superior officers, and in that case he is to make his retreat in good order, and with the best countenance, this being the only means to prevent the enemys pursuing him otherwise than with great precaution. Every retreat that is made in a hurry and in confusion will easily be overpowered and entirely demolished there being nothing to stop the enemy. Every officer is to make it an essential point of his duty to preserve upon all such occasions a good countenance and to exhort his troops to the same as his own honour that of his command and the common safety of both depends upon it.

As these detachments are equally posted at no great distance from camp, every general officer of the day, or other genls. of the army who may happen to be at hand and receive the first accounts of any posts being attacked, he is go there immediately, without waiting or sending for orders from the headquarters, and order up some picquets and even some pieces of cannon to sustain the post, sending only an immediate report by an officer to H.S.H. if any regiments ground have been spoiled by the rain. H.S.H. allows it to look out for better in its rear.

After orders past 7 in the evening.

The baggage and carriages to be loaded, and ready to march off on the first order. The whole to be kept assembled in camp and ready to turn out upon the shortest notice.

The Battle of Vellinghausen, or Kirch Deukern

De Broglie and Soubise had joined hands at Soist, and determined to attack Prince Ferdinand in his position south of the Lippe, between Hamm and Lippstadt; for the allies were actually between them and the Rhine. Prince Ferdinand soon heard of their intentions, and took up a strong position. The River Aest runs a considerable way almost parallel to the Lippe, from which it is not distant in some places more than half a mile. The high road from Lippstadt to Hamm passes between these rivers, and it was of the greatest importance to Ferdinand to secure that important communication, for it was his only advantageous line of retreat, by which he could still retain a command over the adjacent country.

With a view, therefore, of protecting that communication, he established his left wing on the isthmus between the two rivers. The left extremity of that wing stretched as far north as the Lippe, by which it was perfectly secured, as the right flank of that wing was supported by the village of Kirch Deukern, on the River Aest.

At the village of Kirch Deukern another river, called the Salzbach, small but very deep, joins the Aest almost at a right angle.

Behind this river (*i.e.* west of the Salzbach), on a considerable eminence, was placed the centre, under Lieut.-General Conway, and on a continuation of this eminence the right wing, under the hereditary prince, stretched south towards the village of Werle, its flank being well secured by the rugged, bushy, and impracticable ground.

Thus, Ferdinand of Brunswick had a river in front of his centre and right wing, and the left wing was supported by rivers on both flanks.

Prince Ferdinand considered that the French would attack his left wing, and so he placed the bulk of his artillery there; and he was right.

On July 15th, at six in the evening, Lord Granby's advanced posts were attacked with the greatest fury by the French. His division, formed of the Guards Brigade and Townshend's brigade, maintained its ground manfully, defending the village of Vellinghausen by a house-to-house defence—as Prince Ferdinand described it, with "*unbeschreiblicher Tapferkeit*," ("indescribable bravery"). Their task was a hard one, for the French showed all their wonted *élan* in the attack. At last Wutgenau, with his Hanoverians, on the extreme left, reinforced Granby, and the French were repulsed after four hours' desperate fighting, falling back into the woods. Firing ceased at 10 p.m.

During the night Prince Ferdinand shifted the British troops to behind the Salzbach (see sketch), Wutgenau's Hanoverians being told off to hold Vellinghausen. At 3 a.m. the French attacked again, De Broglie commanding in person; and again, Vellinghausen was their main objective. Prince Soubise commanded the French centre and left. For five hours the action raged, the Hanoverians under Wutgenau bearing the brunt and rivalling the conduct of the British.

At 9 a.m. Prince Ferdinand saw that the French were bringing up guns on to an eminence opposite Lord Granby's position; he at once called up his reserve under General Sporken, and, having reinforced his first line, ordered a general advance, the French retiring all along the line in disorder. Soubise, in command of the French left and centre, had not even been able to pass the Salzbach, and had simply

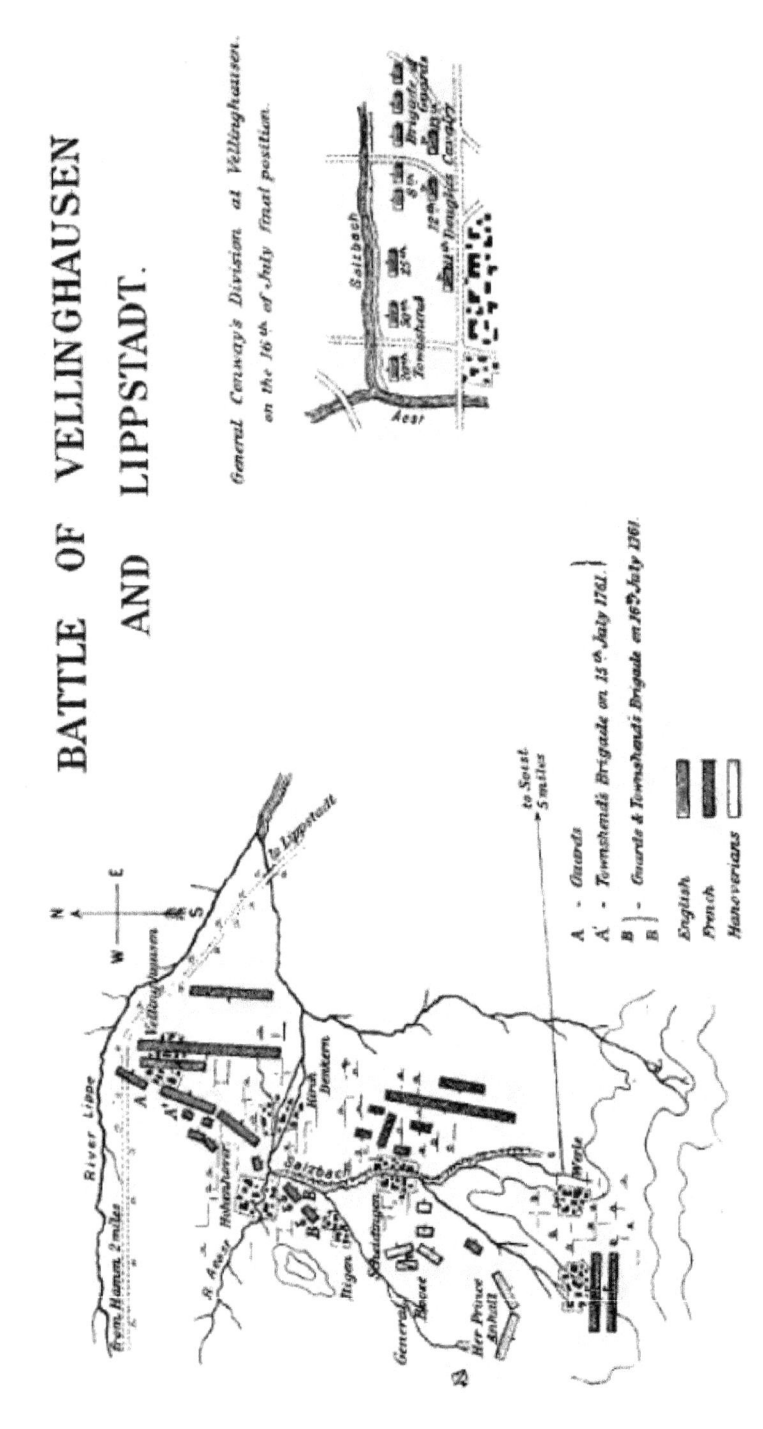

BATTLE OF VELLINGHAUSEN AND LIPPSTADT.

confined his efforts to artillery fire; he promptly followed the example of the French right wing. The close nature of the country, the hollow roads, favoured the French retreat, it is true, but it should have also favoured the pursuit. However, the French were unpursued in their retirement, and so the victory was barren of results.

The allies lost 311 killed and 1,011 wounded, and 192 missing. The French loss was estimated at 5,000 killed and wounded, 9 guns, and 6 colours. The reputation of our British infantry was greatly enhanced in this battle.

Camp at Hohenover 16th July 1761.

Parole. . . .

Countersign . . .

For the day tomorrow Lieut. Genl. Moyston

Major Generals { Cavalry . . . Douglass
{ Infantry . . . . . Bishausen

Divine service to be performed tomorrow morning and the whole army to return thanks to Almighty God for the victory obtained this day over the. enemy, a *feu de joie* tomorrow evening the time for which will be given out in orders, tomorrow. The regiments are to recomplet themselves this evening with cartridges for the field pieces, as well as for small arms.

A return to be given in of the killed, wounded, and missing of the picquets of the British in this day's action.

Morning orders 17th July 1761.

At 6 o'clock this evening, the army and all the detached corps are to be under arms, in the front of the camp to fire the *feu de joie*. The artillery taken from the enemy will begin it, followed by the artillery attached to each corps; the field pieces of the regiments, lastly small arms. The whole to be repeated three times beginning upon the right of each corps.

Camp at Hohenover 17th July 1761.

Parole. . . .

Countersign. . . . .

For the day tomorrow Lieut. Genl. Howard

Major Generals { Cavalry . . . Elliot
{ Infantry . . . Harling

Picquets — *Picquets* { British Guards . Lt. Col. Clark
{ „ Line . Lt. Col. Prescott
Lieut. Genl. Howard's division Lt. Col. Napier
Prince of Anhalt's . Major Swaydorph
Lieut. Genl. Watgenaw's Major Caritzdock

The post of Illingson of a captain and 100 infantry to be relieved immediately by Major Genl. Townshend's brigade. The corps of Lieut. Genl. Conway, Lieut. Genl. Howard, the Prince of Anhalt and Lieut. Genl. Watgenaw's are to order out some workmen, to cut down the hedges and underwood in the front, after which is done, the picquets are to be advanced beyond the Saltzbach, on the other side of which, they are also to cut down the wood and to make good *ouvertures*. A chain to be formed of the picquets under cover of which the regiments may forrage. The field pieces of the regiments are also to be advanced near the Saltzbach. The general officers of the day and field officers of the picquets are to take care that this is done tomorrow. A surgeon from every regiment in the army and detached corps to be sent immediately to Ham to be employed in applying the first dressings to the poor wounded which are in great numbers there.

The glorious victory of yesterday furnishes H.S.H. with a fresh opportunity to testify to the troops which he has the honour to command the highest esteem and perfect consideration he has for them on account of the good countenance which they shewed for so long a time, notwithstanding the redoubled fire of the artillery and musquetry of the enemy and afterwards by the vigorous and intrepid attack by which they overpowered and drove them from all their posts. H.S.H. therefore, hereby makes them his most sincere and perfect acknowledgments and declares to them that as their general he has the utmost reason to be satisfied with that conduct and bravery which the generals, field officers, and others, as also the cause of the different nations have had an opportunity to shew and who have distinguished themselves by their good will and intrepidity, that it is most sensible pleasure to him to make this public declaration of it to them that he will not only remember it as long as he lives, but to retain for them a perpetual esteem and friendship and will not fail moreover to recommend them, to their respective sovereigns, that they may be by them rewarded as they so justly deserve.

H.S.H. further thinks it proper that the army should be acquainted of what passed upon the right, while our left was engaged with the enemy *vizt* that almost Marshall Soubise's whole army manoeuvred opposite the hereditary prince's corps endeavouring to penetrate in several places but that the prince by his prudent manoeuvres, his own personal bravery and that of his troops rendered their attempts ineffectual so that they were obliged to retire with great loss, which contributed not a little to our being able on the left to push with our advantages with more certainty and success with regard to the two princes of Brunswick Frederick and Henry they have well supported by their behaviour yesterday that good opinion, which was with so much justice entertained of them before, having in their first campaign and at their first action they have been in, showing so much presence of mind and so good a countenance and have acted with so much intrepidity.

The eldest at the head of his own regiment and both in places of the greatest danger. H.S.H. feels a particular pleasure in declaring this himself to the army, and to make known to these two princes, his satisfaction and aprobation of them. H.S.H. also looks upon it as an essential a point from gratitude as well as friendship to make his first and most sincere acknowledgements to His Excellency the Count de Lippe for the fatiguable pains in arranging ordering and executing with such surprising expedition everything within his power towards contributing to the glorious success of the day. H.S.H. declares for himself and also in the name of common cause to preserve the most lasting remembrance of and gratitude for it.

The action of yesterday is to take the name of Vellinghausen which is to be declared to the army. Any corps which has taken trophies from the enemy is to report it to Adjutant General Rheden.

After orders 11 at night.

H.S.H. orders the whole army to be under arms in order of battle at one o'clock tomorrow morning. The tents are to be struck and the baggage loaded and ready to march off on the first order.

Camp at Hohenover 18th July 1761.

Parole ....
Countersign.....
For the day tomorrow Lieut Genl. Scheil

Major Generals { Cavalry . . . . Bilbow		
{ Infantry . . . . Townshend		
	(British Guards . . . Col. Wells.	
	{ „ Line . . . Col. Frederick	
Picquets .	{ Lt.Genl. Howard's Division . Major Oaks	
		Prince Anhalt's . „
	(Lt. Genl. Watgenaw's . „	

253

The batt. horses and baggage to return immediately, as soon therefore as the corps and regiments receive their tents they will encamp, the infantry behind their present emplacement, and the brigade of cavalry in the rear of them at a convenient distance.

Major Genl. Braum, Lieut. Col. Phillips and Major Brugmans will park their artillery in the places most suitable either in front or rear of the infantry. They are to leave their artillery that is placed in the works as they are now posted, the detachments guarding the different debouches and bridges are to remain.

The picquets of the cavalry and infantry are not to be advanced till further orders. The commanding officers are to use their utmost endeavours to prevent their men wanting bread. Should any regiment find itself in that situation or that their waggons are not arrived, they are immediately to report it to Captain Polynitz at headquarters.

The duke's headquarters remain at Hohenover those of the hereditary prince are removed to Womble.

After Vellinghausen Prince Ferdinand tried to surprise the French near Cassel, and crossed the Diemel with that purpose; but he did not succeed, and recrossed the river, encamping at Bulme and Corbeke.

In November Prince Ferdinand made a second attempt to surprise De Broglie in his camp at Einbeck; he turned the left flank of the French, and cut off their communications with Göttingen. This obliged the French to leave their entrenched camp and retreat. After this nothing seems to have been done, and both armies went into winter quarters. The cause of the French defeat was the friction between De Broglie and Prince Soubise, divided commands, and divided counsels, for generals as well as doctors seldom agree.

De Broglie wrote to his Court that Soubise delayed attacking until it was too late for De Broglie to continue it, and Soubise said that his rival began before the hour fixed, in the hopes of beating the allies without the assistance of Soubise: the old story of jealousy among officers of an equal rank—the story of the real reason of the French being driven out of the Peninsula by Wellington about fifty years after this campaign.

1762

Nothing was done till June in this year, and in that month Prince Ferdinand advanced again, and attacked Soubise and D'Estrees at

Gravenstein, or Wilhelmstaal. The advanced guard of the allied army was formed by Lord Frederick Cavendish's brigade—11th Foot, 33rd, 51st, and Royal Welsh Fusiliers.

The attack of the allies appears to have been well combined, the French being completely surprised, the attack succeeding at all points. The Marquess of Granby's corps fell on the left wing of the French, and after a short resistance the enemy retreated, abandoning their baggage, but the retirement was well covered by De Stainville's corps, who showed himself to be an excellent rear-guard commander. Two guns, six colours, and one standard were taken by us, the total loss of the allies being 796 killed and wounded.

The name "Wilhelmstaal" appears only, as far as I can see in the *Army List*, on the colours of the 5th Fusiliers, although the above-named regiments of Lord Frederick Cavendish's brigade were present, and also a brigade of Foot Guards. In the brigade with the 5th I find the following regiments were also present: the 24th, 37th, and 12th. Lieut.-Colonel Henry Townshend, of the 1st Foot Guards, was killed in this battle; he was a cousin of George Townshend's, being the second son of the Honourable Thomas Townshend, uncle of the subject of this book. The elder brother of Colonel Henry Townshend was afterwards created Viscount Sydney.

I take the following out of the records of the Grenadier Guards:—

> Colonel Townshend's death was regretted by the whole army. He was second son to the Honble. Thomas Townshend, and had distinguished himself on several occasions. In the previous campaign in Germany he was shot through the arm, and in this engagement he lost his life seeking the post of honour that his duty did not require; he was the only officer of rank killed in this action.

Portugal 1762

General Townshend had left the army in Germany in the spring of 1762, having been ordered to proceed to Portugal with the local rank of lieutenant-general in command of a division in the Anglo-Portuguese Army. Nearly at the end of the Seven Years' War, France and Spain threatened Portugal that, if she did not throw off her alliance with England, she would be invaded. The King of Portugal refused to break with England, and was assisted by us with officers, troops, artillery, munitions of war, and provisions.

I quote letters to Townshend from Charles Townshend (brother to George), then Secretary of State for War, and from Lord Ligonier, the commander-in-chief.

Thursday morn.

My Dear George!

The day after you left me, I received a message from Lord Bute signifying to me that, at your desire, He had, in my absence, recommended you for the Portugal Staff. The next day Lord Ligonier gave it out, and on the Monday, when I went into the closet, the king announced it to me in the most gracious manner. The matter being thus settled and declared as soon as I learnt your intention, I could say nothing, but waited two. days to hear whether the service would actually take place, for some time I thought not, and I still doubt, out, as the staff is public, I judged it proper to send you this express, that you may know how matters have gone.

Lady Ferrers wrote to me yesterday, but I sent her the most prudent answer I could, to quiet her mind and suspend her judgment til she saw you. I owne I was surprized to hear all things so rapidly decided and published, the very day after I heard your sentiments and before I could get out of my bed, but it was thought to be your own desire and carried into execution as such. The troops are talked of for immediate execution, but I know this to be impossible. The Pr: of Bevern will have the command by the appointment of Portugal, our ministers are divided upon the service, the expense is dreaded; the Treaty disputed; the force ridiculed; the object lessened, in my opinion things are in suspense, but, in the meantime the embarkation is preparing for. if things alter, you shall hear again.

    Most aflectly. yrs.

C.T.

P.S. Martinique is now entirely ours without any loss, and little sickness.

London August 27, 1762.

Dear George

I received with great pleasure the favour of your letter—It gave me an insight into the situation of Portugal which I never had before. I hope everything relating to the army, and particularly it's subsistence, is put on a footing conformable to your wishes. We understand that Lord Tyrawley is arrived at Portsmouth.

The newspapers inform us that the King of Portugal has confirmed Monsr. de la Lippe his commander in chief with all the powers necessary to make an army. I should think he will have a little trouble to bring them to the Prussian discipline.

Make haste and thrash the Spaniards, or we will make a peace and prevent your bringing home the Laurels you would gain by the conquest of them.

I send you no news, as I conclude your brother Charles acquainted you with the present state of Great Britain; but I send you my sincere wishes for your success, health and happiness, for I am with great truth and regard

    My Dear George

        Your most faithful and obedient servant

    (Signed)

Ligonier.

The Honble. Majr. Genl. Townshend.

I have a mass of letters and correspondence on this campaign; but I do not propose going into details, for no general actions were fought, and so I do not think that it would interest the public in general to go into matters of commissariat and supply, or dry accounts of marching

A PLAN
of that Part of the Country which was the Scene of Operations in
PORTUGAL
in the Campaigne 1762.
Andrew Frazer Assist. Quart. Master General.
Rio Mondego
COIMBRA
Cam. para Almeida
Ponte de Marcella
Rio Alva
Venda nova
PARTE DA PROVINCIA
Serra d'Estrella
Rio Piqueno
Rio Ducca
Rio Ceyra
Miranda do Corvo
Pedragao Grande
Ponte Cabril
DA
Espinhall
Figueira dos vinhos
Rio Zezare
Pombal
Venda dos muntos
Foz dalge
BEIRA
PARTE DA PROVINCIA
Dornes
Val de Seronne
DA
Rio Fondeiro
Maile
S. Simon
Avanda
Sarzedas

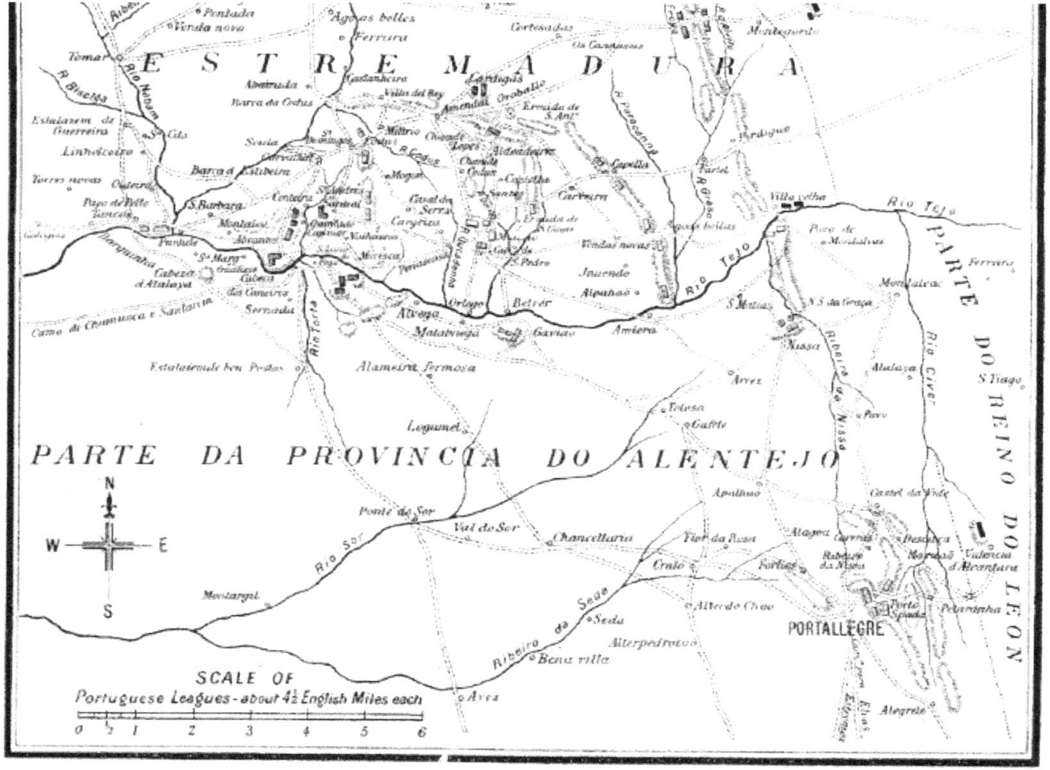

and countermarching.

That famous soldier the Count de la Lippe, who was a pupil of Frederick the Great, commanded the Anglo-Portuguese Army, which was not in sufficient strength to engage the French and Spanish forces in the field.

In August, I find in Townshend's *Diary* that the Count de la Lippe had given him the command of a corps in the Beira Alta. His orders were to cover the province as far as possible, preserving the communication with Oporto, for the defence of which he was to construct some works below the River Douro; he was also to cover the road to Coimbra, and especially to watch and prevent the passage of the river Alva at Ponte Marcellos.

In order to do this, he took up an advantageous position to support Colonel Hamilton in the post of Cerolico, and destroyed the roads and communications, to prevent the enemy subsisting between that place and Ponte Marcellos.

The Franco-Spanish Army was far superior in numbers to the army under Count de la Lippe, who had taken up a very strong and judicious position at Abrantes, with the River Tagus on his right and a mountain on his left. As the enemy could make no impression on Marshal de la Lippe's army without driving General Townshend's corps from the mountains called Sierra da Estrella, every movement could be perceived and was reported immediately, and plenty of intelligence was also constantly brought in by large numbers of deserters. Frustrated at this point, the enemy changed their plan of operations to the Alemtejo, crossing the river Tagus.

On this side the Spanish advanced, the Portuguese falling back, the Count de la Lippe clearing the country of all supplies in front of the invaders in much the same manner as Wellington did prior to retiring to the Lines of Torres Vedras, when Portugal was invaded by Massena forty-eight years later. Indeed, it may well be that Wellington, who was a great student of military history, had read the account of the operations of the Count de la Lippes campaign in 1762. Want of supplies and transport therefore completely crippled the Spanish, who, having no magazines to maintain them in Portugal, had to give up the territory they had overrun, after a few small skirmishes, and retreat across their own frontier on the approach of the winter of 1762.

Thus, ended the campaign, happily for the Portuguese, though the prospects of that country had been gloomy enough when war was declared. A general peace was proclaimed in Europe on November 15th,

1762, and all the special service officers and the 5,000 British troops which had been lent to Portugal returned to England.

Townshend had written to his old Quebec friend, Admiral Saunders, to give him a passage home in one of his men-of-war, and received the following letter in reply:—

My Dear Sir,
As I shall sail for England in two or three days, I have so much business on my hands, that I must desire you will excuse my making use of an amanuensis to inform you that I received the favour of your letter, desiring I would let one of my ships call at Lisbon, on her return to England, to take yourself and family on board: I am sure you know I would do everything You would have me do, that is in my power, to add to the conveniency of Lady Ferrers's return; I go myself in the *Hercules*, with the *Thunderer, Favourite*, and four bombs, the two former are in so bad a condition I can't possibly trust them on the coast, but I have sent the *Favourite* to you; and nothing can be safer on the water; I wish with all my heart there was more room in her, and that Lady Ferrers, yourself and family may have a good passage home, being
    My Dear Sir
        Your most faithfull hble. Servant
                Chas: Saunders.
Gibraltar Bay
24 Dec. 1762.

All the principal officers of the British troops, sent to the relief of Portugal, on taking leave of his most faithful majesty, were honoured with presents, according to their rank, expressive of that monarch's sense of their services. Prince Charles of Mecklinburgh with his majesty's picture, very richly set with diamonds. General Townshend, with a diamond ring, a pair of diamond buckles, and a gold snuffbox, the whole worth £3,000, and those, who embarked for Minorca, with swords of different values, with the arms of Portugal, and a motto in the Portuguese language; signifying, English true faith and bravery, the defenders and security of Portugal—*Annual Register*, vol. vi., 1763, p. 86.

Townshend's wife, Lady Ferrers, had come out from England with her children, and joined him at Lisbon. On their return to England in

George Viscount Townshend

the *Favourite* frigate, they had a very narrow escape of being wrecked at the mouth of the Tagus. The captain of the *Favourite* had shifted some guns to give Townshend better accommodation aft, and in consequence the ship, coming out of the Tagus, could not wear, and drifted broadside on to the bar, where the sea, owing to the high wind, was running "mountains high."

Every effort was made to get the ship to tack. Boats were put out, but they could not get her round, and they were nearly lost. The only hope was to anchor, for, once amongst the breakers, the frigate was doomed. Seeing this, Lady Townshend, with her children, went below. Luckily, the anchor caught in a rock, and held the ship, rolling all night, just clear of the breakers. On the turn of the tide in the morning, they could not raise the anchor, but had to cut the cable and run into a small bay. After this providential escape they sailed for Portsmouth, where they learnt, in the newspaper brought by the Lisbon packet, that they had been all lost.

During his service in Portugal Townshend declined his Portuguese pay, knowing how distressed the Court of Portugal was to pay their troops. He said, at the same time, that he hoped it would not form a precedent for other general officers.

With regard to this subject of money, amongst his letters I found one from an officer to him, whilst he was Viceroy of Ireland, asking for an appointment carrying with it higher pay. Townshend had written across the application:

> If lucre is a man's object let him have it—but then do not let him aspire to those honours, which for the good of the service must be pursued through a different channel.

Viceroy of Ireland

By the death of his father in 1767 George Townshend succeeded to the tide of 4th Viscount Townshend and to the family estates. In August of the same year, on the retirement of the Earl of Bristol, Townshend was appointed Lord-Lieutenant of Ireland—a post then, as now, beset with difficulties of every nature.

In a book such as this, the scope of which is solely to narrate the military side of the life of George Townshend, a description of his political career would be out of place. It will be sufficient to say that in his civil life he displayed the same genius as an administrator that he had shown as a general. While Lord-Lieutenant of Ireland he ruled wisely, with a deep appreciation of the rights and feelings of the people whom the king had placed under his rule. It has been said, indeed, that, thanks to his lenity, wisdom, and moderation, the first ray of liberty dawned upon Ireland during his tenure of office.

No reformer, even in these days of enlightenment, of empire-making, and of army reform, can hope to escape misrepresentation and abuse; and in 1770 the virulence of political opponents was unbounded. Much abuse was naturally lavished upon the young soldier-statesman, who found in Lord Chesterfield a brilliant defender. Chesterfield's celebrated *Essay on the Character and Conduct of His Excellency Lord Viscount Townshend* (printed in 1771) shows at once the indecency of the attacks upon the Lord-Lieutenant and the baseless nature of the charges made against him by the terrible pamphleteers of Grub Street.

He resigned his appointment in Ireland in 1772, after the death of his dearly loved wife, and returned to England; and he was obliged to sell the family estates in Warwickshire to pay off the debts he had incurred in Ireland in the public service. Of these Warwickshire estates, Tamworth Castle alone remained in the family up to a year ago, when that also was sold.

★★★★★★

In Townshend's letter to Lord North, dated July 27th, 1771, asking that the King will allow him to resign his appointment of Viceroy in Ireland (written after the death of his wife), he says:—

> I wish my dear Lord I could close this letter without saying a word upon my own particular situation, but as I am satisfied that when all these arrangements shall have taken place, H.M.'s Government here will be so strengthened and established, that by a steady pursuit of the same system the administration thereof may become most easy and honourable, I shall be extremely obliged to H.M. if he will be pleased to permit me to return into His Royal presence whenever he shall think that some other person may be as usefully entrusted with that important charge.
>
> The truth is that my health, my fortune, and my spirits, since I sustained the late great shock in my family, are all much impaired—my own children and those of my late brother (Charles) who are no less dear to me, call for my utmost attention—nothing but the flattering idea, that in the present peculiar situation in this country, I might possibly appear more useful than another for carrying H.M. Business in the ensuing session of Parliament, could induce me to wish to remain in this kingdom where I hope always to prove that I have H.M.'s Interest more at heart than any other consideration whatever. I am by no means afraid to stay and justify the measures and arrangements which I have recommended, I would only desire H.M.'s permission to retire when he shall judge his affairs will allow him to indulge me in that request"

He was not allowed to leave his post till November 30th, 1772.

★★★★★★

In 1773 Lord Townshend returned to active employment in the army, and fought a duel with Lord Bellamont, in which his antagonist was so severely wounded that his life was despaired of for several months. Lord Bellamont eventually recovered. The aged Lord Ligonier, the Commander-in-Chief, was Lord Townshend's second. A stream of honours now steadily poured upon him. He was given the honorary colonelcy of the 2nd Dragoon Guards, and promoted to full general in 1782. In 1783, he was appointed Master-General of the Ordnance, and on October 30th, 1787, he was raised two steps in the peerage, and became the Marquess Townshend of Raynham, in the county of Norfolk. In 1793, he was made Field-Marshal, and was appointed to the honourable sinecure of the Governorship of Jersey.

Among the last of his recorded public acts are his voting for the acquittal of Warren Hastings and for the legislative union of Great Britain and Ireland. In recording his adhesion to this great measure, he is reported to have said that in his opinion the chief source of the calamities of Ireland was the excessive monopolisation of the land, and the number of bankers, squires, stewards, taxmen, and other persons who stood between the landlord and the tenant—words which show how thoroughly he understood the chief grievance under which Ireland then suffered.

He died in 1807, full of years and honours. His career is thus described in the *Gentleman's Magazine,* vol. xxxvii., 1807, p. 894:—

Sept. 14, 1807. At his seat at Rainham, Norfolk, in his 84th year, the most noble George, marquis Townshend, a field marshal in the Army, Colonel of the 2nd regiment of Dragoon Guards, Governor of Jersey and Lord Lieutenant of the County of Norfolk. He was a godson of George 1st, served under George 2nd at the Battle of Dettingen, and attended the person of William Duke of Cumberland at the Battles of Fontenoy, Culloden and Lafeldt. He was second in command at the memorable siege of Quebec, under General Wolfe, and was consequently the immediate successor of that renowned chief in Canada.

He also served a campaign in Portugal, and commanded the British forces sent to the assistance of that country against Spain. He was appointed Lord Lieutenant of Ireland in 1767, and continued in that high office to the great satisfaction of the Irish people till 1772. His vice-royalty was distinguished by a total change in the Parliamentary constitution of the sister kingdom. On his return to England he was appointed to the Board of Ordnance, which situation he retained for 10 years. He married first in December 1751, the Baroness de Ferrars of Chartley, who died in 1770. His lordship's second marriage was in 1773 with Anne, daughter of Sir W. Montgomery; he had issue by both his marriages. In his private character he was lively, unaffected and convivial. He possessed an acute mind and enlivened his conversation with that original pleasantry which is shown very viably in the works of his pencil when he chose to display it. In the earlier part of his life he frequently indulged in its humours, and was an admirable caricaturist even at the time when Hogarth flourished. No one enjoyed life more than the marquis Townshend. He suffered indeed some heavy inflictions, but he bore them with resignation; and closed a life, protracted beyond the common dale of man, with the general respect and estimation of his country.

By his first wife he has left the Earl of Leicester, now marquis Townshend, Lord John Townshend, and lady Elizabeth Loftus. By his second marriage the marquis has six children: *viz.* Annie Hudson, the Duchess of Leeds, 2 unmarried daughters and 2 sons.

Annual Register, vol, xlix., p. 594:

> The following are stated to be the principal bequests and legacies made in the capital Will of the late Marquis Townshend:
>
>> The family estate of Rainham (the entail was cut off about four years ago) with all the furniture, plate, pictures (including the Belisarius by Salvador Rosa, valued at 10,000 guineas) to his second son Lord C, Townshend, and his Lordships two daughters £15,000 each; and to Miss Walcup £40,000, and his house, library, and furnityre at Richmond. The family estates in Warwickshire and other counties, to the amount of nearly £18,000 per annum remaining entailed go hereditorily to the present *marquis,* who it is generally understood is not named once in the Will.

Appendix

Annual Register, p. 72:

> Feb. 2nd. This afternoon the long subsisting difference between Lord Townshend and the Earl of Bellamont was finally decided in Mary-le-bon-fields, when the latter received a ball in the right side of his belly, near the groin; the event of which the surgeon could not yet decide. They were armed with small swords and a case of pistols, but it was agreed to use the latter first. Lord Townshend fired first, which gave the unfortunate wound, and Lord Bellamont discharged his pistol immediately after without effect.
> The seconds were the Hon. Mr. Dillon for Lord Bellamont and Lord Ligonier for Lord Townshend. Lord Bellamont was immediately taken up and put into a chaise, but from the agony arising from his wound he could not bear the motion; a chair was therefore immediately sent for to carry him to his lodgings, where, when he arrived, he desired to be laid on his back. Mr. Bromfield and other surgeons were immediately called in, who endeavoured, but in vain, to extract the ball.

Annual Register, vol. xvi., p. 85:

> Mar. 3rd. Lord Bellamont has rested well for several nights past, and is now out of danger. The faculty dispairing of finding the ball, have determined to irritate the wound no further by searching for it, but to heal the orifice with all expedition.

Bellamont eventually recovered, after some months in danger from his wound.

Annual Register, vol. xvi., p. 164:

> On the 15th June, General George Viscount Townshend was

appointed Lieut Colonel of the 2nd or Queen's Regiment of Dragoon Guards.

Annual Register, vol. xix., p. 148:

>*June*, 1776. Some experiments were tried at Woolwich before Lord Viscount Townshend, Lord Amherst, Generals Harvey, and Desaguliers, and a number of other officers *with a rifle gun*, upon a new construction by Captain Ferguson of the 70th regiment; when that gentleman, under the disadvantages of a heavy rain and a high wind performed the following four things, none of which had ever before been accomplished with any other small arms; 1st, He fired during four or five minutes at a target at 200 yards distance, at the rate of four shots each minute, 2ndly, He fired six shots in one minute, advancing at the same time at the rate of 4 miles in the hour, 4thly, He poured a bottle of water into the pan and barrel of the piece when loaded, so as to wet every grain of the powder, and in less than half a minute fired with her as well as ever, without extracting the ball. He also hit the bull's eye at 100 yds. lying with his back on the ground; and notwithstanding the unequalness of the wind and wetness of the weather, he only missed the target 3 times during the whole coarse of the experiments. The captain has since taken out a patent for the said improvements. It passed the Great Seal on the 4th Dec following.

Annual Report, vol. xxxvii., pp. 114 and 115, April, 1795.

Trial of Warren Hastings

The Lord Chancellor: 'Is Warren Hastings, Esq. guilty, or not guilty, of the high crimes and misdemeanours charged upon him by the Commons in the first articles of charge? George Marquis Townshend, how say you?'

Not guilty, upon my honour.'

The Marquis Townshend declared the innocence of Warren Hastings on each of the 16 questions.

ALSO FROM LEONAUR
AVAILABLE IN SOFTCOVER OR HARDCOVER WITH DUST JACKET

THE 9TH—THE KING'S (LIVERPOOL REGIMENT) IN THE GREAT WAR 1914 - 1918 *by Enos H. G. Roberts*—Mersey to mud—war and Liverpool men.

THE GAMBARDIER *by Mark Severn*—The experiences of a battery of Heavy artillery on the Western Front during the First World War.

FROM MESSINES TO THIRD YPRES *by Thomas Floyd*—A personal account of the First World War on the Western front by a 2/5th Lancashire Fusilier.

THE IRISH GUARDS IN THE GREAT WAR - VOLUME 1 *by Rudyard Kipling*—Edited and Compiled from Their Diaries and Papers—The First Battalion.

THE IRISH GUARDS IN THE GREAT WAR - VOLUME 1 *by Rudyard Kipling*—Edited and Compiled from Their Diaries and Papers—The Second Battalion.

ARMOURED CARS IN EDEN *by K. Roosevelt*—An American President's son serving in Rolls Royce armoured cars with the British in Mesopatamia & with the American Artillery in France during the First World War.

CHASSEUR OF 1914 *by Marcel Dupont*—Experiences of the twilight of the French Light Cavalry by a young officer during the early battles of the great war in Europe.

TROOP HORSE & TRENCH *by R.A. Lloyd*—The experiences of a British Lifeguardsman of the household cavalry fighting on the western front during the First World War 1914-18.

THE EAST AFRICAN MOUNTED RIFLES *by C.J. Wilson*—Experiences of the campaign in the East African bush during the First World War.

THE LONG PATROL *by George Berrie*—A Novel of Light Horsemen from Gallipoli to the Palestine campaign of the First World War.

THE FIGHTING CAMELIERS *by Frank Reid*—The exploits of the Imperial Camel Corps in the desert and Palestine campaigns of the First World War.

STEEL CHARIOTS IN THE DESERT *by S. C. Rolls*—The first world war experiences of a Rolls Royce armoured car driver with the Duke of Westminster in Libya and in Arabia with T.E. Lawrence.

WITH THE IMPERIAL CAMEL CORPS IN THE GREAT WAR *by Geoffrey Inchbald*—The story of a serving officer with the British 2nd battalion against the Senussi and during the Palestine campaign.

AVAILABLE ONLINE AT **www.leonaur.com**
AND FROM ALL GOOD BOOK STORES